The Girl with the Swansdown Seat

Cyril Pearl

the Girl with the Swansdown Seat

*An Informal Report
on Some Aspects of
Mid-Victorian Morality*

ROBIN CLARK

First published in Great Britain 1955
by Frederick Muller Ltd
Reprinted 1955 (twice), 1956
This edition published 1980 by Robin Clark Ltd.
27/29 Goodge St, London, W1P 1FD
A member of the Namara Group

ACKNOWLEDGMENT

For certain source material used in Chapter IV of this book the author is indebted to an article by Donald MacAndrew, "Skittles or Fair but Frail" (*The Saturday Book*, 1948)

Made and printed in Great Britain by
M C Print Co. Ltd., Stevenage, Herts.
ISBN 0 86072 043 8

CONTENTS

The Victorian Myth

The Victorian Reality

Harlotry Triumphant

A Theme of Fair Women

London Amuses Itself

Dress and Undress

Pornography's Hydra Head

ILLUSTRATIONS

Chapter 1

The Victorian Myth

"THE history of the Victorian Age will never be written; we know too much about it," said Lytton Strachey, in the language of Gilbert Chesterton. He might have said there was no Victorian Age. The two generations and three nations of Englishmen who were Queen Victoria's subjects had little in common but their boundaries in space and time. The landed lord, the city merchant, the factory worker of 1837, inhabited widely different worlds; and their children who saw the dim newsreels of the Queen's funeral in 1901 had lived through more change, material and moral, than half a dozen preceding generations.

The absurdity of the label "Victorian" is never more apparent than in generalizations about "Victorian morality"—a phrase often used to describe a rigid, Puritanical attitude towards sex. In this sense, "Victorian", and particularly "mid-Victorian", are almost synonyms for "virtuous"; the words suggest a tableau of pure women and passionless men, citizens of a solemn, glandless Utopia where duty has routed desire and children are frequently born but never made.

Little research is necessary to show that this pretty picture-postcard oleograph of sex life in nineteenth-century England has no more relation to reality than Edward Lear's description of the domestic habits of the Jumblies. It is questionable, of course, whether the sexual behaviour of a people ever changes much, irrespective of the prevailing moral code. "Of all useless inquiries," observed the *Saturday Review* in 1870, "one of the most unprofitable is whether the moral level of any particular stage or period of society is higher or lower than that of the past. It is easy to make out a case either way." There is certainly no satisfactory method of assessing or comparing sex morality. What are the standards of comparison? The amount of pre-marital or extra-marital sex activity? The percentage of illegitimate births? The facilities for contraception or abortion? The extent and openness of prostitution and the status of prostitutes and mistresses? The licence in dealing with sex enjoyed by novelists and playwrights? The attitude towards nakedness and semi-nakedness on beach and stage? The state of the pornography market? The answers to all these questions, many of which are dealt with in this book, have some bearing on the problem, but it is doubtful if even the patient Dr. Kinsey, despite his unique knowledge of the secret lives of gall wasps and Americans, could deduce from them an effective formula for measuring morality.

What is Victorianism? Without becoming entangled in intangibles, it is possible to examine a period of Victorian life in the light of contemporary evidence and to show how greatly it differs from the accepted idea of Victorian purity; nothing more is attempted in the casual excavations that follow. They deal mostly with the late 'fifties and 'sixties because in these years, it seems, the reaction from early Victorian (or pre-Victorian) Puritanism was at its height. The retreat to respectability which characterized the latter part of Victoria's reign and which continued after her death, began, roughly speaking in the 'seventies, under increasing social and political pressure from the Nonconformists. But the moral code of Victorian Nonconformity, with its specific identification of immorality with sexual irregularity, its deification of duty and its distrust of pleasure, antedated Victoria by many years. It was a product of the religious revival that took place towards the end of the reign of George III—a revival to which the horror of the French

Revolution, the horrors of the Industrial Revolution, and the corpulent torpor of the Established Church all contributed.

Many writers have noted the pre-Victorian origin of Victorianism: "The heyday of what we nowadays call Victorian morality may roughly be placed between 1780 and 1820, the age of the great Evangelists," says Mr. Hugh Kingsmill. "The Victorian era—so far as the expression has any historical value —dawned with the Bourgeois Revolution," says Dr. Wingfield-Stratford. And Mr. Wilson Disher, studying the effect of "the superficial spirit called Victorianism" on the English stage, notes "a slackening" rather than "a tautening" of ideas about virtue. "Piety", he writes, "ran its highest temperature before any influence could be brought to bear on the country by the blithe, alert young woman who occupied the throne."

What is virtue? "I have but a very confused idea of what virtue really is," observes that amiably candid strumpet of the Regency, Harriette Wilson. "Now the English Protestant ladies' virtue is chastity! There are but two classes of women among them. She is a bad woman the moment she has committed fornication; be she generous, charitable, just, clever, domestic, affectionate . . . the Protestant world will have it that all are virtuous who are chaste, even when chastity is to their liking—the selfish, the hard-hearted, the cruel mother, the treacherous friend, the unfeeling mistress—all! all! are called virtuous who are supposed chaste."

Miss Wilson made these observations in 1825, when Victoria was playing with her dolls in Kensington Palace. They remind us that the confusions of morality were just as profound in her time as they were half a century later. When we think of the Regency, or of the years immediately preceding it, we think of Miss Wilson and her sinful sisters entertaining noblemen in their box at the Opera; of the fantastic Pavilion at Brighton and its dissolute Royal Master of the Revels; of elegant dandies and luxurious whores; of gamblers and rakehells, three-bottle men and Corinthians; of the oaths, the cynicism, the jewelled snuff-boxes and the champagne. But it was also the period of Methodism in its most virulent, groanful, impudent form; of fanatics and philanthropists and reformers; of Dr. Bowdler and Elizabeth Fry; of the Religious Tract Society and the Sunday School Society and the Society for the Suppression of Vice—which the Rev. Sydney Smith said should have been called the Society for Suppressing the Vices of Persons whose Income does not exceed £500 per annum—and of a dozen other organizations dedicated to death-worship, self-denial, gloom and a fierce denunciation of worldly pleasures.

"In this country all is contrast," Greville noted in his diary in 1834, "Contrast between wealth the most enormous and poverty the most wretched, between an excess of sanctity and an atrocity of crime," and this in spite of "a strong Puritanical spirit at work and vast talk about religious observances." Writing of *England and the English* about the same time—a few years before Victoria's accession—Bulwer Lytton echoed Harriette Wilson's views on virtue: "Next to our general regard for appearance, we consider morality only as operating on the connections between the sexes." And he noted the remarkable corollary that "out of the exclusiveness of our regard to chastity, arises the fearful amount of prostitution which exists throughout England. . . ."

Good works and bad women: In the same way, when we try to evoke a picture of the mid-Victorian age, we think of genteel homes, family prayers, and sombre Sundays; of purposeful husbands in dundrearies and pallid wives about to be confined; of chaste young men in check unmentionables and simpering virgins in bastions of whalebone and steel; of sentimental songs and sexless courtships; of novelists scurrying under Mrs.Grundy's skirts and playwrights arranging virtue's inevitable triumph; of Miss Florence Nightingale writing: "Life . . . is a hard fight, a struggle, a wrestling with the Principle of Evil"; and of Dr. Arnold grimly doing battle with the Wicked One; of Exeter Hall and its redemptive hosannahs; of Bibles for blacks, hot soup for the clean poor, the Aged Pilgrims' Society, and manifold other good works.

But it was also an age when prostitution was widespread and flagrant; when many London streets were like Oriental bazaars of flesh; when the luxurious West End nighthouses dispensed love and liquor till dawn; when fashionable whores like Skittles and Agnes Willoughby rode with duchesses in Rotten Row and eminent Victorians negotiated for the tenancy of their beds; when a pretty new suburb arose at St. John's Wood as a seraglio for mistresses and harlots, and at popular pleasure gardens like Cremorne and Highbury Barn, prostitution was given a setting of woodland charm; when respectable men bathed naked at seaside resorts and respectable women watched them, sometimes through opera-glasses; when bloods like Waterford and Windham went their raffish way as though "Prinny" were still at Carlton House; when pornography became a well-organized industry and even the most righteous newspapers fed the public appetite for sex and sensation.

The Rev. T. Garnier, rector of Trinity Church, Marylebone, does not seem to have been exaggerating much when in 1858, he said that England was known as "the most religious in pretension but in reality the most immoral and licentious nation under the sun". Yet to Mr. S. M. Ellis, a recent explorer of these times, the word Victorian means "a blessed period of peace and prosperity, port and progress and domesticity in excelsis . . . a good, solid, happy time of English life at its best".

II. MR. MUDIE COMES TO TOWN

Anatomy of a Myth: If both these pictures of Victorianism are valid, why has the myth of Victorian purity prevailed? Partly, because so many of our ideas of life in nineteenth-century England derive from the popular novelist who—enthusiastically or reluctantly 'or indifferently, according to his culture and conscience—accepted the moral code of the middle-class.

Dickens, Thackeray, Trollope and a host of lesser writers emasculated their writings to suit readers like Mrs. General: "A truly refined mind will seem to be ignorant of anything which is not perfectly proper, placid and pleasant." Frederic Harrison wrote approvingly of Dickens: "In forty works or more, you will not find a page which a mother need withhold from her grown daughter." Thackeray confessed that men and women in novels had to be represented according to current convention: "Since the author of *Tom Jones* was buried, no writer of fiction among us has been permitted to depict to his utmost power a MAN ... Society will not tolerate the Natural in our Art." Trollope boasted that he had never written a line which a pure woman could not read without a blush. Literature was tested by this, or by the even more extraordinary touchstone of whether it could be read aloud by a modest man to a modest woman: a procedure that seems to have been devised by Dr. Thomas Bowdler, whose ten-volume de-sexed *Family Shakespeare*, published in 1818, was a popular piece of Victorian furniture. "It has been my study," explained the doctor, "to exclude from this publication whatever is unfit to be read aloud by a gentleman to a company of ladies."

How much of this gentleman-to-lady elocution actually took place? It may have been the Victorian substitute for conversation, as drowsing over the radio or blinking at television is to-day; or it may only have been a useful fiction like the square root of minus one. Certainly, many parents made a ritual of reading each evening to the entire family. T. A. Trollope, for example, writes with some feeling of his father's fondness for this soporific practice: "There was not an individual of those who heard him who would not have escaped from doing so at almost any cost": and Florence Nightingale was equally unappreciative of Mr. Nightingale's regular family readings. In any case, the formula was ruthlessly effective in keeping literature in leading-strings. Writers punctiliously produced what their customers wanted —a formalized, sentimental parody of life purged of all

6

passion and flesh. The customers were the expanding, narrow-minded, uncultured, Nonconformist middle class, who, however they may have behaved in private, in public belonged to a rigidly respectable club where sex was permanently black-balled.

By the middle of the century, the big circulating libraries had become the principal guardians of the novel-reader's morals. Most novels were published in three volumes at 31s. 6d. and most of these were read by subscribers to libraries who paid a guinea a year for the privilege. As the proprietors of the two most important lending libraries in England, Mr. Mudie and Mr. Smith, both hymn-bawling Nonconformists, exercised a censorship as absolute in its way as that of the Holy Office. If they approved of a book, its success was assured: Mr. Mudie approved of George Eliot's *Felix Holt* and bought 2,000 copies of it. If they disapproved, the book had little chance of selling. "I have offended Mudie and the British nation . . . O canting Age!" wrote George Meredith when Mr. Mudie disapproved of *Richard Feverel*. And Mr. Smith and Mr. Day and Mr. Booth and Mr. Mudie, though rivals in the market-place, formed a united front when morality was to be defended. Their tyranny was not challenged till the middle of the 'eighties, when the rebellious George Moore, whose three-volume novel *A Modern Lover* had displeased the libraries, demolished the whole absurd system by publishing his next novel, *A Mummer's Wife* in one volume for six shillings. "Judge Messrs. Mudie and Smith by what they have produced," Moore wrote, "for they, not the ladies and gentlemen who place their names on the title-pages, are the authors of our fiction." And he proudly announced on the first page of *A Mummer's Wife* that it had been placed in the Mudie-Smith "Index Expurgatorius".

The more cultivated Victorian, of course, had no illusions about the paralysis of the contemporary novel. Meredith wrote bitterly to Swinburne of "the restriction imposed on our art by the dominating damnable bourgeoisie" and periodicals which served an intelligent minority often attacked the hypocritical standards of the novelists. "We are by no means prepared to say that in literature, emasculation produces purity," said the *Saturday Review* in the late 'fifties. "Our statistical returns, the nightly appearance of our streets and . . . verbatim reports of trials . . . surely teach us that we are not so immaculate." A few years later, *Vanity Fair* said that London publishers were "as timid as hares" and mistook "the 'Oh, shocking!' of Mrs. Grundy for the deliberate opinion of the intellectual portion of the community". But Mrs. Grundy patronized Mudie's and Smith's, and however damnable was her domination, neither author nor publisher was inclined to antagonize her.

The Victorian biographer was a willing accomplice in this conspiracy against truth. He suppressed or distorted secretly and shamefully. Forster does not mention Ellen Ternan's name in his life of Dickens, though as the legatee of £1,000 she is the first person named in the text of Dickens' will, published as an appendix. Wemyss Reid's biography of Monckton Milnes not only omits all reference to Milnes' passion for pornography but impudently alters the text of his letters; when he describes Queen Victoria as looking "rather cross", Reid changes it to "rather tired". Gosse tampered in the same furtive way with Swinburne's letters.

III. CANDID COLUMNS

No Prudery in Printing House Square: Obviously, to interpret nineteenth-century England in terms of the fiction approved by its circulating libraries is like interpreting twentieth-century America in terms of the fiction approved by the *Saturday Evening Post*. "It must be remembered", said Samuel Butler, as an Apology for the Devil, "that God has written all the books." If the Victorian middle class did not write all the books, nearly all the books were written for them. The popularity of these books, and the relative obscurity of more factual accounts of contemporary life, have done much to consolidate the Victorian myth.

An obdurate facet of this myth is the belief that the Victorians were all as mealy-mouthed as their novelists. Thus Mr. Gerald Heard, in *Morals Since* 1900 observes: "As the First World War drew to a close, the London *Times* for the first time openly mentioned venereal disease. . . . Prostitution and venereal disease became then in the second and third decades of this century matters of general concern and informed discussion." But in the 'forties, *The Times* was advertising Balsamic Pills as "a certain cure for gonorrhea", and a treatise called "The Syphilist" for "those suffering from an invidious complaint so frequently resulting from indiscretion or gaiety". In the 'sixties, it was discussing venereal disease editorially and in the 'seventies, the *Saturday Review* was complaining that "a free and unembarrassed talk goes on between men and women about contagious diseases, prostitution and the Mordaunt scandal [a sensational society divorce in which the Prince of Wales gave evidence]. It is the strangest possible reaction from the mincing prudery of the typical English Miss."

Lord Ernest Hamilton, in *The Halcyon Era*, deploring the "sepulchral dullness" of mid-Victorian newspapers, says they published nothing "to which the degrading term 'sensational' could, by any ingenuity, be applied. . . . They cut out all murders, divorces, burglaries, scandals about rectors, boxing and athletics." Almost any London paper of the period would demonstrate the gross inaccuracy of this statement, irresponsibly set down as social history, for the mid-Victorian Press had a freedom and ruggedness of expression that Fleet Street editors of to-day might envy. Police and divorce reports, even in a paper of such majestic respectability as *The Times*, were full and often clinically frank. *The Times* was well aware of its readers' interest in what Lord Hamilton calls "sensational" news. "You have been lucky in having so many murders," wrote Delane, one of its greatest editors, to his deputy. Its detailed presentation of evidence in unsavoury cases sometimes aroused the indignation of the *Saturday Review*, and its correspondence columns, as we shall see, were just as uninhibited, even when a prostitute wanted to publish a lengthy apologia for her way of life. Nor were its readers surprised to read immediately after the *Court Circular* an announcement such as:

> Mr. Gladstone has had a smart attack of diarrhoea which will probably prevent him from attending Parliament for a day or two.

or to encounter, at the breakfast table, under the heading "The False Modesty of Piccadilly", a Clochemerle-like discussion on whether a urinal should be erected "within view of houses occupied by persons of respectability".

"*A Slice of Bosom, Sir?*": The extravagant nineteenth-century euphemism of legend attained its gaudiest flowering, not in England, but in the United States, where, too, the most violent reaction took place to supposedly indecent English novels, such as *Griffith Gaunt*. When Fanny Trollope wrote of the *Domestic Manners of the Americans*, at the end of the eighteen-twenties, they were pre-eminent in the mass-production of genteelisms. "Hardly a day passed," she wrote, "in which I did not discover that something or other that I had been taught to consider as natural as eating, was held in abhorrence by those around me; many words to which I had never heard an objectionable meaning attached, were totally interdicted, and the strangest paraphrastic phrases substituted." It was "a symptom of the utmost depravity" to mention "shirts", and men and women were not allowed to look at antique statuary together. Thirty years later, a London journalist reviewing Whitman's *Leaves of Grass*, wrote, "It is startling to find the poet acquiring popularity in the country where piano-legs wear frilled trousers, where slices are cut from the turkey's 'bosom', and where the male of the gallinaceous tribe is called a 'rooster'."

Many of the genteel expressions of the Victorians originated, of course, before Victoria was born. "Inexpressibles", that delicious synonym for trousers, came into use towards the end of the eighteenth century to protect the modest from the rude impact of the word "breeches". Peter Pindar refers to it in some verse published in 1790:

> I've heard that breeches, petticoat and smock,
> Give to thy modest mind a grievous shock
> And that thy brain (so lucky its device)
> Christened them inexpressibles, so nice.

and three years later Gibbon uses it in a letter to Lord Sheffield.

"A fine lady can talk about her lover's inexpressibles when she would faint to hear of his breeches," says a magazine writer in 1809.

Goodbye to Mr. Buggey: The case of the sensitive Mr. Buggey is a trivial but amusing example of the candour of the English Press in Victorian times. When a citizen called Buggey advertised that he intended to change his name to Norfolk Howard—a bold combination of the family name and title of the Duke of Norfolk—London newspapers commented good-humouredly on other people who groaned under the burden of grotesque, uncouth or equivocal surnames. A list of such names published in *The Times* included: Bub, Holdwater, Pricke, Poopy, Maydenhead, Piddle, Pisse, Honeybum, Leakey, Pricksmall, Quicklove, Rumpe, Shittel, and Teate; names that an Elizabethan or Restoration dramatist would have delighted in, now, alas, obliterated by the corrosive spread of refinement. Mr. Buggey's change of name had an ironic sequel. In the language of the streets and the pubs, "Norfolk Howard" became a popular synonym for a bed-bug.

Other mutations of mid-Victorian surnames recorded in *The Times* are:

> James Balls to James Woolsy
> John Hogflesh to John Herbert
> Samuel Highcock to Samuel Conden
> Josiah Badcock to Josiah Elliot

The Disappearing Virgin: In 1828, a London Quaker called Jonathan Dymond published a huge treatise on the *Principles of Morality* that went through many editions and was reprinted un-amended as late as 1880. In it he analysed the alarming disparity between the assessment of wickedness according to the Moral Law and according to Public Opinion. He found the comparison "discordant to excess", particularly in the case of male unchastity. Taking the figure twenty to indicate both "the highest degree of reprobation in the Moral Law" and "the highest offence accord-ing to popular opinion," he compiled this instructive table of turpitude:

	Moral Law	Public Opinion
Murder	20	20
Human destruction under other names	18	0
Unchastity, if of women	18	18
Unchastity, if of men	18	2
Theft	17	17
Fraud and other modes of dishonesty	17	6–4 or 1
Lying	17	17
Lying for particular purposes, or to particular classes of persons ..	17	2–or 0
Resentment	16	6 and every in-ferior gradu-ation
Profaneness	15	12 and every in-ferior gradu-ation.

Apart from the melancholy reflection that it provides of the all-pervasiveness of Sin in Mr. Dymond's world—for the mildest infraction of the Moral Law is only 25 per cent. less heinous than murder—the table suggests that his contemporaries viewed the unchaste male with extraordinary tolerance, reserving their Vesuvian wrath for The Woman Who Did, whose sin was regarded as nine times more wicked than the man's. Indeed, if Mr. Dymond is a reliable interpreter of popular *mores*, male unchastity in the early nineteenth century was the mildest of peccadillos, much less reprehensible than lying, or even resentment. Was Mr. Dymond talking through his Quaker hat? It is impossible to say, but twenty years later both Dickens and Carlyle told Emerson that the chaste Englishman was a very rare phenomenom. They were dining together, and the conversation turned on "the shameful lewdness of the London streets at night".

Emerson recorded it in his diary: "I said that when I came to Liverpool I inquired whether the prostitution was always as gross in that city as it then appeared, for to me it seemed to betoken a fatal rottenness in the state. . . . But I had been told that it was not worse or better for years. . . . Carlyle and Dickens replied that chastity in the male sex was as good as gone in our times. . . . Carlyle evidently believed that the same things were true in America. He had heard this and that of New York, etc. I assured him that it was not so with us, that for the most part, young men of good standing and good education, with us, go virgins to their nuptial bed, as truly as their brides. Dickens replied that incontinence is so much the rule in England that if his own son was particularly chaste, he should be alarmed on his account, as if he could not be in good health."

Moralists, if they accept Emerson's tribute to the chastity of his countrymen, will shake sorrowful heads at the decline of innocence in the United States during the last hundred years.

And what of the female in early nineteenth-century England? The intense public disapproval of female unchastity which Mr. Dymond noted does not seem to have acted as a universal deterrent from Sin. A Poor Laws' Commission held about the time of the Dymond survey came to the sombre conclusion that:

... the virtue of female chastity does not exist amongst the lower orders of England, except to a certain extent among domestic female servants who know that they hold their situations by that tenure, and are more prudent in consequence.

Observers were to deplore the unchastity of the lower-class female over and over again throughout the century. And when Mr. Mayhew made his memorable survey of London prostitution in the 'sixties, he found then that even female servants— of whom there were more than a million—were "far from being a virtuous class".

Beware of the Gout: Dickens, despite his satire, despite his eldest son at Eton, despite his mistress, is the voice of middle-class England, the man who, as George Orwell puts it, "identifies with the Puritanical moneyed class against the card-playing aristocracy". You expect Sir Mulberry Hawk to be a rake just as you expect Nicholas Nickleby to go chaste to Madeline's bed. You certainly do not expect Dickens to say that he would be alarmed if his own son were "particularly chaste". Not many years before this talk with Emerson took place, Lord Carlisle, one of the card-playing aristocracy whom Dickens hated, wrote to a friend: "I was afraid I was going to have the gout the other day. I believe that I live too chaste. It is not a common fault with me." Nor, apparently was it a common fault with the middle-class Englishman of 1848. Indeed Carlisle's aristocratic belief that ill-health was a result of chastity was surely less immoral than Dickens' middle-class belief that chastity was a result of ill-health. How genuine, then, was the Puritanism of the Puritanical moneyed class of the nineteenth-century England? The table-talk at the Emerson dinner is a useful starting point for an inquest into the flimsy but enduring legend of Victorian virtue. Before it ends, we will have ridden with the "pretty horsebreakers" of Rotten Row, explored the nighthouses of the Haymarket, looked in the booksellers' windows of Holywell Street, attended a few sessions of the Court of Common Pleas, read some surprisingly candid letters to the Editor of *The Times*, and peeped through the keyholes of those cosy, secluded villas in St. John's Wood, where the Puritanical moneyed stockbrokers and merchants and manufacturers and Empire-builders went for consolation while their wives were busy reading Mr. Dickens' novels and proliferating at home.

Chapter II

The Victorian Reality

"*A VERY Hot-bed of Lust*": While Wesley and his disciples were forging the Nonconformist conscience in the hell-fires of their fanaticism, the early beneficiaries of the Industrial Revolution, undeterred by the whiff of brimstone, were establishing the conditions that produced the great nineteenth-century boom in prostitution. "The almost entire extinction of sexual decency, which is one of the darkest stains upon the character of the manufacturing population, may be traced, to some extent, to this period," wrote P. Gaskell, Esq., a contemporary observer, in 1833.

The first master cotton spinners and weavers, he says, were often men of "coarse habits", sprung from the ranks of operatives and agricultural labourers; intoxicated by their swift acquisition of wealth and power, they took full advantage of "the facilities for lascivious indulgence afforded them by the number of females brought under their immediate control". But they were men of stamina, too:

Many of these might be found, after a night spent in debauchery and licentiousness, sobered down by an hour or two of rest, and by the ringing of the factory bell, going through the business of the day with untiring activity and unerring rectitude ... again to plunge, at the expiration of the hours of labour, into the same vortex of inebriation and riot.

16

Their sons and younger kinsmen, who as mere children were given well-paid positions of authority in the mills, were soon corrupted by the example of their elders:

> Boys ... were thrust into a very hot-bed of lust. ... The organized system of immorality which was pursued by these younger men and boys was extremely fatal to the best interests of the labouring community. ... Chastity became a laughing-stock and a by-word. Victim after victim was successively taken from the mill ... an improper intimacy was rather esteemed creditable than otherwise. The miserable creature was pointed out by her companions, as being particularly fortunate in having attracted the notice of the young master, his nephew, brother or cousin. ... Houses were established in some localities by parties of young men purposely for the prosecution of their illicit pleasures, and to which their victims repaired—nothing loth, it is true—to share the disgraceful orgies of their paramours; and in which scenes were enacted that even put to the blush the lascivious Saturnalia of the Romans, the rites of the Pagoda girls of India, and the Harem life of the most voluptuous Ottoman.

The girls who participated, nothing loth, in these elaborate ceremonies displayed to their less-favoured workmates, "with ostentatious parade", the ribbons, caps, and gowns with which they were rewarded. But Mr. Gaskell notes that other factors than the love of frippery conspired to their seduction. One, he thought, was the stimulus of the heated atmosphere of the mills, which approximated "very closely to that found in tropical climes" and thus produced early puberty. (Despite this, it was unlawful to have intercourse with a girl under twelve, though if she were over ten, it was only a misdemeanour.) Another—which remained a potent incubator of immorality throughout the century—was the foetid congestion of workers' dwellings, in which five or six people often shared a single room:

the father and the mother, the brother and the sister, the male and the female lodger, do not scruple to commit acts in the presence of each other, which even the savage hides from the eyes of his fellow.

The theory that girls are sexually ripened by working in the heat was expounded to Charles Reade when he visited Manchester, note-book in hand, in 1868. It reminded him of a similar observation in the *Germania* of Tacitus.

II. GO WEST, YOUNG MAN

Surfeit of Lamp-posts. In 1703, the Haymarket was described as "a very spacious and public street, length 340 yards, where is a great market for hay and straw". A century and a half later, it was still a spacious and public street, and a great market; but the hay and straw had been replaced by whores and strumpets. "The central fast life of London has migrated to the West, where the aristocracy, middle and trading classes now indulge in nocturnal pleasures, and by their purses, foster carnal desires," said *Paul Pry*, a raffish London periodical, in 1857. For thirty years or more, the Haymarket, as the principal avenue to these pleasures, was the Grand Boulevard of London debauchery.

London night-life in the eighteenth century had swirled around Covent Garden, where taverns, coffee-houses and bagnios clustered:

> *Centrick, in London noise, and London follies,*
> *Proud Covent Garden blooms, in smoky glory;*
> *For chairmen, coffee-rooms, piazzas, dollies,*
> *Cabbages, and comedians, fame'd in story!*

Here, in houses once occupied by nobility, eminent brothel-mistresses like Moll King and Mother Cole received their fashionable clients; and when James Boswell felt sexually adventurous, or Dudley Ryder—before he became a Chief

Justice—"had a mighty inclination to fill a whore's commodity," there were plenty of free-lances to choose from between Covent Garden, the Strand and Fleet Street. Mother Cocksedge's house, where William Hickey boozed and whored, was right next-door to the Bow Street residence of "that vigilant and upright magistrate, Sir John Fielding", a fact which would scarcely be credited, Hickey wrote in his *Memoirs*, "in these days of wonderful propriety and general morality".

The robustious Hickey *Memoirs* were completed about 1813, when the harlots' hegira to the West End was just beginning. To the philosopher sceptical of progress, there is pleasing irony in the thought that one of the reasons for this migration was the improvement in London's street-lighting. When Murdoch's gas-lamps were replacing the glimmer of oil, optimists saw in their bright yellow glow the dawn of a new morality; a verse "On The Gasmakers", written towards the end of the Napoleonic Wars, ran:

> *Our morals as well as appearance must show*
> *What praise to your labours and science we owe;*
> *Our streets and our manners you've equally brightened,*
> *Our city's less wick-ed and much more en-lightened.*

And the *Westminster Review* in 1829 asked: "What has the new light of all the preachers done for the morality and order of London, compared to what has been effected by gas lighting! Old Murdoch alone has suppressed more vice than the Suppression Society." But these tributes to the detergent qualities of coal-gas were offered too soon; old Murdoch made London safer, but not less sinful. Just as cheap printing and greater literacy extended the market of the pornographer, so the spread of gas-lighting through the metropolis gave more scope to the prostitute and the nighthouse keeper.

Rouge and Black Satin: But Covent Garden retained its ambiguous repute well into the nineteenth century. When Renton Nicholson, later to become notorious as the Chief

Baron of the Judge and Jury show, was doing the town in the eighteen-twenties, in company with young Mr. Hayward (who was hanged for burglary in 1827), and such popular ladies of pleasure as Polly Edwards, Fat Glover, the Goddess Diana and Jew Bella, Mother Hoskins' nighthouse was "the greatest rendezvous for the gay city birds, as well as the more fantastic ladies of the West". Her premises were opposite the front entrance of Drury Lane, extending from Bridges Street through to Charles Street—now Wellington Street—and the grand reception room ran the full length of both houses.

Apart from the fashionable brothels, the leading theatres were then the headquarters of casual prostitution. "The boxes and saloons of the playhouses were the marts," says Dr. Acton, "and as the wholesale dealers kept the adjacent taverns and lodging-houses within a moderate radius, the business was, as it were, concentrated and under control." The theatre whores of 1838 were described in Nicholson's scandal-sheet *The Town* as belonging to the "second class of courtesans":

> ... they are looked down upon by the first-rate women who ride about in the carriages of noble protectors. Then the theatre-women think themselves degraded by comparison with those who do the excessively swellish on the *pave*. The dashing Cyprian who treads the aristocratic pavement of Regent Street by day scorns an alliance with those who do the same thing at night and the well-dressed street harlot looks with pitiable contempt upon the ragged, low-life characters.

Using the immemorial journalistic formula of exploiting vice by pretending to rebuke it, *The Town* deplored the immodest appearance of the theatre women, whose "leading characteristics" were "black satin and rouge", and urged them to "have the common sense and decency to attire themselves decorously—it is the least they can do when permitted to mingle with respectable society".

The Cloister and the Harlot: There were prostitutes west of Covent Garden of course, long before the precursive gas-lamps flickered on Westminster Bridge in 1814. Soho, Mayfair and St. James's all had fashionable brothels in the eighteenth century. Somewhere about 1750, Mrs. Goadby, an English pioneer in the art of what is now known as packaging, opened an elegant establishment in Berwick Street, where she introduced some of the refinements that had impressed her during a tour of the more distinguished Parisian houses of pleasure. These refinements, as catalogued by the learned Dr. Ivan Bloch, included a congregation of the most beautiful girls, tastefully dressed, temperate, and skilled not only in satisfying all the "fantasies, caprices, and extravagances" of their patrons, but in singing, playing upon the guitar, and embroidering. Mrs. Goadby, after fulfilling her amiable ambition to refine the Londoner's amorous sports, hitherto conducted on less aesthetic lines, retired to a country estate, a wealthy woman.

Of the many disciples she left to continue her mission of reform, perhaps the most zealous was Mrs. Charlotte Hayes, who established a luxurious salon in King's Place, Pall Mall, under the trade-name of the Charlotte Hayes Cloister. It was a common whimsy at the time to sharpen lechery with the spice of blasphemy by calling a brothel an abbey, and its inmates, nuns. An heresiarch of this strange eighteenth-century cult was "Hellfire" Sir Francis Dashwood, the Father Superior of the dark revels at Medmenham Abbey, near Marlowe, where whores wore religious robes and the sacrament was administered solemnly to a slavering baboon.

Abbess Hayes was an imaginative entrepreneur. Once, inspired by a passage in *Cook's Voyages* that describes certain fertility rites practised in Tahiti, she invited favoured clients to witness "at 7 o'clock precisely" a similar ceremony: "Twelve beautiful nymphs, spotless virgins, will carry out the famous Feast of Venus, as it is celebrated in Tahiti, under the instruction and leadership of Queen Oberea." The abbess herself took

21

the role of Queen Oberea, and twelve athletic youths had important parts.

In the early part of the nineteenth century, when the lights were going on all over London, there were many brothels in the streets near Bedford Square and Bryanston Square—"the tall, dark, dreadfully genteel street" between Portland Place and Bryanston Square where Mr. Dombey lived was probably one of them. The infamous Mother Stewart's juvenile academy was in Charlotte Street, Portland Place. Marie Aubrey, a Frenchwoman with a critical eye for furniture and pictures as well as girls, had her luxurious house in Seymour Place. Other establishments were set up in St. Martin's Lane, Leicester Square, and Exeter Street, where Mother Sparrow achieved a certain notoriety.

Many of the better-class courtesans and procuresses also lived in the West End. In Star Street was Maria Webb, alias Mangerstein, who was said to have been patronized by the Marquis of Waterford and the Duke of Wellington; Mrs. Porter, who had the honour of procuring Harriette Wilson for the Duke, lived in Berkeley Street, and so did Miss Howard, who, before she became the mistress of Napoleon III, had entertained the Duke of Beaufort, the Earl of Malmesbury and the Lord of the Bedchamber, Lord Chesterfield. Mrs. Honey, another recipient of Chesterfield's attentions—he drove her openly to the Doncaster in his carriage—lived in Hertford Street.

"Then Let's to Piccadilly Haste": When Lord George Cavendish bought Burlington House from his uncle, the Duke of Devonshire, he found that residents on the west boundary had a habit of throwing oyster-shells and other useless objects over his wall. His irritation at this unneighbourly practice produced the Burlington Arcade, built on a strip of land cut from the estate. The Arcade, opened in 1819, was a multiple success. Apart from its prime function of keeping oyster-shells out of his garden, it added £4,000 a year to his rent-roll, gave Londoners a short cut from Piccadilly to Cork Street and New Bond Street, and provided street-walkers with a cosy promenade. London has

few arcades, and the girls were quick to take advantage of the new amenity.

Tavern entertainers were soon singing:

> Bazaars have long since had their day,
> Are common grown, and low,
> And now, at powerful fashion's sway,
> Arcades are all the go;
> Then let's to Piccadilly haste,
> And wander through the shade,
> And half an hour of pleasure taste
> In Burlington Arcade.

"The Arcade is the place to get rid of your loose cash in" says the patter that followed the song, "Yes, there's loose fish enough to get rid of anything . . ."

Two beadles, tall and magnificently accoutred, were charged with the preservation of morality in the Arcade, but the loose fish contrived to slip past their brass-topped staffs of office; and for the greater part of the century, the covered walk, with its discreet apartments above the shops, remained a fashionable whoring-ground. "The Burlington Arcade is a well-known resort of women on the long winter afternoons, when all the men in London walk there before dinner," observed Mr. Mayhew in 1862. They were "Cyprians of the better sort":

> They are well acquainted with its Paphian intricacies, and will, if their signals are responded to, glide into a friendly bonnet shop, the stairs of which leading to the coenacula or upper chambers are not innocent of their well-formed "bien chaussée" feet.

A writer in the *Saturday Review* in 1871 described the Arcade "at late afternoon, when the garish gas casts appropriate light on tawdry surroundings" and the "heavy-chignoned brief-skirted" women paraded themselves, as the "Western counterpart of an Eastern slave-market". The purchasers at this "human

23

Tattersalls" were predominantly military men—"Brummagen Lovelaces" and "half-pay veterans", anxious to learn about life:

They certainly get such lessons ... as may be obtained by a study of the photographs of the celebrities of the demi-monde and the stage, or by *viva voce* instructions of some emancipated maid-servant.

Besides these students, there were occasional innocents, straying ignorantly "on contaminated ground":

You meet a respectable country parson, all eyes and boots, creaking out of step between his wife and daughter ... of a sudden general start and shudder. A print in a shop half-way down has turned the hearty rector into a scandal-struck figure of stone.

Many shops in the Arcade sold these petrifying prints, as well as photographs of distinguished harlots, actresses, and later, "professional beauties".

The Rape of Regent Street: Among the fears and confusions of 1848, with half the thrones of Europe toppling, and "every gentleman in London" sworn as a special constable to await the Chartist revolution—over 150,000 gentlemen qualified, including Gladstone and the exiled Louis Napoleon—the removal of 270 iron Doric columns from Regent Street may not have seemed of much importance. Yet the destruction of Nash's splendid Colonnades was as much a symbol of the forces that were reshaping England as the 1,975,486 signatures, many of them spurious, on Feargus O'Connor's giant petition. For it commemorated, in a negative way, the triumph of ugly middle-class utilitarianism, the extinction of aristocratic good taste.

Nash's masterpiece of street architecture, described by a contemporary as "the finest covered promenade in the world" had been erected less than thirty-five years; yet only sixteen years after the passing of the Reform Bill, pinchpenny shop-keepers had sufficient power to lay waste London's most beautiful street.   Nash, under the patronage of the Prince Regent, had built his Quadrant to give fashionable London a pleasant place to shop and loiter in.   But because the prostitutes of the West End also enjoyed the shelter of its balustraded roof, the Regent Street shopkeepers had it demolished.   Whether they were moved by a fear of shrinking sales, and depreciated property values, or whether, as seems more likely, they were simply indulging a passion to harry the harlot, is not easy to decide.

The Times, denouncing the "mercenary cupidity of a set of barbarians", invoked a picturesque curse upon their heads:

> May their ribands fade, may their papier-mâché tea-trays crack, may their cigars be transformed in the night into cabbage-leaves—if indeed, they be not so already—and may every crack, flaw and evil quality of their soiled and spurious wares stand revealed before the customer under the full sunshine which they have dared invite into their windows and shopfronts.

To the cry that the Colonnades at night were "the haunt of those unfortunate creatures with which the streets of London at night are unhappily thronged", *The Times* suggested that the nuisance had been overstated:

> From St. Paul's Cathedral up to Oxford Street, by the Strand ... the long thoroughfare is liable in any of its sections to the same reproach. .... We are much mistaken if the Quadrant shopkeepers will find themselves at all benefited in this respect by the change.

A reader signing himself *Pedestrian* intoned a hearty "Amen, say I," to the maledictions pronounced on the vandals, and then assailed the "shop-keeping Philistine", the "teabord seller and the riband-man", for their "raucous uncharitableness" to the whores:

> It is the curse, sir, of this nation to be beset with a myriad of canting hypocrites, with great pretensions to religion and

morality, but totally devoid of godliness and charity. Sir, I appeal to you, I appeal to every London pedestrian whether they have ever suffered any annoyance, in any way, from the helpless creatures here attacked? No—but this afforded your would-be-saint an occasion to exercise his persecuting spirit too favourable to be lost.

The columns were auctioned at the Café de Paris, Vine Street, and realized £7 5s. and £7 10s. each. *Punch* printed a woodcut showing how a "kind of movable colonnade of umbrellas" had replaced them, and foresaw fearful congestion in Burlington Arcade, "the only covered promenade . . . now left". But as *The Times* had expected, and to the continuing exasperation of the barbarians, vandals, hypocrites and Philistines, the prostitutes did not abandon Regent Street. For many years it remained, by day and by night, one of their most favoured trysting grounds. George Augustus Sala, writing in 1859, pointed out that "the stupid tradesmen, whose purblind, shop-till avarice" caused the columns to be removed, gained nothing by the change:

perambulating Regent Street at all hours of the day and night, as I do now frequently, I see no diminution in the number of moustached, or rouged, or naughty faces, whose prototypes were familiar to me, years agone, in the brilliant Quadrant.

Aldermen and Magdalens: The correspondent of *The Times* who defended the "helpless creatures" of the streets against the "canting hypocrites" of Nonconformity expressed a point of view not uncommon among his more civilized countrymen. While the godly prophets of the bethel were busy consigning their fallen sisters to the flames, other Englishmen, who had inherited some of the worldliness and urbanity of the eighteenth century, regarded them with a tolerance that often shaded into sympathy.

Thus, in 1844, the fathers of the Guildhall rejected a petition from the Ward of Castle Bayard, complaining that the neighbourhood of St. Paul's Churchyard was greatly disturbed by the conduct of the women of the town at night, and Alderman Farebrother—surely a kinsman of the incredible Cheerybles?—was warmly applauded when he said: "These poor creatures must be somewhere; in Regent Street they are infinitely more numerous than they are in St. Paul's Churchyard: why, if acts of disorder are not proved against them, should they be punished with imprisonment or with the hard treatment of being brought before magistrates at all? I for one will not imprison a wretched woman merely because she is brought before me by a policeman."

This belief that a whore should be allowed to ply for hire without interference, so long as she herself does not interfere overmuch with her fellow-citizens, has remained the core of the British attitude towards prostitution, though to-day the Puritanical conscience is sedated by making her life as uncomfortable as possible. Thus a regiment of prostitutes patrolling an unsympathetic pavement is preferred to half a dozen relaxing between their labours in a comfortable brothel.

III. STATISTICS DON'T BLEED

"Old England's Winding Sheet": From St. Paul's Churchyard to Portland Place, from Piccadilly to the City Road, from Ratcliff Highway to the Elephant and Castle, and in towns all over Great Britain, the harlot's cry grew louder and louder through the troubled 'thirties and the hungry 'forties. It was a period of black distress, when agricultural labourers and factory workers were crushed alike in the cogs of social convulsion. Some sought consolation in the bethel. Others, like the Leicester stockinger who cried out at a religious meeting: "Talk to us no more about thy Goddle Mighty, there isn't one!" found it in the bottle or the bed. Gin was cheap, and so were girls.

Though Queen Victoria, to the end of her life, knew almost nothing of the working-class and its sufferings, some rumblings of the wide despair reached Buckingham Palace, where the Prince Consort showed a scholarly interest in the problem of poverty. When a professor of geology gave a lecture on how to serve potatoes economically, the Prince had extracts from the speech printed and distributed; most of the recipients, no doubt, would have preferred a potato to a pamphlet—"but then", as *Punch* commented, "Princes are such wags!" Following the royal example, the Duke of Norfolk advised the poor to allay their hunger with water and curry powder.

The great chef Alexis Soyer, he who had "found the Reform Club *aux gigot* and left it *aux béchamel*", also rose to the occasion. He composed his *Charitable Cookery: or The Poor Man's Regenerator:* which told philanthropists how they could make two gallons of soup for sixpence—including one pennyworth of meat—and warned the well-meaning against putting spices in food designed for the poor, for these only "flattered the appetite" and stimulated it.

There was something waggish, too, about the speech given by Lord John Russell at a City dinner in 1847:

> While the labouring classes and the poorer orders of society have the greatest difficulty in providing for the daily subsistence of themselves and their families, it is the duty, I say, of every master of a household to do what in him lies that that calamity shall not be aggravated by his own waste.

This exhortation was received with cheers which were multiplied when Lord Russell announced that "the highest head of a household in this kingdom—Her Majesty the Queen—has directed that in her own household the utmost economy should be used in the consumption of every article of food".

A London paper published the menu of the dinner which had preceded the Prime Minister's plea for austerity:

MENU

Turtle and iced punch.

Salmon, turbot, fried fish, etc.

Side-board—Petits Patés.

Chickens, capons, turkey poults, larded; hams and tongues, ornamented; ribs lamb, raised ornamented pies, lobster salads, prawns, Chantilly biscuits, ornamented trifles, noyeau and maraschino jellies, pine, strawberry and Italian creams; Genevoise pastry, Swiss and Venice meringues, Chantilly tartlets, creamed tarts, Nesselrode puddings, plovers' eggs, etc.

Remove.—Haunch mutton, chine mutton, sirloin beef, currant jelly, etc.: ducklings, goslings, leverets, turkey poults, pea fowl.

Dessert.—Hothouse grapes, apples, strawberries, oranges, pears, dried fruits, Savoy and almond cakes, mixed cakes, brandy cherries, preserved ginger.

Ices.—Fine, raspberry, strawberry, orange, millefruit, etc.

The Arithmetic of Sin: "This," said Disraeli in 1857, "I believe to be the age of statistical imposture." Mr. Gradgrind was not the only mid-Victorian who was obsessed by facts. In the ugliest days of devil-take-the-hindmost industrialism, when opium was the religion of many of the people—it was retailed by hucksters in the factory towns for a halfpenny a packet— statistics were often the opium of the upper classes. As Koestler has reminded us in our own time, statistics don't bleed; and the incalculable reams of paper which the Victorians covered with figures about pauperism, infanticide, prostitution, crime, insanity and sweating, helped to curtain them from less tidy figures starving in the fetor of the slums. (Sometimes, of course, even the printed page offended; when a Children's Employment Commission in the 'forties published pictures of Yorkshire "hurriers"—mine girls from seven to twenty-one who worked naked to the waist alongside men who were often quite naked—

Lord Londonderry complained that the pictures were offensive, "calculated to inflame the passions", and made him quite sick.)

Underlying this hunger for facts was the vague belief that if you had enough of them, it would be possible, some day, to shuffle them, somehow, into the pattern of a shining new society. Mr. Buckle had almost promised this when he wrote in 1857 that within a hundred years or so "the undeviating regularity of the moral world" would be as well established as that of the material world. So the pursuit of facts went on, tirelessly. By the 'sixties, the statistician could foretell exactly how many Englishmen would forget to address their letters in the following year, just as he could tell you that a London horse deposited each day 38 lb. 2 oz. of excrement and 3 lb. 7 oz. of urine, or that one in every thirty-five persons admitted to the Asylums for the Houseless Poor was a wadding-maker. When this fever for figures was at its height, Elizabeth Browning made her social reformer Romney Leigh say:

> There's too much abstract willing, purposing
> In this poor world. We talk by aggregates,
> And think by systems, and being used to face
> Our evils in statistics, are inclined
> To cap them with unreal remedies. . . .

Unfortunately, but understandably because of its complexities, the evil of prostitution was not faced very effectively by Victorian statisticians. From time to time amateur sociologists attempted a tally, but as the *Westminster Review* said in 1850, "Little is known with certainty, and the estimates, even among those likely to be best informed, vary enormously." In 1793, a magistrate named Colquhoun had estimated that there were 50,000 prostitutes in London, its population then being between 700,000 and 800,000. In 1834, another magistrate put the figure at 70,000. A few years later Lord Gage told a meeting of the Society for the Suppression of Juvenile Prostitution that "exclusive of the City", London had 1,000 brothels and about

100,000 prostitutes. In 1857—the year when Disraeli spoke of statistical imposture—the *Lancet* said that one house in every sixty in London was a brothel, and one female in every sixteen —of all ages—a whore. On this basis, there would have been over 6,000 brothels in London and about 80,000 prostitutes.

This latter figure seems to have been widely accepted; it recurs frequently in discussions of prostitution towards the end of the 'fifties. In *Aurora Leigh*, written in 1856, Romney says that society, "that Phalarian bull"

> . . . *slurs our cruel streets from end to end*
> *With eighty thousand women in one smile,*
> *Who only smile at night beneath the gas.*

And Mr. Mayhew, writing in 1861, said the number of prostitutes in London was "assumed to be about 80,000, probably more". The *Edinburgh Medical Review* in 1859 said that different authorities varied in their guessing from 80,000 to 8,000; it advised the student not to worry about statistics but to walk down certain streets of London, Glasgow or Edinburgh at night:

> his eyes and ears will tell him at once what a multitudinous amazonian army the devil keeps in constant field service. . . . The stones seem alive with lust. . . .

Two years before this, *Tait's Edinburgh Review* had nominated Princes Street, Edinburgh, and Sackville Street, Dublin, as rivals in iniquity to the Haymarket or Regent Street, and published figures of prostitution in other parts of Great Britain in 1840, when Liverpool had 2,000 women in brothels; Glasgow, 1,800; Manchester, 1,500; Leeds, 700; Hull, 300; and Paisley, 250.

Without giving any reason for its scepticism, the *Saturday Review* said in 1860 that it was "certainly not going to trust the very loose and extemporaneous statistics . . . which assure us that there are 360,000 women who live by sin as a trade, of whom 65,000 are to be found in London". As there was no registration of brothels or prostitutes, and no possibility of distinguishing between women who "lived by sin as a trade" and those who prostituted themselves to bring their wages up to the minimum necessary for survival, statistics are necessarily vague. But some unambiguous figures are available in police reports of the arrests of "disorderly" prostitutes between 1850 and 1860. In these ten years, 41,954 were taken into custody in London, an average of nearly 4,200 a year. It is important to remember that these women were not arrested because they were prostitutes, but because they were disorderly, which, as Mr. Mayhew points out, usually means drunkenness or violent behaviour in the streets, and these prostitutes, he says, would represent "the very dregs, the lowest, the most unthinking and vilest of their class", for example, the sailors' whores of Whitechapel or Wapping:

> In the Haymarket there is not much drunkenness and the police are seldom interfered with. If a man, with whom a woman is walking, is drunk, and makes an assault upon the police, the woman will content herself with the innocent, and comparatively harmless amusement of knocking off the policeman's hat, afterwards propelling it gracefully with her foot along the pavement. This pastime is of frequent occurrence in nocturnal street rows, and always succeeds in infusing a little comic element into the affray.

No Kinsey of the day made any attempt to estimate the total turnover in these Smithfields of sin; the equation had too many unknowns. But we can base a rough guess on figures published by Seebohm Rowntree and G. R. Lavers in their study of contemporary *English Life and Leisure*. They estimated that in 1951 there were 10,000 prostitutes in London (population: 8,346,000) who between them had "upwards of 250,000 customers a week".

Lest it be thought that we exaggerate we quote a statement made by a Chief Inspector of the Metropolitan Police. When searching a prostitute's room . . . he found a box containing thirty-seven gross of rubber contraceptives. The woman explained . . . she used them at the rate of a gross a week.

Accepting the more moderate Rowntree-Lavers index of twenty-five customers per prostitute per week, we reach the rather surprising conclusion that the hosts of whoredom in mid-Victorian London received 2,000,000 clients each week— when the male population of London, of all ages, was about 1,300,000.

The Bacchanalian Bankrupt of Birmingham: "The extent to which the frequentation of brothels is carried out among all classes and professions, and even among the married of both sexes, is little suspected by the public at large," said the *Westminster Review* in 1850. "On this topic some frightful disclosures have, from time to time, had to be hushed up."

One of these hushed-up disclosures concerned a bankrupt in Birmingham who had methodically entered the expenses of a rather liberal sex life on his schedule. He stated that he was a constant visitor at brothels, in one of which, in one night, he spent "the enormous sum" of £40 for champagne alone; among other entries in his books there appeared the sum of £2,000 a year for a kept mistress. His solicitor told the court that if his client's examination were pursued "parties now living in happiness with their families may be brought before this court . . . and disclosures made which must inevitably ruin their domestic peace. Some men in this town, respectable in their stations, and holding important positions, must have their names brought before the world as visitors of a brothel."

An equally sombre picture of London life was presented by a writer in the *Lancet:*

The typical paterfamilias, living in a grand house near the Park, sees his son allured with debauchery, dares not walk with his daughters through the streets after nightfall, and is disturbed from his night slumbers by the drunken scenes and foul oaths of prostitutes reeling home with daylight. . . .

Nakedness in Norton Street: During the 'fifties, London began to show some organized interest in what the *Saturday Review* described as "the Cyprian patrol which occupies our streets in force every night". The Haymarket remained the base of these guerillas—it was here that Mr. J. Balfour, a parliamentary messenger and temperance worker, in 1853, saw females smoking cigars—but the solicitation in Coventry Street, Regent Street, and Piccadilly was equally intense, and the clubmen of St. James's Street and Pall Mall, as they stepped from the portico of Boodles or the Athenaeum, were often accosted by flamboyant women who addressed them as "Charlie" and asked "Are you good-natured, dear?"—the quaint inquiry which was the accepted greeting of the mid-Victorian prostitute.

The brothel-keepers, too, were extending their operations. In Marylebone, said a reporter in 1857, "common brothels are as plentiful as blackberries", and "scenes of debauchery and indecency daily and nightly" made infamous "that ugly tract of country bounded by Fitzroy Square, Oxford Street, the Portland Road, and the New Road". Portland Street, said the Rector of Trinity Church, Marylebone, once "an aristocratic place of residence" was "notorious as the favoured walk of harlots" and whole streets in his parish were "abandoned to the reign of profligacy". Of all these abandoned streets, Norton Street was pre-eminent; 80 per cent. of its houses were occupied by whores who:

> were in the habit of appearing naked at the windows, and lounging on the sills to attract the attention of the passer-by. At other times, the same wretched creatures would rush into the streets with only one undergarment on; and it was a common occurrence for them to run out and drag men in as they were passing.

Similar disturbing sights were to be seen in many other parts of London: "They may be witnessed every day and every hour in Wych Street, at the cigar-shops, where gin-bloated unfortunates ply for hire at the doors." The women of Wych

Street were still standing in the doorways "in an undress costume, lascivious and meretricious", at almost all hours of the day, when Mr. Mayhew made his report on harlotry a few years later; and just around the corner, in the Strand, "any afternoon or evening", was "a sight not visible in the chief thoroughfares of any other capital in Europe". Mr. J. Ewing Ritchie describes it in his *Night Life of London*, published in 1858:

> girls whose profession is but too evident from their appearance stopping every man they meet. . . . These girls . . . are dressed in finery hired for the purpose and following them, as a hawk its prey, you perceive at a respectful distance, old hags whose business it is to see these girls do not escape with their fine dresses.

Mr. Balfour told a Select Committee on Public Houses in 1854 that the most disreputable place he knew "as far as females are concerned" was the Eagle Tavern in the City Road, but he had visited a public house called "The Shades", "now extinct", under the arches of the Adelphi, where indescribable scenes were enacted, and in which all the customers, including himself, were "invited to retire with women if they pleased".

Mr. Balfour, of course, visited these places at his own peril; but not even a man of the cloth was immune from the solicitations of the streets. The Rev. T. Beamers complained in 1858 that he had been accosted in French at 2 and 3 o'clock in the afternoon in the vicinity of Queen Street and Sherard Street by foreign women who placed their arms in his.

A Merry Tale from Mr. Mayhew—"A story is told," says Mr. Mayhew, "of a celebrated woman who kept a house of ill-fame in the neighbourhood of May Fair."

> The several inmates of her establishment were dilatory on one occasion and she gave vent to her anger and disappointment by exclaiming: "Twelve o'clock striking, the house full of noblemen, and not a——girl painted yet!"

Mr. Mayhew assures us that he introduces this anecdote merely to show that the best brothels in London, "such as Mrs. C—'s in Curzon Street", were frequented by men of wealth, but it is possible that he found it amusing as well as instructive. After all, he had been one of the founders of *Punch*. He also tells of a Mrs. J—, who having made a fortune by letting temporary accommodation to girls and their clients in a house in James Street, Haymarket, bought a house in Camberwell with the accumulated five-shilling pieces of the amorous, which "she had the questionable taste to call 'Dollar House'."

Solicitation by Her Majesty's Mails: Technically distinct from the brothel, and invested with greater refinement, was the Victorian "introducing house" where the pleasant ceremony of introducing wealthy amateurs to willing girls was carried out with dignity and delicacy. "Introducing houses", says Mr. Mayhew, "are extremely lucrative":

To show how the matter is accomplished let us suppose an introducing house of notoriety and good report in its way, somewhere in the neighbourhood of St. George's Road, Pimlico, a district . . . prolific in loose women. A well-known professional man, a wealthy merchant, an M.P., or a rich landed proprietor, calls upon the lady of the house, orders some champagne, and enters into conversation about indifferent matters, until he is able delicately to broach the object he has in view. He explains that he wishes to meet with a quiet lady whose secrecy he can rely upon, and whom he can trust in every possible way. He would like her, we will imagine, to be vicacious, witty and gay.

The lady of the house listens complacently and replies that she knows someone who exactly answers the description the amorous M.P. has given, and says that she will send a message to her at once . . . if she is out, an appointment will be made . . . a messenger is despatched to the lady who in all probability does not reside at any great distance; perhaps in Stanley Street, or Winchester Street, which streets are contiguous to St. George's Road and inhabited by beauty that ridicules decorum. . . . Some more champagne is consumed, every bottle of which costs the consumer 15s., making a profit to the vendor of at least 70 per cent. When the lady arrives, the introduction takes place, and the matter is finally arranged. . . . The woman so introduced generally gives half the money she obtains from the man to the keeper of the house.

Dr. Acton describes an additional service offered by some introducing houses: "The leading persons in this line of business who keep up regular relations with men of fashion make known to their clients their novel and attractives wares, one might almost say, by circular. . . . A. finds a note at his club, telling him that a charming arrival, *de la plus grande fraicheur*, is on view at Madame de C's . . ."

The Rosewood and Varnish of Vice: Throughout the eighteen-fifties (the period, according to Mr. Michael Sadleir, of a great moral revolution in which "the fire of tolerated licence sputtered and died" and "irregularities", if they survived at all, "were driven underground"), the prostitute and the kept woman were constantly before the public, not only in the ubiquitous flesh, but in equally obtrusive discussions. They were the subject of three full-length sociological studies, of essays, leading-articles, letters, sermons, novels, poems and paintings. William Bell Scott's poem *Rosabell*, the story of a young woman's downfall, inspired Dante Gabriel Rossetti to paint his symbolic *Found*, a picture that haunted him for twenty-seven years and was never finished. In the end, says Mr. William Gaunt, it was "reminiscent of the *Vita Nuova* with a rustic Dante, encountering a bedraggled Beatrice in Central London". While Rossetti was struggling with his first conception of *Found*, Holman Hunt exhibited in the Royal Academy of 1854, *The Awakening Conscience*—later called *The Awakened Conscience*—a picture of peculiar interest because of the significance that critics saw in details of

37

the background. "It represents", wrote Archdeacon Farrar "the showily furnished room of a suburban house into which a man of wealth and rank has beguiled his victim":

The fatal gloss of all the new furniture, the fresh lustre of the rosewood piano, the youthfulness of the maiden, tell their own tale. The seducer has a sort of evil handsomeness, and is full of eager vivacity. . . . His right arm is lightly thrown around the girl's waist, and he has begun the song:

> *Oft in the stilly night*
> *When slumber's chain has bound me,*
> *Fond memory brings the light*
> *Of other days around me.*

But the words have touched, have startled the slumbering conscience of the sinning woman. She has turned from him with open lips and dilated eyes, and the expression of anguish and horror is passing convulsively across her features as she recalls the parents and the pure home which she has abandoned for this evil and callous wretch.

The critic of the *Athenaeum*, who described this moving tableau as a picture "drawn from a very dark and repulsive side of modern life", was also impressed by the "wonderfully true" furnishings, "hard, varnishy and new, unconsecrated to the domesticities by long use", and Ruskin, in a letter to *The Times*, expounded the moral of this sinister glitter and polish:

There is not a single object in all that room—common, modern, vulgar . . . but it becomes tragical, if rightly read. That furniture so carefully painted, even to the last vein of the rosewood—is there nothing to be learnt from that terrible lustre of it, from its fatal newness; nothing there that has the old thoughts of home upon it, or that is ever to become a part of home?

Holman Hunt went to the shores of the Dead Sea to get faithful atmosphere for his picture of *The Scapegoat*, and no less daring, paid several visits to St. John's Wood to study the *mise en scène* of metropolitan sin. The accuracy of his observations is attested by all the critics, but it is difficult to-day for us to perceive this eloquent relation between furniture and fornication. How, one might ask, would the respectable Victorian married couple, setting up home with a virtuous rosewood piano, escape the suspicion of its fatal newness and fresh lustre?

"Poor Little Jenny, Good to Kiss": The Awakened Conscience and *Found* both belong to Victorian mythology, but Rossetti's poem *Jenny*, written mostly in 1858 though unpublished till 1870, has a warm flavour of living flesh. It is a monologue, addressed to a Haymarket whore who sleeps with her head on the poet's knee.

> *Lazy, laughing, languid Jenny*
> *Fond of a kiss and fond of a guinea*

is a very different whore from the shuddering shadows of Victorian fiction; and a generation nurtured on the lilt of "Elaine the fair, Elaine the lovable, Elaine the lily maid of Astolat" must have responded curiously to the frank sensuality of lines such as:

> *Why, Jenny, as I watch you there,—*
> *For all your wealth of loosened hair,*
> *Your silk ungirdled and unlac'd*
> *And warm sweets open to the waist*
> *All golden in the lamplight's gleam—*

Ruskin, who had approved whole-heartedly of *The Awakening Conscience*, did not approve of *Jenny* at all. He thought most people would be offended by the "mode of treatment". He thought the speaker of the poem "altogether a disorderly person", apparently because he leaves some gold coins in the sleeping whore's hair; and he would not accept "guinea" as a rhyme for "Jenny". But the beautiful and gifted Marie Spartali was one of many who openly admired the poem. It remains to-day, a clear cry of sexual emotion echoing from a muted age. Rossetti described it to his mother as "a perfectly truthful delineation of commonplace fact".

Trouble in the Strand: Chief Baron Nicholson, presiding over his bawdy Judge and Jury show in Maiden Lane, had a keen sense of topicality. In 1858, "in consequence of the excitement in the public mind upon the subject", he made the "social evil" the theme of a mock trial. The treatment was sufficiently realistic to offend members of the profession, one of whom, a vigorous crone called Hannah McCarthy, showed her displeasure by assaulting Mr. H. G. Brookes, an associate of the baron's, as he was sauntering up the Strand, where, as a follower of juvenile prostitutes, she earned her living.

"Entrance Fee": Under this heading, you may recall, Alexander Woolcott relates the charming legend of Cosette, the beautiful courtesan who charged 5,000 francs for a night's entertainment, and the amorous but poor cadets of Saint-Cyr who dreamed of her. So they held a sweepstake to which one thousand cadets each contributed five francs. The winner, after paying his respects to Cosette, and her fee, shyly tells the story of how the money was raised, and Cosette is so moved that she hands him back his five francs.

Superintendent James of the Leeds police told a Select Committee on Public Houses in 1854 of a similar sweepstake, but the setting was less elegant and the happy climax lacking. He described a beer-house where a number of boys from sixteen to eighteen assembled every evening after leaving the factories, with young girls of about the same ages:

> It came to my knowledge, from private sources, that twelve of them were in a habit of putting down a penny piece, and then throwing dice in a basin or milk-bowl, and the one who threw the highest number was the winner of the prize, and that prize was, that he select one of those girls, and take her up stairs for prostitution.

This practice went on for some time before the inspector was able to penetrate the publican's defences, and get sufficient evidence to convict him of harbouring prostitutes. With unconscious humour, one member of the Select Committee asked whether he had been charged with keeping a gaming-house.

West End Wolves: That the amorous buccaneer whom modern idiom terms a "wolf" was a familiar sight in mid-Victorian London, is clear from a correspondence in *The Times* during January, 1862. It began when "Paterfamilias from the Provinces" protested to the Editor against the "cowardly lasciviousness" of "ill-conditioned blackguards" in the guise of gentlemen who followed young ladies and dared to speak to them, with sinister intent. Two members of his own seraglio, down to enjoy the refinements of urban life, had been thus affronted, and "Paterfamilias" promised to discover the responsible wretch, and to give him in retribution "the sorest skin of bones in all London".

This letter drew from "Puella" a spirited defence of her metropolitan countrymen. She pointed out that she herself had frequented Oxford Street for eighteen months without having any embarrassing encounters, and suggested that if the young ladies of Pater's household were modestly dressed they, too, would not be pestered. But if they wore "red cloaks and porkpie hats with white feathers", they could not hope to escape the notice of a "few despicable idlers". To this, "Paterfamilias" replied indignantly that his ladies were not so adorned, but were dressed "in plain mourning, like all loyal people at the time" (the Prince Consort had died three weeks before). And he found an eloquent supporter in "A London Man", who gave more instances of this "national disgrace". As for "Puella", if she had really escaped molestation in Oxford Street, this circumstance would drive any man who knew London, to "an uncomplimentary inference", for no "good-looking girl or woman" was safe. "The cause of this gross stain upon our manners", "London Man" explained, "is that the experience some London young men have of a certain class of women is applied to all." The philosophy of these young men seems to have been identical with that of the footpath philogynists of to-day: "The conviction is hugged that impudence ever receives its reward, and that the rebuff is a harmless contingency." Nor did a sober garb guarantee immunity. "The shrewder Hetairae have discovered this speedily, and have learnt that the simplest toilette, and the most demure manner, are in these days, the surest bait to the lounger of the pavement, while the accompaniment of a respectable-looking female servant, or the loan of a well-dressed child, amply repays any expense attending them, and that even the assumed repulse of modesty will but add piquancy to the pursuit." (It is unfortunate that Mr. Mayhew, in his monumental study of the extraordinary occupations of the London poor, did not report on this practice of hiring-out well-dressed children as accessories to harlotry.)

The *Saturday Review* commented unsympathetically on the plight of "Paterfamilias'" daughters, which it regarded as the "natural consequence" of their ignorance of the "moral geography" of the West End. It appeared that they had innocently tripped down the "tabooed" side of Regent Street. "There is a perpetual complaint coming up from the respectabilities of both sexes of the unsolicited advances which lie in ambush for them between Pall Mall and the Regent's Park. Country virgins passing in maiden meditation fancy free, and middle-aged lawyers stumping up from the Court, suffer equally from proffers of affection which they have not the least desire to reciprocate." The problem would be solved if the interested parties, male and female, got together and left the others alone. On the question of dress, the *Saturday Review* disagreed with "A London Man". "If they will be seen in well-preserved coverts," it advised the affronted daughters, "it is for them to be careful that they do not look like game. . . . Let them dress thoroughly unbecomingly. Let them procure poke-bonnets, stint their skirts to a moderate circumference, and cultivate sad-looking underclothing."

The Sights of London: "A stranger on his coming to London," writes Mr. Mayhew, "after visiting the Crystal Palace, British Museum, St. James's Palace and Buckingham Palace, and other public buildings, seldom leaves the capital before he makes an evening visit to the Haymarket and Regent Street," where "the brilliant illumination of the shops, cafés, Turkish divans, assembly halls, and concert rooms, and the troops of elegantly dressed courtesans, rustling in silks and satins, and waving in laces," would impress him profoundly.

These thronging streets displayed samples from every stratum of the great London sex market, from "the first class, of kept women . . . supported by men of opulence and rank . . . to the bloated women who have become grey in prostitution . . . or invalid through venereal diseases". The majority in the Haymarket belonged to the "second class"; they were streetwalkers, but "better educated and more refined", often with respectable middle-class connections. Among them were a considerable number of French girls, and a few from Belgium and Germany:

> You see many of them walking along in black silk cloaks or light grey mantles—many with silk paletots and wide skirts, extended by an ample crinoline, looking almost like a pyramid, with the apex terminating at the black or white satin bonnet, trimmed with waving ribbons and gay flowers. Some are to be seen with their cheeks ruddy with rouge, and here and there are a few rosy with health.

Below these, in Mr. Mayhew's careful classification, were the "third class" whores, most from the "lower orders of society", servant-girls, daughters of labourers, and "some of a still lower class":

> Some of these girls are of a very tender age—from thirteen years and upwards. . . . Many of them are dressed in a light

43

cotton or merino gown, and ill-suited crinoline, with light grey or brown cloak, or mantle. Some with pork-pie hat, and waving feather—white, blue or red; others with a slouched straw hat. . . . Some have a look of artless innocence and ingenuousness, others very pert, callous and artful. . . . They prostitute themselves for a lower price, and haunt those disreputable coffee-shops in the neighbourhood of the Haymarket and Leicester Square where you may see the blinds drawn down, and the lights burning dimly within, with notices over the door that "beds are to be had within".

The fourth and lowest class, the worn-out prostitutes, cadged not only from the fashionable people in the streets, but from the superior prostitutes who would gladly pay sixpence to be free from their embarrassing company:

These faded and miserable creatures . . . sometimes retire for prostitution into dirty low courts near St. James's Street, Coventry Court, Long's Court, Earl's Court, and Cranbourne Passage, with shop boys, errand lads, petty thieves and labouring men, for a few paltry coppers.

"*The March of the Dead*": One stranger who visited London in the 'sixties was the French historian Hippolyte Taine. The "deplorable procession in the shade of the monumental streets" he found sickening:

I recall the alleys which ran into Oxford Street, stifling lanes, encrusted with human exhalations; troops of pale children nesting in the muddy stairs; the seats on London Bridge, where families, huddled together with drooping heads, shiver through the night; particularly the Haymarket and the Strand in the evening. Every hundred steps one jostles twenty harlots; some of them ask for a glass of gin: others say, "Sir, it is to pay my lodging." This is not debauchery which flaunts itself but destitution—and such destitution . . . it seems to be a march of the dead.

44

Observe the Cold Fowl: An Englishman's description of "that strip of pavement between the top of the Haymarket and the Regent's Circus"—now Piccadilly Circus—appeared in *Household Worlds* in 1857; it is one of the few references to the wickedness of London streets that Dickens permitted in his "gentle mouthpiece of reform". The writer was Albert Smith:

> By day, the greater part of the shops and houses betray the character of the locality.... Observe the stale drooping lobsters, the gaping oysters, the mummified cold fowl with the trapping of flabby parsley, and the pale fly-spotted cigars, and then look into the chemist's windows and see, by the open display, in which direction its chief trade tends.... It is always an offensive place to pass, even in the daytime; but at night it is absolutely hideous, with its sparring snobs and flashing satins, and sporting gents and painted cheeks, and brandy-sparking eyes, and bad tobacco and hoarse horse-laughs and loud indecency....

There might also be "a brass band forming a dam before the gin-shop, with tawdry bacchantes blundering about the pavement to its music". Smith, claiming an extensive Continental experience of cities, said he had never anywhere witnessed such open ruffianism and unrestrained profligacy.

"It is indeed a striking sight," said the *Saturday Review*, "one which no foreigner who wishes to study our national morality ... ought to overlook:

> The pavement is occupied in force by crowds of men and women, who saunter about in the blaze of gaslight which issues from the aggregation of gin-palaces and oyster-shops of which the street consists. They enjoy themselves, on the whole, after the manner of English people, *moult tristement*, occasionally dancing and shouting, but more generally simply lounging. Their conversation, it is needless to say, is frank and candid.... There is no room for any charitable self-delusion as to the character of this assemblage of men and

women or the nature of the deities in whose service they are engaged. Some intrusive respectability, too sleepy and anxious to get home to be eager for the service either of Silenus or Cytherea, may perhaps find his way into the street. But unless he is anxious for unsought caresses, under whose ambiguous importunity either lust or larceny may lurk, he will carefully avoid the footway and stick to the middle of the street. Sharp granite edges, or muddy pools, or the danger of being run over by a cab, are light risks compared to the certainty of being hustled, bonneted, and probably robbed by the half-tipsy, half-amorous sirens of the pavement."

That curious symbol of sin, the mummified cold fowl, was invoked again by Mr. Ewing Ritchie, in his description of the Haymarket about the same time:

We are standing in the very temple of vice—its ministers are all around us. Not one unholy appetite but can be gratified here; gamblers, blacklegs, prostitutes surround us on every side. Here law, and order, and decency are alike all violated. If it be in the prohibited hours, we can go into coffee-houses and get as much brandy as we like, which of course, is easily removed when the signal is made that the inspector is coming, and is again brought out when he is gone.

But let us knock at this door, the glare of gas indicates that there is something going on, though the cold fowl in the window and the cigar shop close by, scarcely inform us what. . . .

In a burst of prophecy, Mr. Ritchie sees "that girl in satin and rouge, in another hour . . . lying on the stone pavement with an unmeaning grin" and "that fine manly lad, out to see life," sleeping "where the mother now praying for him in tenderness little imagines". Overcome by this apocalyptic vision, he flees from "this moral dungeon" reflecting that in a few

46

hours the police will have retired, the debauchees have gone home to bed, the oyster-houses and gin-palaces will be deserted, the place will have a serious and quiet air, and bishops will ride past in their cushioned carriages to make speeches at meetings or the promotion of the Gospel in foreign parts.

The lords spiritual and temporal had been similarly rebuked by the *Lancet* a few years before: "Noble lords and bishops . . . weep over the depravities of the Feejee Islands . . . but they will then start with horror from the pollutions of Exeter Street." At the end of the 'sixties, the *Morning Post* was still making melancholy comparisons between the savagery of the Haymarket and the civilization of darkest Africa:

> Is there any capital in Europe where such undisguised profligacy is permitted? . . . Children of tender years are handed about for the most profligate purposes. . . . We permit these gross orgies to take place every night of our lives and on some of the morrows we attend meetings to subscribe for missionaries to distant climes for the civilization of savages! Bushmen at the Cape, the most untutored denizens of the remotest isles in the Indian Ocean, have far less real need of such aid than the habitual frequenters of that locality which has earned for itself the infamous sobriquet of "Hell Corner".

"For Love, Lust or Lucre": But if the bishops were indifferent to these abominations, the lesser clergy were not. In 1857 and 1858, the clergymen and vestrymen of St. James's Westminster, St. Martin's-in-the-Fields, and St. Marylebone met many times to seek, with the aid of the Home Secretary, Sir George Grey, "effective measures to put down the open exhibition of street prostitution . . . carried on with a disregard of public decency and to an extent tolerated in no other capital city of the civilized world". While all agreed on the extent and flagrancy of the evil, there were irreconcilable differences about how it could be cured. Mr. Taverner, of St. Marylebone, even dissented from

47

the remark made by the Rev. Chairman J. E. Kempe, rector of St. James's, that his parish was a Sodom and Gomorrah. On the contrary, said Mr. Taverner, the exhibitions on the streets were "the very means of preventing the crimes of the cities of the plain"; and he pointed out that driving prostitutes from one street to another, which was about the only practical suggestion that anyone had to offer, would not solve the problem. "The upper classes lavish such large sums upon those who minister to their illicit pleasures," he said, "that they can afford to pay excessive rents and to establish themselves in the most expensive neighbourhoods." What was wanted was a reformation beginning with the upper classes.

The Rev. T. Garnier observed that there were two extreme views to be avoided—one, that prostitution could be eradicated by legislation; the other, that the Government should license brothels and thus "take vice under its direct patronage and protection". This question of the recognition of whoring by some form of registration was the rock against which discussions of prostitution in England were ever to be shattered. The *Saturday Review*, which vociferously and indefatigably championed the Continental system of licensed houses, dismissed the argument that this was alien to the "English habit of mind" by recalling that

> this matter was very carefully attended to in darker ages than ours ... the regulations of the Southwark stews are the foundation of much of the present municipal legislation on the subject on the Continent.

Another advocate of registration was Dr. Acton, who spoke from experience gained as an externe of a female venereal hospital in Paris. But he realized that "the national love of liberty" was "anterior to law and logic".

> We may by no means deprive the female of the right to abandon herself privately for love, lust or lucre ... [or of]

48

her right to see and be seen in the streets with all well-conducted Christian women.

The Times entreated the clergymen and gentlemen not to hurt their chances of success by aiming at the unattainable:

> It is no business of theirs to hunt men and women who are bent on vicious indulgence from corner to corner. So long as they keep themselves from giving public offence and do not violate any law, they must be left to settle the matter, each man with his own conscience, and according to his own views of right and wrong.

The Rev. Garnier and his colleagues formed a society to carry on their mission of purification, without noticeable results, though it seems to have been fairly active in its field-work. Thus at the annual meeting in 1859, Mr. Garnier reported on the importation of whores from across the Channel, and described "a room with seats placed round it" where brothel-keepers attended auctions of these foreign girls. (A few years before a London rabbi had written to *The Times* about a reciprocal traffic in young girls between Liverpool and Hamburg. Hull was the port used by operators who exchanged batches of English girls of fifteen or sixteen for German girls of the same age.)

The Rev. Mr. Baptist Noel was active, too, in the early 'sixties, with his Midnight Meeting movement, a successor to the London-by-Moonlight Mission that had been founded in 1847 by Lieutenant Blackmore, R.N. Their technique was to hold street meetings in the centres of prostitution and distribute tracts and invitations to a "Morality tea", at which repentance was preached against a background of hymns, cakes and tea-cups. After holding twenty meetings, preaching the gospel to 4,000 girls and circulating 23,000 scripture cards, tracts, and sermons, the Mission was able to report that upwards of thirty girls had given evidence of a change of heart.

Miss Janet Dunbar, in a study of *The Early Victorian Woman*, quotes this piece from a woman's journal of the 'forties:

Apropos of the midnight meeting of the erring sisterhood of St. James's Restaurant, an Englishwoman makes this proposal: "Might I venture to suggest that a meeting be called of the other sex, that they might be lectured and prayed with about the awful sin and misery that lie at their door. I will bear my share of the necessary tea and toast. When the demand ceases the supply will soon be stopped."

What a Young Girl Used to Know: In the Victorian legend, the young middle-class girl of these times, her eyes focused dewily on her *potichomanie* or her drawn-thread work, her lips shyly whispering the words of *I'd Be a Butterfly, Born in a Bower,* knew nothing of the sinfulness of so many of her sisters —and, as a necessary corollary, brothers. But the evidence suggests that she was far more aware of prostitutes and of kept women than is the girl of to-day. Even if she were screened by vigilant parents from all the discussion of the "social evil" that appeared in newspapers and periodicals, she could scarcely escape the candid spectacle of the streets: "The daughters of Dives," said the *Lancet* in 1857, "knowing all about the plot of the *Traviata,* visit the Opera to witness the apotheosis of a consumptive prostitute, and drive home through the Gehenna fair nightly held in the Haymarket—yet we are expected to credit that they lay their heads upon their pillows without considering what it all means." (Bertrand Russell's mother, Kate Stanley, who was the daughter of a lord, was taken to *Traviata* when she was sixteen, and liked it "a great deal better than the Somnambula".)

About the same time, Miss Dinah Mulock, the future Mrs. Craik of *John Halifax, Gentleman,* in a book addressed to the "ordinary middle-rank of unmarried females", wrote frankly of "that deplorable phase of womanhood which, in country cottages as in city streets, in books, newspapers and daily talk, meets us so continually that no young girl can long be kept ignorant of it". To avoid mention of it, she said, was to give a "one-sided and garbled view of life". And she counselled her readers to a tolerance worthy of Whitman:

> We have not to construct human nature afresh, but to take it as we find it and make the best of it. . . . We have no right, not even the most sensitive of us women . . . to treat as impure what God has not made impure or to shrink with sanctimonious ultra-delicacy from the bald mention of things which . . . we must know to exist.

Miss Mulock also queried the popular theory, sown and nourished by the witch-doctors of Dissent, that when a woman lost her "honour" she lost everything, and became an abject, tormented dweller in the Pit.

Romans VI, 23: Though the Victorians were fond of the text "The wages of sin is death", few could have believed in it. A statistically-minded age must have noted that the wages of industry seldom conduced to long life, especially if one were industriously employed in say, a slop-shop or a bleaching factory. (In 1856 the House of Commons rejected a Bill to regulate the hours of labour in bleaching factories where young girls worked from eighteen to twenty hours a day in a temperature between 90 and 130 degrees, and four years later Brougham told the House of Lords that infants of seven and eight years old were working in these factories, sometimes for four nights without sleep.) On the other hand, there was conspicuous evidence that sin in its most toxic form, that is, sexual anarchy, was often rewarded with silk and jewels, a secluded villa, a comfortable annuity, or even a social marriage.

V. LIBERTY, NOT LICENCES

Army of Occupation: The contemplation of this continuing interest in the prostitute led the *Saturday Review* to repeat its campaign for some form of control. "No set of people have enjoyed so large a share of public attention as the woman whom we hesitate to bring under the regulations of the police for fear of recognizing their existence," it wrote, early in 1862:

> They have been the subject of angry complaint, philanthropic tenderness, and cynical comment, until they have a right to look upon themselves as one of the most interesting classes in English Society. The fast man makes love to them; the slow man discusses them; the fashionable young lady copies their dress; the Evangelical clergyman gives them tea, toast, and touching talk at midnight; and the devout young woman gives herself up to the task of tending them in some lovely and sequestered retreat . . . while they are resting between the acts of their exhausting lives. But we still flatter ourselves that our national morality is benefited by the fact that we recognize them only in the newspapers and are silent about them in the statute-books. Meanwhile, under cover of our decorous ignorance, they have seized upon the West End like an army of occupation. . . . The principal streets are in their hands. The pavement of the Haymarket they rule with a sway no prudent passenger will care to challenge after the sun has fallen. Portland Place is occupied by a French detachment of voluble habits, and by no means backward manners; and in Regent Street they have come to a compromise with respectability, mixing freely on both sides, but claiming that one . . . [the sunny side] as exclusively their own. . . . Men are generally safe till after dark; but female intruders . . . are liable to insult, or at least, unflattering observation, at any hour of the day.

A Statute for Stew-Holders: There had been licensed brothels in London at least as far back as the reign of Henry II. Regulations for controlling them were placed in the statute-book in 1161. Stew-holders—brothel-keepers—were forbidden to charge more than fourteen pence a week for a woman's board, to open their doors upon holy days, or to receive any woman of religion, or any man's wife. Two clauses in the Act gave the customer some protection, in purse and person:

> No single woman to take money to lye with any man, except she lye with him all night, till the morrow.
> No stew-holder to keep any woman, that has the perilous infirmity of burning; nor to sell bread, ale, flesh, fish, wood, coal or any victuals.

The Southwark brothels were controlled by the Bishop of Winchester, and displayed their names on signboards, like taverns—"The Boar's Head", "The Bell", "The Cardinal's Hat". In the time of Richard II, the stewhouses belonged to William Walworth, Mayor of London, and were farmed by whores imported from Flanders. But this official recognition was ended by Henry VIII, who a year before his death, in a spasm of Puritanism induced perhaps by his rampageous poxes, had them suppressed with an order proclaimed by sound of trumpet. The suppression was no more successful than many other attempts to put down prostitution. "But tho' the Sin was no longer allowed in this Place, yet the same Sin still remained," says John Stow. The Rev. Father Latimer, "in his blunt but honest way of preaching", told Edward VI: "I hear say, there is such whoredom in England as never was seen the like. . . . There is more open whoredom, more stued whoredom, than ever was before."

The Blessings of Syphilis: It was over 300 years before another attempt was made to control prostitution in England. Early in the 'sixties, The British Army Medical Department recommended the introduction of the Continental system by which prostitutes were licensed, inspected and, if necessary, forced to have medical treatment. This system had been operating in France since the beginning of the nineteenth century. In 1864, the British Government passed a temporary Act "for the prevention of contagious diseases in certain naval and military stations". On a declaration, not necessarily an oath, that a woman who was a common prostitute was suffering from a contagious disease, she had to submit to examination, and might be detained three months in hospital. This Act, applying to eleven garrison towns, was extended in 1869 to seventeen towns, in which 2,121 prostitutes were registered. A committee of medical men recommended that it be further extended to any locality in which the inhabitants applied for it, providing there was sufficient hospital accommodation, moral and religious instruction and police, to carry out its provisions. The opposition to this suggestion, and to the existing Acts, produced one of the most remarkable campaigns of the century, led by one of its most remarkable women, Josephine Butler. Among her first supporters were Florence Nightingale, who denounced the licensing system as disgusting and unworkable, and Harriet Martineau. When a doctor proposed attaching a number of whores, under religious instruction, of course, to each regiment, Miss Nightingale observed that "prostitutes who survive five years of this life should have good service pensions".

The Ladies' National Association for the repeal of the Acts waved a fierce torch of protest throughout the kingdom. "In Edinburgh", said the *Saturday Review* in 1870, "the feminine excitement about the Contagious Diseases Act is extreme. Old maids ask if it does not mean the cattle plague."

Miss Butler and her colleagues argued that the law was one-sided and punished one sex, leaving unpunished the sex which was the main cause of prostitution; to which the *Saturday Review* retorted that the Acts were not punitive at all:

They do not profess to punish the female fornicant for her sin but to cure her. . . . We do not punish a sewer when we clean it, nor do we punish a diseased prostitute when we seclude and heal her. You cannot catch the men, but you can catch the women; *quae corpore suo quaestum facti.* . . . We should be extremely glad to seclude infected persons of either sex, if we knew how.

The Ladies' National Association also deplored the fact that the State, by its inspection of prostitutes, made the path of evil easier for England's sons and provided conveniences for the practice of sin. "If this means anything at all," said the *Saturday Review*, "it means that syphilis, as a moral restraint, is a blessing, and therefore ought to be encouraged." This pious view was, in fact, held by many who opposed the Acts, including some medical men. "Far from considering syphilis as an evil," said Mr. Solly, one of the Council of the Royal College of Surgeons, "I regard it on the contrary as a blessing, and believe that it is inflicted by the Almighty to act as a restraint upon the indulgence of evil passions."

But for the most part doctors supported the inspection system. In 1873, 2,300 declared themselves in favour of continuing it; it was infatuation and hypocrisy, they argued, for the Government to shut its eyes to what went on, and to fail in its duty to protect the health of the armed forces. Against them were ranged 1,600 clergymen who objected to the Government conniving at sin, stripping vice of its consequences, and accepting the idea that immorality was necessary.

The clergymen won, though public opinion was curiously divided. When Miss Butler was campaigning in Colchester in 1870, there was such intense hostility to her interference that she was in danger of mob violence, and hotel-keepers refused her accommodation because they were afraid the house would be burnt down if she were in it. But when Parliament was debating the repeal of the Acts in 1883, a crowd of women not far from the House spent the night on their knees in the street— "ragged and miserable women from the slums of Westminster . . . side by side . . . with ladies of high rank in their splendid dresses,"—praying for repeal.

The Royal Assent to the Repeal Bill was not given till 1886, but seventeen years of strenuous crusading had not abated Miss Butler's fervour. She continued to fight, unceasingly and uncompromisingly, till the end of her life, thirteen years later, for the abolition of regulated prostitution throughout the world. By this time, her former ally, Florence Nightingale, had changed sides. Faced with alarming figures of the spread of venereal disease, Miss Nightingale now supported some system of inspection and control.

VI. HUNGER AND WHOREDOM

Silk, Stuff and Nonsense: These symposia on the sinfulness of the streets went on and on, but of all the theologians and vestrymen who contributed to them, only one, according to the reports, detected some association between hunger and whoring. He was Mr. Watkins, of Chelsea, who thought that the slop-making system was one cause of vice, since young women were unable to maintain themselves upon the pittance they earned from their needles.

Tom Hood sang *The Song of the Shirt* in 1844, but the slop-system of sublet and re-sublet contracts for needlework was one of the most tenacious evils of Victorian individualism. In 1850, there were 11,000 girls in London under twenty trying to live as sempstresses; by working seven days a week from 5 o'clock in the morning till midnight, sewing and button-holing full-fronted shirts, they could earn 1s. 3½d. In 1864, Mrs. Gladstone wrote to *The Times* of needlewomen who receive 7d. a gross for stitching collar-bands; after paying for their own cotton, they made 2¾d. a day. There were then about 287,000 slop-workers, dressmakers and milliners in England, most of them wretchedly paid. At the end of the century, when Victorianism had flowered into triumphant, swaggering Imperialism, London was still a vast sink of sweated female labour.

Historians, bemused by the manifest prosperity of the Victorian middle-class, are inclined to overlook the continuing mass poverty behind the ornate façade of material progress. "The mid-Victorian age smiles like a flowery meadow between the discontent and prodigality of the indignant 'forties and the 'eighties . . ." says Mr. Michael Sadleir prettily. The small minority of English people who enjoyed the fragrance of this meadow were similarly myopic: "The increase of the wealth of England is so enormous," said the *Saturday Review* in 1858, "that it is as easy for a large number of families to buy silk dresses now, as it was for them to buy stuff dresses thirty years ago." But this increase went to the man who sold the silk and the man who sold the dress and perhaps to the man who contracted to have the dress made; the sempstress who made it still worked for a few wretched pennies.

Despite the promise of the millenium that the Crystal Palace held in its glittering walls, the standard of living of the English working-class actually declined between 1851 and 1865, and by 1870 it was only 10 per cent. higher than it had been in 1850. It had been predicted in that year that if the foreign trade of the United Kingdom were to rise by 50 per cent. pauperism would disappear. In 1864, Mr. Gladstone told the House of Commons that the country's foreign trade, imports and exports together, totalled £444,855,915, about 2½ times the figure of 1850 but there were 840,000 registered paupers in the kingdom—and this did not include people who were receiving private charity but only those driven "by the last necessity to the poor-house". "What is human life," asked Mr. Gladstone, "but in the great majority of cases, a struggle for existence?" And what the poor-house meant in 1865, twenty-eight years after the publication of *Oliver Twist,* is shown by the answer of an eighteen-year-old boy who was asked why he smashed windows in the "Chelsea Workus";

> Because, please, they gives us four pounds of oakum to pick in the house in the day and it scrubs our fingers and we can't do it, and in the prison we only get two pounds and far better vittles.

In 1868, the number of registered paupers had reached a

million, and even the society paper *Vanity Fair* thought it a "monstrous state of things".

> ... that the people of this rich England, who lay the whole world under contribution for the flower of its products, and who are a byword among the nations for plethoric wealth ... should yet have to confess the shameful fact that one in thirty of them has not wherewith to support bare existence.

When Alfred Russel Wallace wrote in 1898 of *The Wonderful Century*, he found that one of its most prominent features had been "the enormous and continuous growth of wealth, without any corresponding increase in the well-being of *the whole people*". London then had about 1,300,000 people below the "margin of poverty"—the absolute minimum required for the necessaries of life. Mr. Sadleir's flowery meadow had become an even more tenuous mirage.

VII. UNFORTUNATE BUT UNREPENTANT

"Eve's Family": Perhaps the most valuable result of all this agitation was a series of letters published in *The Times* in 1858, in which the viewpoint of the prostitute was presented. The first, headed *The Delicate Question*, was written by a street-walker who, alarmed at the possibility of police interference, pleaded that the lower-class prostitute be left alone; the professional courtesans, she said, were "the pitfalls for the males of good family", not the women of her own class, with whom the reformers seemed to be solely concerned; these women, she reminded the readers of *The Times*, were of "Eve's family, as your mother was, and as your wife and daughter are—aye, and as even your Queen is":

> Why begin with the most abject and unprotected? ... Why should the virtuous indignation of the present day be all expended on ... the poor creature without a friend, while

her more fortunate sister, whom I will call harlot, stares impudently out from her luxurious brougham?

The writer of this letter, which occupied over a column of small type, said she had been a governess in a highly respectable family but could not give her name, "having so disgraced it", nor her address, as it was "disreputable". She signed herself *One More Unfortunate*. In a second equally long letter she asked the gentlemen who "seduce, keep, abandon, and then patronize us indiscriminately" to "be careful how you legislate for the suppression of one portion of your victims".

A benevolent reader signed *Amicus*, who later revealed himself as Mr. John La Touche, Great Cumberland Street, Hyde Park, offered his help, and received "the most heartrending tales of misery rendered the more harrowing by the fact that the narrators were once in luxury and affluence". But the most remarkable reply came from another harlot who called herself *Another Unfortunate*, and who bitterly assailed the first unfortunate not only for her class hostility but also for her shame at her profession. *Another Unfortunate* proudly claimed to be one of the "real prostitutes of the true natural growth of society" and refused to be judged by the standards of "a mere chance intruder in our ranks". Her letter ran to more than 3,500 words. The autobiographical part is worth quoting at length:

My father's most profitable occupation was brickmaking. . . . My mother worked with him in the brickfield, and so did I and a progeny of brothers and sisters; for, somehow, or other, although my parents occupied a very unimportant space in the world, it pleased God to make them fruitful. We all slept in the same room. There were few privacies for family secrets in our house. Father and mother both loved drink. In the household expenses, had accounts been kept, gin and beer would have been the heaviest items. We, the children, were indulged occasionally with a drop, but my honoured parents reserved to themselves the exclusive privilege of getting drunk. . . . I give you a chapter of the history of common life which may be stereotyped as the history of generation upon generation.

I was a very pretty child, and had a sweet voice; of course I used to sing. Most London boys and girls of the lower classes sing. "My face is my fortune, kind sir, she said," was the ditty on which I bestowed most pains, and my father and mother would wink knowingly as I sang it. The latter would also tell me how pretty she was when young, and what a fool she had been, and how well she might have done had she been wise.

Frequently we had quite a stir in our colony. Some young lady who had quitted paternal restraints, or perhaps, been started off, none knew whither or how, to seek her fortune, would reappear among us with a profusion of ribands, fine clothes and lots of cash. Visiting the neighbourhood, treating indiscriminately, was the order of the day on such occasions, without any more definite information of the means by which the dazzling transformation had been effected than could be conveyed by knowing winks and the words "luck" and "friends". Then she would disappear and leave us in our dirt, penury and obscurity. You cannot conceive, sir, how our young ambition was stirred by these visitations.

Now comes an important event in my life. I was a fine robust healthy girl of thirteen years of age. I had larked with boys of my own age. . . . I had seen much and heard abundantly of the mysteries of sex. . . . For some time I had coquetted on the verge of a strong curiosity and a natural desire, and without a particle of affection I lost—what?— not my virtue, for I never had any. . . . You reverend Mr. Philanthropist—what call you virtue? . . . I repeat that I never lost what I never had—my virtue. According to my own ideas at the time I only extended my rightful enjoyment and opportunity was not long waiting to put my newly acquired knowledge to profitable use. In the commencement of my fifteenth year, one of our be-ribanded visitors took me off, and introduced me to the great world, and thus commenced my career as what you better-classes call a prostitute. I cannot say that I felt any other shame than the bashfulness of a novitiate introduced to strange society. Remarkable for good looks, and no less so for a good temper, I gained money, dressed gaily, and soon agreeably astonished my parents and old neighbours by making a descent on them. Passing over the vicissitudes of my career, alternating between reckless gaiety and extreme destitution, I improved myself greatly, and at the age of eighteen was living partly under the protection of one who thought he discovered that I had talent, and some good qualities, as well as beauty, who treated me more kindly and considerately than I had ever before been treated. . . . Under the protection of this gentleman, and encouraged by him, I commenced the work of my education; that portion of education which is comprised in some knowledge of my own language and the ordinary accomplishments of my sex; moral science, as I believe it is called, has always been an enigma to me, and is so this day. I suppose it is because I am one of those who, as Rousseau says, are "born to be prostitutes". Common honesty I believe in rigidly. I have always paid my debts, and though I say it, have always been charitable to my fellow-creatures. . . .

She had looked after her parents, buried them decently, paid for the defence of a brother "who had the folly to be caught in the commission of a robbery", apprenticed another brother to a good trader and helped him into a little business, and when drink frustrated this effort, had used her influence with a very particular *friend* of hers to get him into the police force. She had brought out all her sisters and started them in the world:

The elder of the two is kept by a nobleman, the next by an officer in the army, the third has not yet come to years of discretion and is having her fling before she settles down.

Now what if I am a prostitute, what business has society to abuse me? Have I received any favours at the hand of society? If I am a hideous cancer in society, are not the causes of the disease to be sought in the rottenness of the carcass. Am I not its legitimate child, no bastard, sir. Why does my unnatural parent repudiate me? . . . I have neither stolen (at least not since I was a child) nor murdered, nor defrauded. I earn my money and pay my way, and try to do good with it, according to my ideas of good. I do not get drunk, nor fight, nor create an uproar in the streets or out of them. I do not offend the public by open indecencies. I go to the Opera; I go to Almack's; I go to the theatre. I go to quiet, well-conducted casinos. . . . My milliner, my silk-mercer, my bootmakers, know, all of them, where I am and how I live, and they solicit my patronage as earnestly and as cringingly as if I were Madam, the lady of the right rev. patron of the Society for the Suppression of Vice. We come from the dregs of society, as our so-called betters call it. What business has society to have dregs—such dregs as we? You railers of the Society for the Suppression of Vice, you the pious, the moral, the respectable, as you call yourselves, who stand on your smooth and pleasant side of the great gulf you have dug, and keep between yourself and the dregs, why don't you bridge it over or fill it up. . . .

Why stand you there mouthing with sleek face about morality? What is morality?

The Significance of Seduction: For a prostitute to be rhetorically unrepentant and eloquently without shame was sufficiently alarming to the custodians of mid-Victorian *mores,* but even more seditious was *Another Unfortunate's* assault on the popular belief that seduction was the principal cause of prostitution. This belief was the keystone of the respectable Victorian's moral structure. In fulminating about the wickedness of the individual he was able to forget about the wickedness of society; "More

Prayers" was a much safer slogan than "Less Poverty". Among the lower orders, too, the seduced girl was an important symbol. The popularity of seduction as a theme in early Victorian melodrama—the theatre of the people—was probably a reflection of the class bitterness of the times. The pure maidens foully betrayed like Agnes Primrose and Maria Marten who knocked 'em in the Whitechapel Road were poor but honest victims of the rich man's whim. A shiny top hat was the seducing villain's badge; to assail it with catcalls and execrations must have been an enjoyable catharsis for workers who in real life had to salute it humbly.

But *Another Unfortunate* denied that seduction was "the root of the evil" of prostitution. It was "scarcely a fibre of the root":

> Seduction is the common story of numbers of well brought-up, who never were seduced, and who are voluntary and inexcusable prostitutes. . . . Vanity and idleness send us a large body of recruits.

And thousands of women were driven on the streets by poverty: "These poor women toiling on starvation wages, where penury, misery and famine clutch them and say, 'Render up your body, or die.' "

Not surprisingly, this letter attracted some attention. The *Saturday Review* doubted its authenticity: "If it were possible for a female Arab to expand into [its] striking style and choice language . . . the common-sense conclusion would be, that the life of a prostitute is the best educational discipline in England." But *The Times* reassured readers that the letter was genuine ("We are not endeavouring to palm off a cunningly executed literary imposture.") and analysed it in a leading article.

The observations on seduction were described as "a new view of the Great Social Evil . . . worth the attention of all persons who are endeavouring to deal with it". They were, indeed, as important in their way as the works on Natural Selection that Darwin and Wallace published in the same year. But they were slow in gaining acceptance. Eight years later, the *Saturday Review* endorsed them:

> the fact is that for one case of one-sided seduction there are fifty cases of mutual and consentient unchastity.

but when the Rev. G. P. Merrick issued a pamphlet on prostitution in 1890, he proclaimed as a new, surprising, and painful discovery, that the "common impression" about prostitutes being victims of seduction was "altogether wrong". Of 16,022 women whom he had interrogated, only 4 per cent. had been seduced. Most told him frankly that they had become prostitutes because they liked the life.

Another Unfortunate had been equally frank on this aspect of prostitution. *The Times* realized the significance of this, too:

> the writer ... bids us ... to dismiss from our apprehension all the crudities with which the divines, and philosophers, and romance writers, have surrounded it. ... The great bulk of London prostitutes are not Magdalens *in esse* or *posse,* nor specimens of humanity in agony, nor Clarissa Harlowes. They are not ... cowering under gateways, nor preparing to throw themselves from Waterloo Bridge, but are comfortably practising their trade. ... They have no remorse or misgivings about the nature of their pursuit. On the contrary, they consider the calling an advantageous one, and they look upon their success in it with satisfaction. They have their virtues, like others; they are good daughters, good sisters and friends.

Should Parsons be Paid? In 1868, when Dr. Acton took part in a debate on prostitution at a meeting of the London Dialectical Society—a philosophical body "founded upon the principle of absolute liberty of thought and speech"—he was pleased to find ladies participating. Lord Amberley, later the Vice-President, noted some of the observations in his journal:

> Mr. Acton rejoiced in the change of tone that had occurred

since he first began to write on this subject, when he could hardly get anyone to discuss it. Now it was discussed here with ladies present. Formerly, Lord Shaftesbury when appealed to, had said that he knew little of it, and wished to know less. Mr. A pointed out that these women do not remain prostitutes long, but marry, etc.

Mr. Fox Bourne, who began the debate, said "there was a great deal of unreasonable prejudice against prostitutes":

They did not lead as bad a life as was supposed. Their health was better than that of other women. . . . There was quite as much moral worth among them as among other people. . . . If these women ought not to take money for the particular service they render, neither ought doctors or parsons to accept pay. Moreover, these women performed a providential function, that of a staying population.

Dr. Drysdale, who summed up, said that *a priori* theories of morals were nonsense.

Prostitutes were far healthier than sewing women, and better off; they have better food and clothing. He had heard a surgeon observe that they seemed to have all virtues but the single one of chastity.

In his book on *Prostitution*, Dr. Acton had expressed similar views. "Fresh experience in London," he said, had strengthened his dissent from "the vulgar error that early death overtakes the daughters of pleasure" as well as his impression that "the harlot's progress as often tends upwards as downwards".

I have become daily more convinced that far from perishing in hospitals, workhouses, or obscure degradation, she generally in course of time, amalgamates with the populace. Young persons are, I believe, generally led to believe that the class of unfortunate females are, with few exceptions, Messalinas or Delilahs living in riot for a little season—dying neglected and miserable—of most dreadful diseases, or by violence or suicide—upon dunghills or in ditches. . . . But . . . this is as gross a fallacy as that every prostitute is a *Dame Aux Camelias*.

These heresies, of course, would never have reached the aseptic shelves of the circulating libraries. But the correspondence and comment in *The Times* must have been sufficiently alarming to Mr. Mudie's readers, for whom the life of the prostitute had hitherto been represented as a sort of Walpurgis-night phantasmagoria, lit with red fire, in which Mrs. Gaskell's Esther, "naught but skin and bone, with a cough to tear her in two", lay dying on the ground with feverish, glittering eyes, while Mr. Dickens' Martha stumbled wildly through the ooze and slime, moaning "Oh, the river! Oh, the river!" and beseeching Mr. Peggoty to stamp upon her and kill her.

VII. THE NOVELIST AND THE STATESMAN

Who is Derry, Indeed?: Mrs. Gaskell when she wrote of Esther and Ruth may not have known better. But Dickens was obviously dishonest when he luxuriated in the agony and abasement of his Martha and Little Em'ly—whose apostrophe clings to her as maddeningly as her remrose. He knew that many of his friends had mistresses who did not spend all their nights writhing in Millbank mud, and that prostitutes had at least as good a chance of happiness as factory girls with phosphorous-rotted jaws.

But it was proper to believe that when a woman lost her virginity outside of marriage, she was damned. In a letter to his friend de Cerjat, Dickens said he concurred "with a sore heart" that the prostitute's return to virtue was cut off:

I have been turning it over in my mind for some time, and hope, in the history of Little Em'ly (who *must* fall—there is no hope for her) to put it before the thoughts of people in a new and pathetic way, and perhaps do some good.

It is hard to see how an hysterical caricature, in which all the Puritanical mumbo-jumbo about immorality is consolidated, could do any good to any one except, perhaps, the publisher and author. Yet while he was writing this unrealistic nonsense Dickens was realistically—but secretly—grappling with the problem of redeeming prostitutes.

For many years, he was associated with Miss Burdett Coutts, whose great fortune and long life—she was born in 1814 and died in 1906—were devoted to good works. Dickens, who met Miss Coutts in 1835, acted as her almoner and adviser; when she turned from Ragged Schools to the reclamation of whores he helped her plan a rescue home and showed a sensitive understanding of how it should be conducted. "These unfortunate creatures are to be *Tempted* to virtue," he wrote to Miss Coutts in 1847. "They cannot be dragged, driven or frightened." Nine years later, when the home, under the name of Urania Cottage, had been established, he was still concerned with details of its administration. He complained that a material called Derry, which it was proposed the inmates should wear, was a "mortal dull colour":

> Colour these people always want, and colour . . . I would always give them. In these cast-iron and mechanical days, I think even such a garnish to the dish of their monotonous and hard lives, of unspeakable importance. One colour, and that of the earth earthy, is too much with them early and late. Derry might just as well break out into a stripe, or put forth a bud, or even burst into a full blown flower. Who is Derry that he is to make Quakers of us all, whether we will or no!

Here was the real Dickens, compassionate, exuberant and life-loving, at war with the grim institutional mind that would condemn the whore to a dress of mortal dullness because a stripe or bud or flower might give her pleasure; a Dickens who knew that a whore was still a woman and capable of being

67

happy. Why, then, did he hide this aspect of himself from the public? Why were his activities with Miss Burdett Coutts kept secret? Una Pope-Hennessy suggests that some "native instinct" warned him not to "invalidate the magic in his books" by disclosing his practical philanthropy. It is simpler to assume that Dickens concealed his sympathy for prostitutes, because he knew that his women readers, at least, had little sympathy for them. They preferred the twisted satisfaction of imagining their fallen sisters in agony. " 'Serve them right'," said the pre-Raphaelite poet William Bell Scott, "is the verdict of the sweetest and gentlest of creatures."

The Grand Old Manner: Gladstone was no less a public figure than Dickens, but he made no secret of his compassion for "the unfortunate ministers to the great sin of great cities". He had discussed plans for reforming them when he was at Oxford in the early eighteen-thirties, and his diaries and account books show how much time and money he devoted to this work—in which Mrs. Gladstone helped enthusiastically—until he was past eighty.

Often, on his way home from the House, Gladstone would talk to a prostitute in the street; and on one occasion, at least, with his wife's full approval, he brought a girl home for the night. These open activities caused his friends some anxiety, because his political enemies did not scruple to spread the most sinister stories about them. Some of these stories reached Queen Victoria; when Gladstone mentioned her coldness towards him to Lord Stanmore, he was told that the Queen suspected him of "immoral behaviour with common women". "If the Queen thinks that of me, she is quite right to treat me as she does," said Mr. Gladstone, in the grandest manner.

Not a Sixpence or a Situation: One night in May, 1853, Gladstone left the House after the division on the Nunneries Bill, to attend the Opera. He was forty-four, and had recently presented his first Budget, in which, despite violent opposition, he had retained the "temporary expedient" of the income tax, which was fixed at 7*d.* in the pound. The Nunneries Bill was designed to give the Home Secretary power to inspect any of the seventy-five nunneries in England and Wales when there were reasonable grounds for believing that a woman was confined against her will. Its sponsor, who pointed out that lunatics, sailor-boys and parish apprentices enjoyed this protection, said his object was not to invade religious liberty but to protect civil liberty. By a majority of twenty-three, leave was granted to introduce the Bill, and Mr. Gladstone drove off to Covent Garden, where Grisi, Mario and Ronconi were appearing in *Lucrezia Borgia*. When he arrived at the theatre, he dismissed his brougham, and at the end of the performance, set out by way of Long Acre to walk to his house in Downing Street.

About midnight, as he was entering Panton Street from Leicester Square, he was accosted by a young woman who "earnestly begged his attention to her story". She seemed to be in great distress, and though it was obvious she was a prostitute, Mr. Gladstone stopped politely to listen to her. As she began to talk a man approached and said something in a loud voice which Mr. Gladstone did not comprehend but which so frightened the girl that she seized him by the arm. He told her not to be alarmed, and offered to escort her to her home in King Street, Soho. The man followed them along Coventry Street and Oxenden Street, announcing in a loud voice that he knew who Mr. Gladstone was and intended to accuse him of "being in company with the woman for an immoral and improper purpose".

With great restraint, Mr. Gladstone continued quietly on his way, and saw the girl, who enjoyed the protection of his left arm, safely to her door. The man remained in attendance, ignoring the suggestion that he should go away. Mr. Gladstone resumed his homeward walk, turning this way and that in an attempt to discourage his follower, who, however, kept close behind and went on talking: he declared that though he admired Mr. Gladstone's public character much, he must now expose him, and would do this in the columns of the *Morning Herald*, thus greatly discomfiting the whole of the Conservative Party. If, however, Mr. Gladstone would make it right with him, such as by getting him a Government appointment in Somerset House, his lips would be closed. "Sir," said the Chancellor of the Exchequer sharply, "do exactly as you please. I will give you neither a sixpence, nor a situation!"

The man continued to follow Mr. Gladstone, repeating his threats, and Mr. Gladstone, his anger rising, repeated his terse reply. Finally, in Sackville Street, he hailed police-constable C187 and stated his desire to be rid of his unwanted companion. The constable invited them both to accompany him to the station house. On the way, the man again warned Mr. Gladstone that, for his own sake, he had better do something about the Government job. "I told him", Mr. Gladstone said in court later, "that I had no wish to conceal any act of mine and that he was not justified in imputing to me the intention on which he had founded his claim; an intention which, being on oath, I solemnly deny."

The persistent job-seeker was arrested on a charge of attempting to extort money. He was a young out-of-work Scotch traveller named William Watson. While he was awaiting trial, an anonymous correspondent wrote to *The Times* an account of how Gladstone not long before had redeemed two "unfortunates" whom he had met in the Haymarket, and extolled him for his humanity. Mr. Bodkin, when he opened the case for the Crown, also referred to Mr. Gladstone's labours among the fallen: "His benevolence," he said, "particularly in reference to this unfortunate class of society, was well known to all who had the honour of his acquaintance."

Mr. Gladstone was equally benevolent towards the accused Watson, who, because there was no evidence of premeditation, escaped with a sentence of twelve months' imprisonment. In a statement made to the police, he said he would not mind if he were transported, as long as his name was associated with that of Mr. Gladstone, "one of the greatest men of the day".

"The Top of the Tree": Ten years later, Gladstone's work among the fallen again involved him in some embarrassment. He had negotiated the redemption of a twenty-year-old harlot, no slattern of the slums, but a young woman of "singular character" who was, in his own words, "at the very top of the tree". When she gave up her sinful trade, she also gave up the open carriage and pair, hired from a livery stables in Cheval Place, in which she had driven daily from her house in Brompton Square to the Park. The proprietor of the stables then wrote to Gladstone, asking him to pay the lady's outstanding account of £40, on the grounds that the man responsible for her giving up her mode of life, should also be responsible for her debts incurred by it.

IX. ALAS FOR AMARYLLIS!

"Nymphs That Breathe The Rural Air . . .: The stones of the city streets, as we have seen, were "alive with lust". But so, alas, were the Meadows trim with Daisies pied; the hawthorn bush with seats beneath the shade; the crowded Corn-field, blooming Mead; the willow's marge of murmuring brook; and the pensive shadows of the grove. "It is a romantic and false notion," wrote a country vicar to *The Times* in 1858, "that while the city is the favourite seat of vice, virtue loves to dwell in the country. Poets and dreamers have taught many to imagine that where the wood-bine and ivy twine, simplicity and innocence make their blest abode, in happy ignorance of the pollutions of the world, the flesh and the devil." The rural districts, he said, were the "chief nursery" of urban prostitution, and he described a typical household of his parish:

> We are in a small apartment which serves all the purposes of cooking and living, kitchen, scullery, bake-house, laundry and sitting-room for a family of six or eight, parents and children. . . . Upstairs . . . on the same space as below are arranged two bedsteads, and what is called a "Bist", pronounced with the

"i" long. In these are couched every night, six, eight or ten warm and throbbing bodies of different sexes whose ages vary up to sixteen, seventeen or eighteen.

The *Saturday Review,* a few years later, agreed with the country vicar that the prostitution of the cities was mainly recruited from the country where, "by the deliberate choice of the woman, a sort of bundling is the rule of English life".

. . . *nor So Chaste as Fair":* In 1865, when London bloods, described as "gentlemen" on the charge-sheet, were still wrenching knockers from front doors, and curling their whiskers with a cunning instrument known as a bostrokizon, and merchants of erotica were doing a brisk business in obscene meerschaum pipes and valentines, Mr. J. Percival, returning from a tour of Cumberland and Westmorland, reported on the immorality of "these beautiful hills and valleys", which he found "disfigured by bastardy" and sunken deep in vice. In an anguished letter to *The Times* he said that in both counties chastity was a matter of little concern and one out of every nine children was illegitimate. *The Times,* in a leading article, expressed the view that this figure was a "delusive minimum", and comparing the classical concept of Arcadian life with the modern reality, said, "Statistics prove with inexorable logic that virtue, and especially female virtue, is on much the same level in town and country, and that the great sin of the great cities is also the great sin of rude and secluded villages."

In his aetiology of village vice, Mr. Percival included the "traditional licence" of Martinmas and Whitsuntide holidays; he suggested that female servants should be compelled to return from these junketings before dark, and that employers should refuse to engage either a male or female who had been guilty of unchastity. *The Times* urbanely disagreed with this: "We cannot desire it", it said, "that ruin should be the inevitable doom of female frailty in the lower ranks of society even if it be right that it should still be so in the upper." Mr. Percival had also been shocked to observe that women were anxious to marry rustic profligates and that neighbours spoke gently of a woman's fall.

The Times attributed much of this immorality to overcrowding and to the promiscuous association of boys and girls in factories. Quoting a bulletin from Staffordshire, it pointed out that modesty had become a byword with female operatives who, it seemed, enlivened their hours of toil by singing, "unblushingly, the most disgusting songs". A master in the Staffordshire brickfields said of the thousands of girls whom he had met in his work, one in every four by the age of twenty had had an illegitimate child; some, three or four.

Bombardment with a Pop-Gun: Mr. George Moore, a wealthy and philanthropic Cumbrian who as a poor boy had walked thirty-four miles to see a man hanged, and as a rich man was the subject of one of Mr. Samuel Smiles' admiring sagas of self-help, called a special early morning session of the Evangelical Union to discuss Mr. Percival's melancholy charges. It was held at the Queen's Hotel, Keswick, and attended by the more important clergy and gentry. Little came of the conference, but after a substantial breakfast, Mr. Moore announced that he would award two prizes, of £10 and £5, for the best essay on "The Excessive Immorality of the Two Counties", the judges to be four clergymen and one member of the laity. A correspondent to *The Times* suggested coldly that the reverend gentlemen would have been better occupied working among their fallen flock than proposing resolutions at the breakfast-table, and the *Saturday Review* said, "Directing a prize essay against vice is like bombarding Gibraltar with a pop-gun."

Mr. Percival was Right: The industrious returns of the Registrar-General for the years 1845 to 1848—the only ones I have been able to consult—suggest that Cumberland was then the most sinful county in the kingdom. While the all-England (and Wales) average for illegitimate births was 67 in every 1,000, the figure for Cumberland was 108 per 1,000, and for Westmorland

87 per 1,000. Next to Cumberland came Norfolk, 105 per 1,000, followed by Hereford, 100 per 1,000. It is significant that Middlesex comes at the bottom of the list with only 40 per 1,000. The inference is, I fear, that contraception, abortion and infanticide were more widely practised in the cities. In London between 1855 and 1860, inquests were held on the bodies of 1,130 children under two years of age, all of whom had been murdered —an average of 226 a year.

"Stow All That Trash!": "Although the Strephon and Daphne of the English counties make love openly and grossly," said the *Saturday Review* in 1869, "there is at bottom not much more immorality in their intercourse than in that of young Boots and his Traviata." And did Daphne, when she became a London Traviata, lament her abandoned hedgerows? That often remarkable, sometimes ridiculous, Victorian, Ouida, answers this question in *Under Two Flags*. "The Zu-Zu"—a country girl who has done well for herself with the Guards—"was perfectly happy":

> . . . and as for the pathetic pictures that novelists and moralists draw, of vice sighing amid turtle and truffles for childish innocence in the cottage at home where honeysuckle blossomed and brown brooks made melody, and passionately grieving on the purple cushions of a barouche for the time of straw pallets and untroubled sleep—the Zu-Zu would have vaulted herself on the box-seat of a drag, and told you "to stow all that trash!" Her childish recollections were of a stifling lean-to with the odour of pigsty and strawyard, pork for a feast once a week, starvation all the other six days, kicks, slaps, wrangling, and a general atmosphere of beer and washtubs; she hated her past and loved her cigar on the drag.

"The Zu-Zu is a fact," says Ouida, "the moralist's pictures are moonshine", and the Zu-Zus, in 1864, were "daily becoming more prominent in the world, more brilliant, more frankly recognized, and more omnipotent".

"Melancholy, Groans and Sighs": That witty and worldly clergyman, the Rev. Sydney Smith, who made an enlightened study of the antics of the "impious coxcombs" of Methodism, foresaw, at the beginning of last century, how the "madness of the tabernacle" would spread over England: and he feared that when, as a result, happiness had been destroyed, reason degraded and fanaticism become "too foolish and too prurient to be endured", a long period of the "grossest immorality, atheism and debauchery" would follow. Perhaps he over-estimated the intensity of the reaction which did take place from the "wretchedness, melancholy, groans and sighs" of Dissent; but there is no doubt that the desire to escape from this Stygian cave-world of "no theatre, no cards, no Punchinello, no dancing dogs, no blind fiddlers," encouraged many Victorian girls, even without the sharper goad of hunger, to become prostitutes. Sydney Smith had not been dead many years when the *Saturday Review* asked:

> What is the life of a young provincial servant-girl, a young factory-girl, milliner's assistant, or daughter of a small tradesman? It is one dreary routine of work, work, stitch, stitch, church-and-chapel going.

And it saw the "garish harlotry of our metropolitan streets" recruited by "poor girls whose first corruption was a natural reaction against the formal Puritanism which clouded their days with a gloomy alternation of work and sermons, sermons and work".

A year or so later, the *Spectator* attributed the spread of profligacy in England in part to that "pernicious drawback of English life—its tendency to be humdrum" which had been intensified "by the dullness of the Court, by the passion for accumulation, and by the wide spread of a pseudo-asceticism inculcated by Calvinists ignorant of Calvin":

Bourgeois manners have reigned and bourgeois manners are

regulated on the assumption that life ought to be dull, that half the amusements man has invented are wicked and the other half frivolous.

Of a Caledonian, Stern and Wild: In Scotland, the excoriatory fires of Calvinism blazed with an even fiercer glare, and so, it seems, did the inextinguishable fires of lust. When some eminent Glaswegians in 1859 asked the House of Commons to withdraw Government subsidies from art schools that used nude models, the *Saturday Review* commented sardonically on the state of morals north of the Border:

Glasgow bears an evil name, even among great cities, for drunkenness and profligacy; but at least its godly ministers have wiped out the scandal of their toil-worn parishioners visiting green fields on the blessed Sabbath. . . . Scotland vindicates her principles of sobriety by a peculiar law which closes every tavern on the Sunday; but that law seems in no way to interfere with a very large number of excellent persons who may be seen between services staggering down the Cannongate in Edinburgh, in what must be called a very unmanageable condition of spiritual ecstasy. Something of the same policy our Puritan neighbours are pursuing in the matter of licentiousness. The Cyprian patrol which occupies our streets in force every night, and subjects every passenger to a flying interrogatory, is scarcely less formidable in Scotch cities than in London, and the constant scandal of pregnant brides prevails in Scotland to an extent which would put even our own rural districts to the blush.

The Scottish attitude towards sex and the Sabbath is pleasantly illustrated in an anecdote from Lord Amberley's papers that have been published by his grandson, Bertrand Russell. Towards the end of the 'sixties, Amberley outraged Sabbatarians by introducing a Bill to allow secular lecturers to charge admission for meetings held on Sunday. When the Bill was defeated, a sympathizer sent him an encouraging letter, and enclosed this story "as embodying the sublimated sanctified cant" of those who had opposed it:

SCOTCH SABBATH PIETY
IN ITS "NAKED" SIMPLICITY

Being in Edinburgh once during the strict religious festival of the Year, I went out on the Sunday evening to take a stroll. Before long I found myself the companion of a full-grown carmine-haired "lassie" who, tho' pious enough in her way, had a freedom of manner and conversation that, to a stranger —like me—was very agreeable. She proposed supper in her rooms, which I agreed to, and away we went. Whilst she was "putting things straight", I turned my back to the fire, split my coat-tails and began to whistle an air. This attracted her instant attention, she stopped suddenly, and turning round with features pale and distorted by terror, asked:

"*What are you doing?*"

"Doing? Nothing?"—and I went on with my melody, as if I had not been interrupted. I saw that there was something unusually the matter with her, but I took little, or no notice and continued. She, again, called out with that particular hoarseness indicating the action of great fear:

"*Ye're whustlin!*"

"Yes; but what of that? Whistling's nothing."

"*Whustlin's naethin! D'ye ca tha naethin?*"

"Of course I do; it *is* nothing."

Then she raised her hands above her head, looked piteously on me, turned her large, bright blue eyes up to the ceiling and exclaimed in an agony of holy terror:

"*Sweet Edinboro' and Scotland's Kirk, an he ca's that naething! Jist button up yer breeks, and gang yer gate, my chick: — G—d for sakes! ma man; I'm na goin to fornicate the nicht wi a man who whustles on the Sabbath!*"

The lady was obdurate, and as I walked along, meditating

on the all-pervading character of Scotland's religious feeling, as so beautifully exemplified in this incident, I returned to my hotel a "disappointed"—*a wiser man.*

"A Frightful Lot of Cads": Puritanism, with its frenzied recoil from sex, so indelibly conditions the Anglo-Saxon cortex, that its agonized twitchings often survive, like a phantom limb, long after the religion that engendered it has been amputated. Frederic Harrison provides a good example. Harrison was an ardent prophet of positivism, an agnostic who had rejected all the trappings of Christianity, yet he remained as pathologically sensitive about sex as any louse-ridden anchorite of the second century. "The immitigable offence in his eyes was sex," says his son, Austen Harrison.

The positivists, in their passionate cult of man as the measure of all things, devised a calendar in which the days and months were named after illustrious poets, philosophers and scientists. It is strange to think of so fervent a worshipper of humanity as Harrison telling his son (perhaps on some balmy spring morning in Sophocles) that the man who could not control his sex urges was foul, anti-social and contemptible, a wrong-doer, a beast and a cad. Austen Harrison reports the conversation he had with his father when, as a youth, he asked some timid questions about morality:

"What is a fellow to do who cannot marry and falls in love?"

At these words, my father bounded up and moved across to the fire-place. He looked grave and perplexed.

"Do!" he cried. "Do what every gentleman does in such circumstances. Do what your religion teaches you. Do what morality prescribes as right. . . . A man who cannot learn self-control, is a cad. What more can I say?"

"There must be a frightful lot of cads," I ejaculated.

"There are," responded my father. . . . "You know the difference between good and evil."

"But is it evil," I interrupted, "I mean is love only right in marriage?"

"Certainly. A loose man is a foul man. He is anti-social. He is a beast."

"Positivism, then, takes the theological view about morality?"

"Of course," said my father. "Even more so. . . . A man who gives way to the flesh is a wrong-doer. I regard vice with contempt."

And the philosopher of humanity impatiently ended the discussion by saying it was not a subject to be discussed by decent men.

XI. IN SEARCH OF HISTORY

That Blessed Word "Sublimation": "The real, central theme of history," says Mr. C. M. Young, who views the nineteenth century through the bow-window of a comfortable club, "is not what happened, but what people felt about it when it was happening." Then let us invoke the historians, including Mr. Young. They will tell us much about the Irish Question and the Oxford Movement; about Disestablishment and Ritualism; about stuffed doves and prevenient grace and auricular confession and baptismal regeneration; about what happened to Don Pacifico's house in Athens and to the lorcha *Arrow* in Canton; about brave deeds in Jigdulluk Pass and braver words in Downing Street. But it is reasonable to assume that millions of Englishmen felt nothing at all about these elements of history, even if they were ever aware of them.

And what will the historians tell us about the sex life of these millions, which, it is also reasonable to assume, they did feel something about? Very little, and that very vaguely. When they do not ignore it, they are usually at pains to prettify it. Lord Cecil, for example, says: "Any respectable Victorian looked on sexual irregularity as a sin so heinous that he hardly dared look at it at all." But how many were "respectable"? The inference is, of course, that as it was an age of "respectability", a majority of Englishmen recoiled in horror from "sexual irregularity". Mr. R. C. K. Ensor develops this argument, rebuking writers who depict the Victorians as hypocrites and suggest that "behind a façade of continence, their men were in fact profligate and over-sexed". Though it may be backed by "particular instances", says Mr. Ensor, this view as a generalization misunderstands the age:

> The religion-ruled Englishmen then dominant in the govern-ing, directing, professional and business classes spent, there can be little doubt, far less of their time and thought on sex inter-ests than either their Continental contemporaries or their twentieth-century successors, and to this saving their extra-ordinary surplus of energy in other spheres must reasonably be ascribed.

Let us pass over the assumption that the morality of the "dominant" classes—say ten per cent. of the population—is the only one worth studying. A more dubious assumption is that these upper-class Victorians must have been chaste because they were busy—inventing, manufacturing, building, buying, selling and exporting the Law to lesser breeds. It would be as valid to argue that Marlowe's contemporaries were more chaste than Masefield's because the Elizabethan age, too, was one of expan-sion, energy and achievement. But the theory of sublimation, the belief that sexual energy can be switched from the art of love to say, the love of art, as electrical energy can be switched from a radiogram to a potato-peeler, is quite unproved. It might be shown that a mystic will see more incandescent visions if he suppress his sexual impulses, but it would not be easy to show that sleeping alone confers equivalent benefits on a soap-manufacturer, a poet, a statesman or a judge. "Certainly," says the untiring Dr. Kinsey, "no one who actually knew the sexual histories of particular artists would have thought of using them as illustrations of a sexually sublimated people." Was Turner, for example, with his mistresses and his bastards and his prodigious output—he left a fortune of £140,000 from his painting— a sexually sublimated person? Dr. Havelock Ellis, I recall, returned with a similar conclusion from his more leisurely voyagings on the sea of sex.

A casuist might argue that Mr. Ensor means the Victorians spent little "time and thought on sex interests" because they lived busy sex lives, whereas a St. Jerome must have spent much time and thought on those ghostly bands of naked girls who pirouetted inaccessibly round his earthen couch, while his fleshly companions were scorpions and wild beasts. (*Letter to the Virgin Eustochium.*) In this sense, the blessed St. Aldhelm of Malmesbury, who passed chaste and mortifying nights between two corporeal girls, *unam ab uno latere, alteram ab altero,* must have spent even more time and thought on sex. But I do not think this is what Mr. Ensor means.

Dr. Wingfield-Stratford, is more realistic:

> The Victorians [he writes] as a general rule, managed to conceal the coarser side of their lives so thoroughly under a mask of respectability that we often fail to realize how coarse it really was. Could we have recourse to the vast, unwritten literature of bawdry, we should be able to form a more veracious notion of life as it really was in those not so very remote times. . . . There was a great and flourishing underworld of vice. . . . The era of respectability was also one of high play and fast living.

And, in another place, the doctor says:

> Victorian morality . . . reposed upon the belief that if you could not be virtuous, you could at least be respectable. Though the streets of London swarmed with harlots and a male virgin was regarded in the smoking-room as a rather poor-spirited fellow, the pretence of chastity was to be kept up.

These observations are closer to the truth. They err, I think it can be shown, in over-estimating this pretence of respectability. There is evidence, especially among Mr. Ensor's "dominant" classes, that many Englishmen with an appreciative eye for a mistress or a whore, cared little or nothing whether the massed congregations of all the bellowing bethels in the kingdom knew about it.

Fancy Work at Badminton: Mr. E. F. Benson tells an illuminating story of the eighth Duke of Beaufort as related to him by the Duke's daughter-in-law Lady Henry Somerset. (It was the seventh Duke, in his ardent youth, who had to be dragged by paternal arms from Harriette Wilson's bed.) This happened in the 'seventies: there was a house-party at Badminton, the Beaufort seat, but the Duke was away. One day the butler told the Duchess that a picture had arrived for His Grace; where should he hang it?

> So the whole party went into the corridor . . . to see the picture and there found the portrait of a very pretty young lady whom everyone knew to be the Duke's mistress. Was that an awkward situation? Not in the least. The Duchess with complete self-possession looked admiringly at it and said, "Is it not charming? A fancy portrait, I suppose," and without a grin or a wink or a whisper, they all looked at the fancy portrait and liked it immensely. It would do very well, thought the Duchess, just where it was, hung on the wall there. Then as they moved quietly on, she changed her mind. "His Grace might like it in his own room, perhaps," she said to her butler. "You had better hang it there."

Soon after, the Duke's mistress abandoned him for another protector, and, tearfully, the Duke told his sons and daughter-in-law of his sad loss. "Being a thoroughly religious man," Mr. Benson says, "he sought spiritual consolation in his trial, so the order went forth that next Sunday every groom and coachman and helper in the Badminton stables should attend church and receive the Sacrament with their master. This was quite characteristic of the time; a man could be a sincere and devout Christian and yet be keeping a mistress."

Equally pious was a notable Oxford professor of whom Mr. Benson also tells. The professor, a devout Tractarian, was very upset when he learned that his mistress had not been confirmed. He persuaded her to "repair this shocking omission" and "their relationship was renewed with nothing to mar its brightness".

Love among the Bohemians: Artists and writers are notoriously gay dogs and Mr. Ensor warns us against "particular instances". But it is impossible to avoid them. The nineteenth century provides no annals of anonymity, no Kinsey catacombs of tabulated tumescence, no jagged statistical alps of what he rather insensitively calls "outlets", to explore. For the most part, it is only when a Victorian becomes news and merits the attention of a court reporter or a biographer that we can learn anything about his sexual habits. And then, perhaps, we can borrow Mr. Young's divining-rod and find out what other people felt about him.

What did Thackeray feel about the sexual gymnastics of those friends of his whose morals were as flexible as caoutchouc? As one of Lord Cecil's "respectable" Victorians, he suckled Mr. Mudie's subscribers on milk-and-water; but did he avert his respectable eyes from the brilliant young politician Charles Buller, Judge-Advocate-General in the administration of 1846, whose mistress for many years was a "beautiful improper female" from the Baker Street bazaar; or from his other close friend, Saville Morton, who died at the end of a carving-knife wielded by a man he had cuckolded? "He is always in some feminine mischief," Thackeray wrote to Miss Carmichael-Smyth of Buller; "he is shocking with women. . . . He lusts after [a girl] and leaves her." Tennyson, too, the singer of Elaine, and Fitzgerald, were intimate friends of Buller.

Or did Dickens' friends reject him when the great chronicler of the pure and pullulating domestic hearth abandoned the mother of his children and established young Ellen Ternan in her bower in Ampthill Square? Did Ellen herself as a good Dickens' character would, sink to the tips of her pretty ears in a morass of shame and degradation when she became his mistress? There was, Dickens wrote, "no hope" for Little Em'ly, the victim of a crafty seducer; but Little Ellen, who crept into Dickens' bed with her eyes open, so to speak, did very nicely, and apparently lost no caste; after his death she married respectably, and a clergyman and school-teacher at that, the Rev. George Wharton Robinson, Principal of the High School, Margate.

Did Dickens slam the door in Wilkie Collins' face when his young friend set up house with Mrs. Caroline Greaves, the woman in white whom he picked up one summer evening walking home from dinner with Millais? Collins' bedroom permutations were fairly complex, even by the coney-like standards of Sunset Boulevard, Hollywood, Cal.; the *Dictionary of National Biography* calls them "intimacies formed as a young man". He lived with Mrs. Greaves for about nine years, and adopted her daughter. When Mrs. Greaves married again, he consoled himself with Martha Rudd, later known as Mrs. Dawson, who bore him three children. Not much is known about Mrs. Dawson, but she lived in Bolsover Street, one of London's less virtuous addresses. Then Mrs. Greaves returned and lived with Collins till his death, nearly twenty years later, but not to the complete excommunication of Mrs. Dawson whose third illegitimate child was born four years after Mrs. Greaves' return. Collins acknowledged all these children in his will.

Puzzling Questions: Whether or not Charles Reade slept with Mrs. Seymour, the actress of "Hebe form" and "handsome looks" who lived in his house for twenty-five years is, like what song the *Syrens* sang, or what name *Achilles* assumed when he hid himself among women, a puzzling question, though not beyond all conjecture. The conjecture, however, is not germane. It is sufficient to note that Reade retained his status as a respected and successful novelist in spite of his tenancy of what seemed to be a shameless love-nest.

George Eliot was splendidly defiant about her "irregular" relations with George Henry Lewes—whose wife Agnes had two children by his friend Thornton Hunt while they were all living together like the *dramatis personae* of the early Coward's brave new world. "That any unworldly, unsuperstitious person who is sufficiently acquainted with the realities of life can pronounce my relation to Mr. Lewes immoral I can only understand by remembering how subtle and complex are the influences that mould opinion," she wrote. These were heroic words for a woman to use in 1855; but they seem to have been echoed by her many devoted friends, who included Tennyson, Browning, Trollope, Burne Jones, Millais, Lord Acton, Lord Houghton, Herbert Spencer, Thomas Huxley and Frederic Harrison—all very distinguished and some very "respectable" Victorians. And Miss Eliot's open defiance of the Podsnap code did not deter her old friend, J. W. Cross, from marrying her after Lewes died.

Nor, before she set up house with Lewes, was she shocked by the fact that Dr. John Chapman, editor of the *Westminster Review*, kept his beautiful mistress, Elizabeth Tilley, in the same house as his wife. On the contrary, when Miss Eliot joined the Baker Street *agape*, she immediately fell in love with Chapman, and though their relations seem to have been innocent enough, Chapman's wife and his·mistress joined forces to drive her from the household—surely one of the most curious alliances in English history.

"Oh, Go Along Risetty!": Benvenuto Cellini said of his young girl-friend Caterina: "I keep her principally for my art's sake, since I cannot do without a model; but being a man also, I have used her for my pleasures." This attitude was not uncommon in the Renaissance; some of its most spiritual madonnas were portraits of the painter's mistress. In the folk-lore of the pub and the pavement, the legend survives of the dual-purpose woman, model by day, mistress by night, as a gadget to be found in every well-equipped studio.

Dante Gabriel Rossetti openly followed Cellini's example.

Two loves, at least, he had of comfort and despair; his wife, Elizabeth Siddal, ethereal, refined, remote, quiescent, and his mistress, Fanny Cornforth, vulgar, assertive, greedy, stupid. His attachment to the comfortable Fanny lasted for a quarter of a century and softened his despair at Elizabeth's suicide. Her real name was Sarah Cox, and William Rossetti describes her as a "pre-eminently fine woman, with regular and sweet features, and a mass of the most lovely blonde hair". *Fazio's Mistress* is a good portrait of her, and she was the model for *Bocca Baciata*, *Lady Lilith*, and *Monna Vanna*, that sumptuous tapestry that William Gaunt calls a "flaming stunner, rich in barbarous splendour of gown, ornament and countenance". To Swinburne, who preferred women in anapests to the flesh, she was "a bitch, at the other pole of her sex" from Lizzie Siddal. Look at *Monna Vanna*, and then at *Beata Beatrix*—the portrait of Elizabeth painted after her death—and you will see these two poles of womanhood, the flesh and the spirit, charted in paint.

William Bell Scott says Fanny was standing in the Strand "cracking nuts with her teeth and throwing the shells around when Gabriel first saw her and that she threw some nuts to him". It is a pleasant picture of a poet meeting his Blessed Damozel—"her hair that lay along her back was yellow like ripe corn" and I am sorry William Rossetti rejects it. Fanny's own story of the meeting—or one of them—is also picturesque. She says she was at Surrey Gardens during a firework display, an impoverished village maiden from Sussex, celebrating Florence Nightingale's return from the Crimea, when Rossetti, in company with Burne Jones and Ford Madox Brown, faked a collision with her and thus knocked down her mass of beautiful hair; after apologizing, the designing young men made her promise to call at Rossetti's studio next day.

She called, she stripped, she conquered. She became not only Rossetti's model and mistress, but after his wife's death, the hostess and domestic dictator of Cheyne Walk. Rossetti's pet name for her, "Elephant" was inspired by the amplitudes of flesh to which her splendid body expanded. A quaint correspondence survives, in which Rossetti writes of sending "a tidy cheque for the poor Quadrupin", or "a small cheque for the Elephant's trunk". Once, when he missed a piece of blue china, he wrote: "Hullo, Elephant, just you find that pot. Do you think I don't know that you've wrapped your trunk around it and dug a hole for it in the garden?" Or more affectionately: "Good Elephant, do come down. Old Rhinoceros is unhappy."

A vivid daguerrotype of their life together is preserved in William Allingham's journals. One day while Rossetti, in lyrical mood, was telling Allingham that Fanny's lips were "not really red at all, but with the bluish pink bloom that you find in rose petals", Fanny was sprawled buxomly on a couch, giggling coyly, and saying "Oh, go along Risetty!"

Butterfly in Bed: Whistler, who lacked the excuse of Latin blood, had at least four mistresses before, at the age of fifty-four, he married widow Godwin. Two were diversions of his student days in Paris; Fumette, or La Tigresse, and the dancer Finette, "une créole de moeurs légères", who later had the honour of introducing the cancan to England. In London, he lived with the red-haired Joanna Heffernan for ten years—Courbet painted her as *La Belle Irlandaise* and Whistler as *The White Girl*—and she was succeeded by another redhead, Maud Franklin. One of his two known bastards attended his funeral.

'Enrietta was well: Not only dukes, writers and artists were able to enjoy the licence of the unlicensed bed without loss of reputation. Henry Labouchere of *Truth*, "the Christian member" for Northampton, lived with Henrietta Hodson, a burlesque artist whose father kept the "Duke's Arms" at Westminster, for some time before they were married. When he was addressing election meetings during this companionate period, Labouchere was often asked by good-humoured hecklers: "Ow's 'Enrietta?" He opened one meeting by politely anticipating this inquiry. "I wish to convey to you all," he said, "the gratifying intelligence that Henrietta is quite well."

The Way of All Flesh: My last "particular instance" is that unpleasant fellow Samuel Butler, who, as you would expect from a man who studied book-keeping so as to keep elaborate household accounts, measured out his sex-life by double-entry. For many years, he and his shadow, Henry Festing Jones, shared a mistress, Madame Lucie Dumas, of Handel Street. They paid her £1 a week each, even when they were out of town, and were punctual and punctilious in their attentions. Butler visited her regularly every Wednesday afternoon, and Festing Jones on Tuesdays. "I have a little needlewoman," Butler told J. B. Yeats, "a good little thing. I have given her a sewing machine." Mr. Alfred Cathie, Butler's manservant, told Malcolm Muggeridge that his master would say to him: "Oh bother, Alfred. It's Wednesday, and I've got to go to Handel Street. . . ." "The Governor'd leave about 2.30 and be back by five," Mr. Cathie explained. "She was a fine woman, dark and large, not a regular street-walker, but receiving gentlemen in her room. . . . I took her out once or twice myself."

> *Oh, lyric love, half Henry's and half Sam's*
> *And all a wonder and a wild desire.*

XII. MARRIAGES AND MORALS

Economics of Sin: Snobbery and conformity were the josses of an ascendant middle class which had acquired, in Chesterton's phrase, every possession but self-possession, and which proclaimed as its eleventh beatitude: "Blessed are the respectable." But here again the daemon of history perversely bites itself in the pants; this passionate cult of respectability led to one of the most heinous violations of its moral code. For respectability, in the domestic sphere, meant keeping up with the Joneses', having as grand a house, as shiny a carriage, as bejewelled a wife, as the man next door, and under this compulsion to maintain appearances, marriage became a matter for delay and deliberation. On economic grounds, then, the harlot or the mistress was often preferred to the wife. "With the increase of civilization or rather of luxurious civilization, there is a diminution of marriage, except in the patrician class", said the *Lancet* in 1857, pointing out that the marriage-rate in England had declined progressively from 1,716 per 100,000 females between 1796 and 1805, to 1,533 per 100,000 between 1836 and 1845. "It is thought impossible in a large class of society now to marry unless you have £1,000 or £1,500 a year," said *The Times,* the same year. And Miss Mulock believed it was "hardly possible to over-calculate the evils accruing to individuals and to society from this custom, gradually increasing, of late and ultra-prudent marriages".

A correspondent to *The Times*, signed Theophrastus, wrote in 1857 that these restraints on marriage among young men of the middle class were the "real cause of most of our social corruption":

The father of the family, has, in many instances, risen from a comparatively humble origin to a position of easy competence. His wife has her carriage; he associates with wealth greater than his own. His sons reach the age, when, in the natural course of things, they ought to marry and establish a home for themselves. It would seem no great hardship that a young couple should begin on the same level as their parents, and be content for the first few years with the mere necessaries of life; and there are thousands who, were it not for society, would gladly marry on such terms. But here the tyrant world interposes; the son must marry on much the same footing as his father. If he dare to set the law at defiance, his family loses caste, and he and his wife are quietly dropped out of the circle in which they have hitherto moved. Thousands of young men live in sin. In the face of the powerful tyranny of social laws in this country it is difficult to suggest a general remedy for the evil. But the mischief is on the increase with our increasing worship of money.

The Times agreed with Theophrastus. Though not advocating "love in a cottage"; it pointed out that it was not necessary for happiness;

> that a man should live in a house near the parks, or that he should even keep a manservant, or a brougham, or that he should ride in Rotten Row, or that he should rush down with his family every three months by railway to Brighton, or Hastings, or Dover, for the benefit of his health . . . this undue, artificial, and unnatural postponement of marriage ends in a great blot on our social system.

Modern caution, said *The Times,* had outstepped all reasonable limits. The hesitant bridegroom was offered the example of two great lawyers:

> Lord Cottenham formed early in life the resolution not to marry till his practice was £4,000 and he married at forty. Lord Eldon married upon nothing at twenty-one. . . . Lord Cottenham was not aided by late marriage, and Lord Eldon was certainly not impeded by his early one.

"Produce! Produce! Produce!": But even those who followed Lord Eldon's example and married young, found another Victorian convention inducing them to sin. This was what Dr. Wingfield-Stratford calls the Cult of the Double Bed—that secret but sanctified altar of philo-progenitiveness around which Victorian married life revolved. " 'Produce! Produce!' was the cry, not only of the prophet Carlyle, but of the age itself," says the doctor. And "however romantically chivalrous a husband might be in other ways, he was the most austere taskmaster in exacting the punctual succession of children that so often overtaxed his wife's strength."

The Queen, who had the excuse of being a very busy woman, set a modest example by having nine. (Her uncle, William IV, had sired the same number, but they were all bastards.) Loyal subjects, such as Mrs. Charles Dickens, with ten children and at least two miscarriages in fourteen years, and Lady Durham, who died when she was thirty-five after having thirteen children in seventeen years, were typical sacrifices to Victorian fecundity. The effect of this almost perpetual cycle of pregnancy on a husband who was lusty as well as loyal was easy to predict. The Cult of the Double Bed led often to the Cult of the Double Life. While Mamma was presenting Papa with a pair of bouncing twins, Papa might be presenting Mabel with a pair of frisky ponies; the little lover's villa in St. John's Wood became a necessary annexe to the bulging family mansion in Belgravia. So the procrastinating upper-class bachelor and the proligenous upper-class husband between them produced the resplendent upper-class whore, whose emergence as a member of a recognized English *demi-monde,* publicly courted, imitated and discussed, was a phenomenon of the 'sixties.

Chapter III

Harlotry Triumphant

I. ENTER THE HORSEBREAKERS

"*CUPID*" *at the Helm:* In 1860, Queen Victoria had been on the throne for twenty-three years—more than a third of her reign—but statesmen who had begun their careers in the reign of George III and who had drunk and gambled and whored through the Regency, were still in public life. The Prime Minister, Lord Palmerston, had been a junior lord of the Admiralty two years after Trafalgar and Secretary at War six years before Waterloo. Harriette Wilson tells of him dropping in at one of her sister's parties to share a tray-supper of chicken, champagne and claret with Beau Brummell and Lord Alvanly. She reports also that he once did her "a pecuniary service" without being asked. Now, as Victoria's first Minister, he had as little respect for the Queen's moral code as he had for her views on foreign policy. He had never shown much reticence in his sexual enterprises. He was Lady Cowper's lover while her husband was still alive and when he married her as a widow it was generally accepted that he was the father of her beautiful twenty-year-old daughter, Lady Jocelyn, who was one of Victoria's ladies-in-waiting. He had even had the effrontery to attempt to seduce Mrs. Brand, another of the Queen's ladies, while enjoying the royal hospitality at Windsor Castle; an abuse of guestship which soon reached the unsympathetic ears of his hostess.

Palmerston was middle-aged when he received his most famous nickname "Cupid", and in his eightieth year he was co-respondent in a divorce suit brought by the husband of a "jolly, short and stout Irishwoman with fine black eyes and darkly pencilled eyebrows", who had been in Lady Jocelyn's employ. The suit was dismissed on a technicality, but there seems little doubt that this was contrived to save scandal. William Hardman gives a succinct account of the affair in a letter to his friend in Melbourne, Edward Holroyd:

> The potent septuagenarian nobleman proved irresistible to the easy-virtued nursery governess. Hence a connection which resulted in various letters, sundry banknotes, and equivalent copulation.

It is not surprising that the septuagenarian nobleman was, in Greville's words, "always asleep both in the Cabinet and the House", a practice he tried to conceal by wearing his hat over his eyes.

As he nodded over his *Morning Post* one sultry July morning in 1860, Palmerston may have seen an article complaining of the shameless way "fine young English gentlemen" associated openly with London's elegant harlots, even to the point of riding with them in the parks. "We see them descend from their mother's box at the Opera to exchange persiflage with notorious individuals," said the writer. "We detect them rising from their chairs in Rotten Row, by the side of Lais and Aspasia, to chat with Lady Alice or Miss Fanny over the rail." The remedy was for hostesses to decline the acquaintance of these young men. If this were done, "they would no longer openly court their mistresses in the presence of their sisters. . . . Such things were not done even under the dissolute society of the Regency; they certainly should not be done in the respectable reign of Victoria."

The plaint was reprinted, according to current journalistic practice, in *The Times*, and evoked a reply from a reader who signed himself "A Young Englishman". He blamed the *grandes dames* of English society, with their insistence on fashionable and opulent marriages, for the prevalent evil, and timidly suggesting that one day a parallel might be drawn between London and Athens, quoted Grote's comment on Athenian ladies: "Their society presented no charm or interest which was accordingly sought in the company of a class of women entitled Hetairae, or courtesans, who . . . supported themselves by their power of pleasing." The parallel between the fashionable London harlot and the Greek courtesan was to be made often during the 'sixties. It flattered the cultivated reader and appeased Mrs. Grundy when journalists wrote of Aspasia and Lais in London—"those" as *The Times* said in a leading article, "for whom to the credit of the English language, a Greek name is the most appropriate".

A Flutter of Soiled Doves: But the English language was soon to prove capable of evolving an attractive English term for attractive English whores. For a decade or more they were known in the most august columns of journalism as "pretty horsebreakers". The inventor of this charming phrase is unknown; it suggests at once the good-humoured, even affectionate, tolerance with which, by the upper classes, at least, these enterprising creatures were regarded. Surprisingly, though the phrase was very widely used, even by the leader-writers of *The Times*, it is not included in Murray's massive dictionary. Neither is "Anonyma", another synonym for a high-class harlot that was current about the same time.

Students of semasiology discussed the social implications of these and other coinages. "The very fact that we have lost sight of the old-fashioned language . . . is significant," said the *Saturday Review* in 1860. "We purposely used the term 'street-walker' just now; but nobody else uses the phrase, nor that of prostitute, to say nothing of more homely language. The term 'Social Evil' by a queer translation of the abstract into the concrete has become a personality. 'Unfortunates' and 'fallen sisters' are the language of the sentimental." There was a current story of a young woman in the street who was given a tract by an evangelist and entreated to go home and read it; she looked at him bewilderedly for a moment or two, and exclaimed: "Lor bless you, sir, I ain't a social evil, I'm waiting for the bus." The *Saturday Review* commented that the society that supplied these euphemisms had done something to break down the barriers of virtue.

"The straightforward names that our fathers used have been repudiated by the delicacy of the age," it said, in 1862. "In coarser times words were employed to represent facts; but in proportion as the facts became more numerous, and more obtrusive, the words which represent them have become obsolete and shocking":

> Many circumlocutions have undoubtedly been invented to describe . . . the highly-tinted Venuses who form so favourite a study of the connoisseurs of the Haymarket . . . But on the whole, the nicest, the softest, the most poetical designation we have heard is that which the Penitentiaries have invented—"soiled doves" . . . The time will no doubt come when this, too, will be thought too coarse and too direct.

A few years later the *Saturday Review* suspected they had "a good deal more of the soil than of the dove about them", and suggested it would be better if we used more Saxon speech when we spoke of the courtesans of the day.

"Traviata", another pretty substitute for the Saxon, became popular after the opera was performed in London in 1856. "It is nicer phraseology than that of coarser days when port wine drinkers and bluff parsons called such persons courtesans or harlots," observed *Vanity Fair*. "It might perhaps be said . . . that the terms have become more delicate . . . because the subjects of them have preliminarily become more refined, and that the Anonyma of 1869 would probably vote Lady Bellaston not fit to sit down to dinner with."

Venus Holds Court: There were "pretty horsebreakers" in London before the 'sixties, of course. Men who had learnt the facts of life under George the Bad were not likely to forget them because an austere wind blew through the court of Victoria and Albert the Good. It was only thirty-five years since Harriette Wilson's *Memoirs* had sent a shiver through the clubrooms of St. James's Street and Pall Mall. It was only eighteen years since Greville had penned his memorable description of the last days of the "ostentatiously crapulous" Lord Hertford:

> Between sixty and seventy years old, broken with various infirmities, and almost unintelligible from a paralysis of the tongue, he had been in the habit of travelling about with a company of prostitutes who formed his principal society, and by whom he was surrounded up to the moment of his death, generally picking them up from the dregs of that class, and changing them according to his fancy and caprice. Here he was to be seen driving about the town, and lifted by two footmen from his carriage into the brothel, and he never seems to have thought it necessary to throw the slightest veil over the habits he pursued.

"There can be no disguising the fact", said a writer in *Paul Pry* in 1857, "that at the West End, at Brompton, at St. John's Wood, Foley Place, Portland Road, Regent's Park, and intermediate spots some of the most magnificent women in London live under the protection of gentlemen."

But it was not till the end of the 'fifties that the London Aspasias became conspicuous in the fashionable life of Hyde Park, where their skill as equestriennes and drivers suggested the new title of "pretty horsebreakers". Hyde Park during the high season—from May to mid-July—was then a spectacle of unexampled brilliance, "a large open drawing-room", a contemporary writer called it, where people loitered for hours watching London society on parade—the ponderous family carriage, with its gleam of brasswork, its solemn cock-hatted coachmen on the hammer-cloth and brace of flunkies on the splashboard; the fashionable victoria, open to the summer sun: the new, perhaps too shiny, barouche bearing the new, perhaps too shiny, escutcheons of the City magnate: the mail-phaeton, fast and raffish, with a blood at the ribbons and a cockaded tiger at the back: and the riders on horseback, with their sleek and beautiful mounts.

Into this glittering pageant the fashionable whores of the 'sixties boldly insinuated themselves and very soon, by their dashing appearance dominated it. Writing of London, in 1859, George Augustus Sala described them in prose as florid as his famous nose:

> The Danaës! The Amazons! The lady cavaliers! The horse-women! Can any scene in the world equal Rotten Row at four in the afternoon and in the full tide of the season? Watch the sylphides as they fly or float past in their ravishing riding-habits and intoxicatingly delightful hats; some with the orthodox cylindrical beaver, with the flowing veil; others with roguish little wide-awakes, or pertly cocked cavaliers' hats and green plumes. And as the joyous cavalcade streams past ... from time to time the naughty wind will flutter the skirt of a habit, and display a tiny, coquettish, brilliant little boot, with a military heel, and tightly strapped over it the Amazon-ian riding trouser.

All the sylphides did not canter out of the pages of Debrett. Some of the most attractive, and the most eagerly awaited, were ladies of the town:

> You may chance to have with you [said Mr. Sala], a grim town Diogenes . . . who pointing with the finger of a hard buck-skin glove towards the graceful *écuyères*, will say: "Those are not all countessess' or earls' daughters, my son. She on the bay, yonder, is Lais. Yonder goes Aspasia, with Jack Alcibiades on his black mare Timon; see, they have stopped at the end of the ride to talk to Phryne in her brougham. Some of these dashing delightful creatures have covered themselves with shame, and their mothers with grief, and have brought their fathers' grey hair with sorrow to the grave. All is not gold that glitters, my son."

Newspaper readers and writers continued to express alarm at the invasion of good society by these wantons, and the open acceptance of them. "It is said that hetairism, with its Phrynes and Aspasias, is so far becoming a recognized institution that patrician matrons and aristocratic maidenhood allude to the subject with more simpers than blushes," said the *Saturday Review* in 1860. The gallant Captain Gronow, who had spent his "hot youth" in the reign of George III was writing his *Recollections* at this time, and he, too, deplored the habits of fashionable young ladies who seemed "to have taken for ideal a something between the dashing London horsebreakers and some Parisian *artiste dramatique* of a third-rate theatre". The object of their ambition was "to be mistaken for a *femme du demi-monde*" and "to discuss the merits of Skittles and her horses or the latest scandalous story fabricated in the bay window of White's". Skittles was the *nom de lit* of the doyenne of London's demi-monde. Writing of her in 1861, a correspondent to *The Times* asked rhetorically: "Who drives the most rampageous ponies? Whom do all the best girls ape in dress and deportment and equipage, if they can; aye, and in talk, too? Who first set the fashion of the 'pork-pie' hat? Who restored the ancient chimney-pot?"

Skittles' arrival in the Park was the awaited climax of each day's parade. After she and her colleagues had displayed their elegant wares—their hacks, their habits, their chignons and their carriages, they held an open-air *levée*, usually near the thirty-ton statue of Achilles, which was attended by many of Belgravia's most distinguished sons—and fathers. Music-hall comedians sang of it in a popular ballad:

> *The young swells in Rotten Row*
> *All cut it mighty fine,*
> *And quiz the fair sex, you know,*
> *And say it is divine.*
> *The pretty little horsebreakers*
> *Are breaking hearts like fun,*
> *For in Rotten Row they all must go,*
> *The whole hog or none.*

Not many years ago [said *London Society* in 1867], it would have been considered to be the very acme of indecency and impudence ... for any young man ... to appear even to notice in public any of those fair "unfortunates". .... They would have been distressed beyond measure at the idea that their mothers or sisters would suspect, much more know, of their having formed any liaison so dangerous and disreputable. But ... such regard for the proprieties of life scarcely remains. It is no uncommon thing for a young man to appear in the Park escorting a "celebrity" of this kind, and as he passes some lady of acquaintance, to lift his hat in courteous recognition of her, as though there was nothing to be ashamed of in his companion.

A writer in another number of *London Society*, noting the "rapid increase of the *demi-monde* in the Park" suggested that the police should have "peremptory orders" to exclude them: "A man hardly feels easy in conducting a lady into the Park and answering all the questions that may be put to him respecting the inmates of gorgeous carriages that sweep by," he complained. "These demi-reps make peremptory conditions that they shall have broughams for the Park and tickets for the Horticultural and even for the fêtes at the Botanical Gardens."

Fortunately for those who enjoyed the spectacle of vice caparisoned and carefree, no one took any notice of this tettish appeal to the police, who, indeed, even had they possessed the power to remove a well-behaved young woman from the Park, might have been embarrassed to find that she enjoyed the patronage of a Cabinet Minister, or someone still more exalted. Mr. Mayhew, in his patient examination of London prostitution in the 'sixties, hints at this possibility.

"There", he says, "is Lais under the protection of a Prince of the Blood; Aspasia, whose friend is the most influential nobleman in the kingdom; Phryne, the *chère amie* of a well-known officer in the Guards, or a man whose wealth is proverbial on the Stock Exchange." And he observes that "the prevalence of this custom, and the extent of its ramifications, is hardly dreamed of". These women not only had their villas, their carriages, and their box at the Opera; at times, through the influence of their aristocratic friends, they obtained vouchers for "the most exclusive patrician balls". Their condition, says Mr. Mayhew, "is the nearest approximation to the holy state of marriage and finds numerous defenders and supporters".

With a Whip or a Wink: In 1865, the Paris correspondent of the *Morning Post* attended, in the line of duty, a ball given by France's most eminent harlots. He reported that the saloons were crowded with princes, dukes, marquises, and counts, and that "some English peers and Members of Parliament were present and seemed to enjoy the animated and dazzlingly improper scene". Choice Yquem, Johannisberg, Lafite, Tokay and champagne flowed throughout the night, and the "sardanapalian entertainment" was rounded off at seven in the morning with a vigorous *cancan d'enfer*.

A few years later, the *Pall Mall Gazette* recognized the fact that the *demi-monde* now formed a regular set in London life, "having establishments and holding receptions such as distinguish a corresponding class in Paris". And it repeated the complaint of the frank way in which young men of fashion met these women in public resorts: "The yellow-chignoned denizens of St. John's Wood and Pimlico draw up their carriages or horses close to the rails and are chatted with as candidly as if they had come from some dove-cot in the country watched over by a virtuous mother. The audacity of these *réunions* is unprecedented." The notion that the loose women could not be distinguished from their virtuous sisters was preposterous: "In the Park, at least, there is no difficulty in distinguishing the carriage that anybody may pay for, or in guessing the occupation of the dashing *equestrienne* who salutes half a dozen men at once with her whip or with a wink, and who sometimes varies the monotony of a safe seat by holding her hands behind her back while gracefully swerving over to listen to the compliments of a walking admirer."

Smoke Got in Their Eyes: In the 'sixties, too, another assault was made on the traditions of the Park. Because of the example of the young Prince of Wales, smoking began to be tolerated on Rotten Row. A critic of the innovation recalled a character in Lord Lytton's *My Novel,* published in 1853, who had said: "I no more dare smoke this cigar on the Park at half-past six when all the world is abroad, than I dare pick my Lord Chancellor's pocket or hit the Archbishop of Canterbury a thump on the nose."

Shapes that Passed in the Night: Far removed from the enticing Loribelles of Rotten Row were the battered whores who inherited the Park after dark. "Park women," says Mr. Mayhew, "are those degraded creatures, utterly lost to all sense of shame, who wander about the paths most frequented after nightfall ... and consent to any species of humiliation for the sake of acquiring a few shillings." They were to be met in Hyde Park until the closing of the gates, and in the Green Park all night:

> These women are well known to give themselves up to disgusting practices, that are alone gratifying to men of morbid and diseased imaginations. They are old, unsound, and by their appearance utterly incapacitated from practising their profession where the gas-lamps would expose the defects in their personal appearance, and the shabbiness of their ancient and dilapidated attire.

Mr. Mayhew was told of one of these old women who earned a precarious livelihood haunting the by-walks of Hyde Park near Park Lane, though her front teeth were "absolutely wanting".

II. LAMENT FROM BELGRAVIA

Two Dozen Virtuous Daughters: The rivalry between the pretty horsebreakers and the virtuous daughters of Albion was the theme of a series of letters published in *The Times* during June and July, 1861. The first, though signed "Seven Belgravian Mothers" was almost certainly written by James Matthew Higgins, who for many years amused himself by sowing controversies in the correspondence columns. Higgins was a wealthy man-about-town and a Quixotic amateur of letters—a "guerrilla journalist", *The Spectator* called him—who tilted with his pen under a bewildering variety of disguises; "Jacob Omnium", "A Thirsty Soul", "Paterfamilias", "Mother of Six" (to whom he replied as "Father of Four"), "John Barleycorn", "Rose du Barri", were some. He combined a light, ironic style with a crusading zeal that ranged from the reform of the public schools to the emancipation of London's street horses by the introduction of steam-rollers. His friends, among them Thackeray, knew him as "the genial giant"; he was 6 ft. 8 in. high.

The "Seven Belgravian Mothers", mostly noblewomen, declared that they had between them twenty-four daughters to dispose of at the altar. No opportunity had been missed to guide them into the nuptial bed, "balls, bazaars, breakfasts, concerts, scientific conversazione; churches and chapels; the Opera; Epsom; Ascot; Volunteer reviews; even the Crystal Palace". But all in vain. None of the two dozen accomplished virgins had received an offer of marriage that could be seriously entertained. "Marriage in our world seems to be repudiated," the seven sorrowing mothers lamented. Eligible young men danced with the daughters, flirted with them, ate their parents' food and drank their parents' claret. But they would not marry. And why? Because of what the "simple-minded" daughters called "the pretty horsebreakers". "These bad rivals of our children are no longer kept in the background," said the "mothers". "Neither Row nor ring, church nor chapel, opera nor concert, are wanting in their evident, recognized presence. . . . Our husbands have been at their balls—the best dancing, they say, and perfect decorum."

Low Cost of Love-Nests: Among the many readers of *The*

Times who replied to the "Belgravian Mothers'" lament was a clubman signing himself "Beau Jolais" who offered an economic interpretation of the pretty horsebreakers. These "frail young beings", he said, were the result of "the hollowness, worldliness and insincerity of the age". Years before, when Beau Jolais had sounded his "soul's idol" as to her expectations in marriage, she intimated blandly that her aspirations were of the humblest order. . . . "Just a brougham and pair, a saddle horse (necessarily implying two), a house in a quiet part of Belgravia, a cottage in the Isle of Wight, and an occasional box at the Opera." Her fortune was under £2,000 and his income at the time, £500. "Girls," said Beau Jolais, "are now so expensively, thoughtlessly, brought up, and led to expect so lavish an outlay on the part of the husband . . . that hundreds have been forced to abandon all notion of a connubial alliance, taking up instead with a simple and more economical arrangement, temporary or permanent. . . ."

As an example of the advantages and amenities of such an arrangement, Beau Jolais described the establishment of a friend with whom he had dined the day before, and a "more comfortable, a more elegant *ménage*" he had never beheld. The hostess was apparently as efficient at home-making as at horse-breaking. Her conduct was as faultless as that of any high-born lady, and unlike the typical *chère amie* of Mr. Mayhew's survey, she was well educated, conversed with ease in three languages, sang, played, and drew really well, was familiar with the topics and writers of the day, and witty in repartee. With all these useful accomplishments, and others no doubt equally endearing, she supervised admirably the management of her protector's cuisine and cellar. Yet this delightful synthesis of culture, charm and comfort cost Beau Jolais's friend less than the rigours, repressions, and compromises of bachelorhood. Out of an income of only £600 he had a larger balance left at the end of the year, than when he was dwelling alone in chambers at the Albany. Beau Jolais advised the mothers of England to bring up their daughters with less extravagant ideas; "Teach them economy and let them prove to the rising generation that virtue may be rendered less costly than vice. . . . Thus and thus only can Lais and Aspasia, Blondelle and Loribelle, with all their pretty sisterhood, be effectually disarmed."

The suggestion that virtue should be encouraged to challenge vice on economic, rather than on moral, grounds was an interesting reflex of the commercial spirit of the age. This pragmatic acceptance of unhallowed fornication evoked a sharp comment from "An Old-fashioned Parson" who wrote: "We seem to be going back to the morality of last century. Illegal connection is no longer called adultery but a 'temporary engagement'. This is much the same kind of euphemism as I observe in your city articles where robbery is called 'defalcation'. I suppose it would be very vulgar to quote the seventh and eighth commandments in reference to these questions, but a spade is a spade for all that."

Market Report: The *Saturday Review* joined the forum with a light-hearted review:

The market is absolutely glutted with unsaleable young ladies. Heiresses, of course, are still brisk, and something is done in pretty orphans. A little inquiry has been made for motherless articles of prime quality, the absence of a mother-in-law increasing the price considerably. But buyers will not look at the ordinary, well-chaperoned, pink-and-white, unexceptionable young lady. Whole rows of them may be seen undisposed of in any ballroom, wrapped up in their own weight of tarlatan. Many various reasons have been assigned for this melancholy stagnation of an interesting trade . . . the favourite theory attributes the cause to the unusual fascinations which are on all hands ascribed to the present race of "pretty horsebreakers".

Mothers preparing their daughters for the wife-market made the mistake of assuming that what a man looked for in a wife was "a bad imitation" of a pretty horsebreaker. The training of daughters was concentrated on making them "eligible objects for young men to make love to". But the stratagem "of entrapping men to make wives of their daughters by fitting them to be their mistresses" broke down in practice for two reasons:

In the first place it is idle for the amateur to compete with the professional. In the second place, men are not quite such lunatics as the fashionable mothers appear to think. They know that the power of amusement may beguile odd evenings during a few years of life. But to pass a whole life with a woman who can do nothing but amuse is like dining for life on sugar-candy.... St. John's Wood offers him the real thing, Belgravia offers him a washed-out and imperfect imitation. But Belgravia insists that he should tie himself to the inferior article for life; while St. John's Wood is content that he should change whenever he think fit.

So in St. John's Wood—the Grove of the Evangelist, smart people called it—the moneyed men of the 'sixties decreed their sprightly pleasure domes. A new suburb arose, dedicated to Cytherea, of pretty little villas, screened from Victorian gigmanity by shrubs and trees and convent walls. Here, the pretty horsebreakers rested after the fatigues of Rotten Row, and here the bachelor refugees from Belgravia and their errant husbands of Mayfair, dined on sugar candy with their Aspasias and Loribelles and Mabels and Nellies and Kates.

III. SENSATION IN DRURY LANE

"*Railroad to Ruin*": The elegant harlot was in the Park and in the news; it was inevitable that she should make her bow in the theatre. Her stage début was arranged by Mr. Dion Boucicault, the industrious actor-manager and author of about 150 plays, including the very successful *Colleen Bawn*. Boucicault was an Irishman of French descent who was supposed to look like Sir Kenelm Digby.

In 1869, early in August when London was "deserted", Mr. Chatterton, manager of Drury Lane Theatre, announced a sensational new Boucicault melodrama: *Formosa, or The Railroad to Ruin*. The play opens in Oxford just before the University Boat Race. Sam Boker, a virtuous ex-pugilist and his equally virtuous wife, keep a modest riverside pub. They have a pretty daughter called Jenny who they believe has a respectable domestic situation in London, though at times as when the play begins, she comes home and helps them in the bar. Little do they realize that Jenny is known to half the House of Lords as Formosa; she is, as the dramatic critic of *The Times* put it, "one of those meteoric beauties who frequently change their names, inhabit superb villas, and whose public scene of action is Rotten Row".

Nor does the handsome, imprudent and susceptible undergraduate Tom Burroughs, who meets her in her parents' pub, recognize in the modest Jenny the notorious London *demi-mondaine*. But unfortunately Tom's cousin and heir-presumptive, a cad called Compton Kerr, does; and with a curl of his wicked mustachio, resolves to cash in on his knowledge. For Tom, who has fallen in love with Jenny, is the stroke of the Oxford Eight, and Kerr has wagered heavily and recklessly on Cambridge. Oxford is strong favourite (having won every race from 1861 to 1869) and Kerr is ruined if it wins again. So he hisses in Jenny-Formosa's little ear that unless she helps him to promote Tom's ruin before the race, he will expose her London life to her noble, trusting parents. To save the ingenuous couple from shame, Formosa agrees.

The curtain rises on the second scene to disclose Tom "travelling express on the railroad to ruin". He has been playing baccarat at Formosa's luxurious Fulham villa, surrounded by painted and bejewelled harlots, powdered footmen, champagne, and card-sharps. Cousin Kerr and an evil accomplice called

Major Jorum have not only fleeced him at play but forged his name to I.O.U.s. In vain has honest young Lord Eden pleaded with him to remember the interests of the Oxford Eight; on the very eve of the race Tom lies asleep on a sofa in Formosa's boudoir, besotted, and about to be arrested for debt. Suddenly, into this masque of Fortuna, Bacchus and Cytherea, burst Formosa's bewildered parents, who have been looking for her all over London. Formosa, overcome with shame and contrition— "her leap from vice to virtue is sudden and sublime", said *The Times*—immediately sells her valuables, spoils of her sinful past, to liberate Tom from the bailiffs, and leaves her Fulham villa with her parents, never to brighten its doorstep again. Tom is released from the sponging-house just in time to stroke the Dark Blues to victory. He marries an old sweetheart, who had been forgotten in a sub-plot, and Formosa marries a wealthy and devoted admirer, though returning with Mr. and Mrs. Boker to the beer pumps.

This lush and lively melodrama was highly praised by *The Times*' critic, who predicted a long run for it. "The man of the world will start at the magical transformation of Formosa from a 'goblin-damn'd' into an angel of light," he observed. "But the belief that in the lower orders there is a latent principle of virtue that no circumstances of social humiliation can overcome is the cherished faith of a vast portion of the public, to whom a gallon of sentimentality is more tolerable than a homeopathic dose of cynical truth."

Harlots and Heroines: The sentimentally-inclined public, to the satisfaction of Messrs. Chatterton and Boucicault, endorsed the verdict of *The Times*, but less sympathetic critics soon reached for their pens. The first was an old Oxonian who complained to *The Times* about an Oxford stroke moving up to the eve of the race in "the very vortex of dissipation". There were two categorical objections to this, he pointed out:

(1) He would not be permitted to do this.
(2) If permitted, he would be simply incapable of rowing.

This specialized but not very serious objection was followed by a 3,000-word polemic from an angry reader who signed himself "Amateur Critic", in which Mr. Boucicault was accused of corrupting the English stage. "Not only is a harlot the heroine of the piece," he wrote, "but her harlotry is made one of its most prominent features. To assist the effect, there were three or four subordinate harlots":

I have never before seen or heard of anything like this open introduction of harlots and harlotry on the stage in an English play and I have hitherto always fondly believed that this was one of the best recognized and not least important distinctions between the dramas of the two nations, that however necessary it may be to exercise caution in Paris, one can in London always take one's unmarried sister or country cousins to a theatre without risk of prostitution, in all the glory of paint, powder, costly jewellery and superb dresses, being flaunted before them.

Mr. Chatterton replied to this letter from the managerial viewpoint. He offered to show his box-book, "crowded with names of ladies, the most respectable in London". Ladies, too, were in a majority in the stalls. It was obvious that they approved of *Formosa*. Yet for seven lean years, Mr. Chatterton had lost money staging Shakespeare, Byron, Milton and Goethe. These enterprises, though supported cheerfully by the pit and gallery had been sadly deserted by the boxes and stalls. "I am neither a literary missionary nor a martyr", Mr. Chatterton wrote. "I am simply—the manager of a theatre, a vendor of intellectual entertainment to the London public, and I found that Shakespeare spelt ruin and Byron bankruptcy."

The Nude Language of Newspapers: In a much longer reply, Mr. Boucicault carried the war right into his assailant's home. He asked whether "Amateur Critic" expurgated *The Times* before leaving for his club, or whether his young daughters were left to pore over its sensational divorce reports. Why were such scenes reproduced in the theatre an abomination, when described in nude language in the columns of *The Times*, they were fit for the digestion of the innocent? From the Press, Mr. Boucicault turned with gusto to the Opera, a place of entertainment especially devoted to the young females of "Amateur Critic's" class.

"Last season's favourite operas", he wrote, "were Norma, Don Giovanni, Rigoletto, Traviata, Lucrezia Borgia, Faust, and the Somnambula." What were the themes of these popular entertainments?

Norma is a vestal priestess who has been seduced. She discovers her paramour in an attempt to seduce her friend, another vestal priestess, and in despair contemplates the murder of her bastard children. *Don Giovanni* is the proverbial hero whose career represents the romance of successful adultery and debauchery. *Rigoletto* exhibits the agony of a father obliged to witness the prostitution of his own child. *La Traviata* is the progress of a transcendental harlot. *Lucrezia Borgia* is the history of adultery not unassociated with incest. *Faust* is the most specious apology for seduction, ending with the apotheosis of crime—Margaret, who murders her mother and her illegitimate child, is carried up to Heaven. *The Somnambula* is the most idyllic, the most innocent, of the Italian *repertoire*, and perhaps the most popular. In this play, we see a young girl, on the night before her marriage, entering the bedroom of a gentleman just as he is retiring to rest. She is in her night-dress and carries a flat candlestick. She gets into his bed. In this situation she is found by her intended husband. . . .

Mr. Boucicault suggested that "Amateur Critic" believed in a limited obscurantism, with a line drawn between the English Theatre on the one side, and the Press and the Italian Opera on the other. "I decline to accept the moral disfranchisement," he declared resoundingly. "The production of *Formosa* was calculated and deliberate. I, at least, have submitted long enough to a ridiculous restriction. I have broken down a barrier which prejudice had established. I have proclaimed a literary thorough-fare, with the full approbation of the public. And I mean to keep it open."

Sin on the High Cs: The dramatic critic of *The Times* had approved of the demolition of these literary road-blocks, but the editor could not overlook references to the nude language of his columns. He had already dealt briefly with Mr. Chatterton's economic defence of his theatre policy; now a second and formidable editorial bull was released against Mr. Boucicault and his moral arguments:

"We readily admit", said *The Times*, "that our columns occasionally contain reports of cases that are not less offensive, and references to others that are infinitely more offensive, than even Mr. Boucicault, with all his courage, would dare to put on the stage." But in no family with pretensions to be well-conducted were young girls allowed to read such reports—though, of course "a girl may read them on the sly, taking her risk of being discovered, as she may go to her father's library to read Peregrine Pickle or Don Juan." They were published, not for the study of young girls, but because it was the opinion of the nation and the age that publicity in such matters was on the whole preferable to secrecy. As for the "nude language", it was amazing that a man of Mr. Boucicault's ability did not see that this very nakedness made them harmless: "Our police reports frequently contain brief biographies of such ladies as Formosa, but told in plain language, they do anything but attract. It is when affecting situations, jewels, powdered foot-men and fine phraseology are thrown in . . . that the story becomes morally mischievous."

Mr. Boucicault had a better case, *The Times* conceded, when he turned from the Press to the Opera, but pointed out, without underrating the task of defending the Opera, that it stood on an entirely different footing from the Theatre. It was a "Utopia in Fairyland", and its morals were not to be judged by the standards of real life. "The mere fact that all the sinning is done to tune, and that one class of crime is usually assigned to the bass and another to the tenor, would alone suffice to destroy all resemblance between it and our unmusical matter-of-fact world."

Descent to the Mud: Meanwhile, stimulated by this and similar publicity in other newspapers and reviews, the show went on. "The immediate result of 'Amateur Critic's' letter will be an enormous run on the piece," a writer in *Vanity Fair* observed. Analysing the *Formosa* boom, he came to the conclusion that though society was not any worse than it had been twelve years before when *La Traviata* was the rage, morality had sunk "many fathoms nearer the mud" since his father's day. "Men, twenty years ago," he wrote, repeating a now familiar plaint, "were not seen sitting side by side with their cocottes in the boxes and stalls of our theatres. If they had their little weaknesses, they did not dare openly flaunt them before the public. . . . Society, rotten at the core as it has long been, is now so at the surface, and until the ban of ostracism is set on those men who flagrantly outrage decency, it will remain so."

Vice Behind the Footlights: "Amateur Critic" nakedly revealed his amateur status when he wrote of harlotry on the English stage as something novel; he had never encountered the long line of stage harlots, the Blandas, the Prisses, the Frails, the Shave'ems, the Mistress Frigbottoms, Cicely Bumtrinkets and Penelope Whorehounds, who minced behind the candles of the Elizabethan and Restoration Theatre.

Sixteen years before the Lord Chamberlain permitted the production of *Formosa*, he had refused to license an English stage version of Dumas' *La Dame Aux Camelias*. At the time, George Henry Lewes, later to violate convention by taking George Eliot for mistress, applauded the Lord Chamberlain for prohibiting "this unhealthy idealization of one of the worst evils of our social life". Paris might delight in such pictures, he wrote, "but London, thank God! has still enough instinctive repulsion against pruriency not to tolerate them". But within three years, packed houses at Her Majesty's were applauding the opera *La Traviata* in which Verdi had transformed Marguerite Gautier into Violetta, and given sin its aseptic habiliments of song. *The Times*, reporting Piccolimini's triumphant début, said Violetta was "a reigning belle, more celebrated for beauty than for virtue", but made no other comment on her morals. And in 1858, Dumas' original play was presented in English at the Lyceum.

IV. MAD WINDHAM AND BAWDYHOUSE BOB

Wedding in St. John's Wood: The symposium about pretty horsebreakers in *The Times* was read with particular interest by a young man called William Frederick Windham, who belonged to an old Norfolk family and was heir to its seat, Felbrigg Hall, and considerable estates. His mother was the daughter of the first Marquis of Bristol; his father was dead, and at the time of the "Belgravian Mothers'" lament, he was within a month of attaining his majority, and succeeding to his inheritance. He was an uncouth, irresponsible fellow, of gross habits and low tastes, and given to wild and offensive pranks. In Norfolk, he was known as "Mad Windham", a title conferred on him at Eton. He was now living in Duke St., St. James, and amusing himself in raffish adventures round town; principally in the vicinity of the Haymarket, where he liked to pose as a policeman, and thus to threaten with arrest the ambulant prostitutes of the nighthouses and the pavements. In this diversion he was not discouraged by the genuine police, who treated him with the good-humoured tolerance traditionally shown by the London constabulary towards the caprices of wealth and rank.

When Mr. Martin, the bailiff of the Windham estates, came to town to stay with his young master in July, 1861, Windham drew his attention to what he called the "capital" letters in *The Times:* and declared emphatically that he would rather marry a pretty horsebreaker than a lady. Martin did not take this announcement seriously, but soon after Windham told him that he was about to marry Agnes Willoughby, one of the most attractive and most celebrated of London's high-class harlotry. Miss Willoughby, whose real name was Rogers, and who claimed to be a clergyman's daughter, was then living elegantly in Blenheim Place, St. John's Wood, under the patronage of a Mr. Roberts who allowed her £2,000 a year. At a time when 18,000,000 of England's population of 20,000,000 had incomes of less than £100 a year, when agricultural families of seven were living on 13s. a week, and London needlewomen were stitching cotton-bands from dawn to dusk to earn 3½d. a day, less the price of the cotton which they had to supply, Miss Willoughby's annuity was not ungenerous. It enabled her not only to dress becomingly, but to exercise her skill as a horsewoman; she kept a string of high-class hunters, rode during the Season in Hyde Park, and followed the Queen's staghounds in Buckinghamshire. Roberts, who introduced Windham to his mistress, and then graciously agreed to relinquish his interest in her, was a well-known man-about-town. He had an income of £5,000 a year, lived in a mansion in Piccadilly, and maintained his four-in-hand, his brougham, and his hounds. Windham had a great affection for him and like his other intimates, called him "Bawdyhouse Bob", in playful recognition of the fact that Roberts owned a string of fashionable brothels in Shepherd Street.

The faithful Martin tried to prevent the marriage, but Windham ridiculed his objections, and quoted the names of two noblemen who had recently married harlots. Windham came of age on 9th August, 1861. Three weeks later he and Agnes Willoughby were married in All Saints' Church, St. John's Wood. His income was then £3,000 a year, reduced by certain deductions to £1,300. He made his wife a perpetual, not merely a life, settlement of £800 a year, to be increased to £1,500 in 1869, when he would succeed to additional estates worth about £5,000 a year. He also bought her £14,000 worth of jewellery, in compensation, he said, for having given her a "foul disease". For unexplained, but apparently sentimental reasons, and with Windham's approval, Miss Willoughby passed her pre-nuptial night under the roof of her retiring protector, but afterwards denied that she had shown him any valedictory courtesies. It is charitable to assume that the last hours together were devoted to a discussion of the notable news of the week—the Queen's visit to Ireland; the female Blondin's hazardous journey across the Thames on a single wire; President Lincoln's proclamation of a state of insurrection in the Southern States.

De Lunatico Inquirendo: Windham's uncles, Lord Bristol, Lord Alfred Hervey and General Windham, heard of these extravagancies with a disquiet that was not allayed when Roberts arrived at Felbrigg Hall to cut down all the timber on the property, claiming that Windham had sold him the rights. Family lawyers were consulted, and it was decided to ask for a Commission in Lunacy to declare that young Windham was insane and incapable of managing his valuable estates. A panel of eminent counsel and a great number of witnesses were mobilized to prove that Windham's transactions with Miss Willoughby and Mr. Roberts were characteristic episodes in a long history of lunacy.

There was certainly abundant evidence that his conduct since childhood had been at least idiosyncratic. Before he went to school he had known no companions but the stablehands and servants of Felbrigg Hall. As a child he had been so fond of life below stairs that his father, also an eccentric, had fitted him with a Windham livery—blue coat, red waistcoat, red plush breeches and dress buttons—in which he would wait at dinner, from soup to dessert. At Eton, his conduct was alternately that of a buffoon and a savage. Many bewildered tutors in turn tried to nurture in him an appreciation of Homer, Horace, Virgil and Lucian, but were frustrated by his unorthodox responses, which included screeching, howling, slavering, carpet-biting, and over-eating to the point of disgorging on the table. His contempt for scholarship was unconcealed, and the only enthusiasm he displayed, apart from food, was for horses and railway-engines. In his mingled and enduring passion for these two forms of locomotion, Windham was a curious symbol of the overlapping centuries. He belonged, at the same time, to the age of the aristocratic coachdriver, and to the age of the humbly-born engineer. His greatuncle William Windham, a hard-living eighteenth-century blood who had been Secretary at War under the younger Pitt, would have understood this aspect of his kinsman, though he would have recoiled in fastidious disgust from the young man's slovenly habits.

As a youth, the Victorian Windham stole a mail-cart and tried to drive it into a menagerie, a whimsy that involved him in a fight, and two black eyes. Years later, he took to driving a Norwich coach, assuming a broad East Anglian accent to fit the role. But he always derived his greatest satisfaction from an association with trains. When he was at Eton, he used to ride in the guard's van whenever possible, or he would run round the grounds with a lamp, imitating a locomotive, or play guard with a whistle and the study doors. Back in Norwich, an old Etonian, he provided himself with a guard's uniform and its appendages, ticket-bag, whistle, and pouch. Dressed in these, he would install himself at the local station, take the luggage from passengers, put it in the van, and jump in after it, repeating the process at every stop. This necessarily involved some co-operation from the railway employees, and Windham's relations with them, as with the London police later, became so cordial that he soon progressed from guard to stoker, and ultimately, to engine-driver. It was a logical development from the days when a Sir John Lacey took the ribbons of the Brighton coach, though it is doubtful whether the passengers whose lives were in "Mad Windham's" hands would have appreciated the historic parallel.

The Queen Was Not Amused: When "Bawdyhouse Bob" Roberts heard of the projected Commission in Lunacy, he composed a placard, which Windham signed, and of which 500 copies were stuck up round London, calling upon the men and women of Great Britain to attend a preliminary meeting at the Freemasons' Tavern, and afterwards a monster demonstration in Hyde Park, to protect Windham from a conspiracy to defraud him of his property. The placard also invoked the intervention of Queen Victoria. There was no response from the Palace or the public. The demonstration did not take place, and the printer of the placards was not paid. Meanwhile, Mrs. Windham had left her husband. Their married life together had lasted two months.

"*The Notorious General Windham*": The Commission, comprising the Master in Lunacy, Mr. Samuel Warren, Q.C., and a special jury of twenty-one, began its hearing on 16th December, 1861. It sat for thirty-four days, at a cost assessed by an eminent contemporary mathematician of nearly £3 3s. a minute. The Prince Consort had died three days before the Commission opened, but even this tremendous event, and the elaborate obsequies that followed, did not overshadow the long daily reports of the Windham affair in the London press.

The petitioners were handicapped somewhat by the reputation of General Windham, both as an officer and a gentleman. "The notorious General Windham, of Crimean pseudo-fame, and Indian disgrace", was William Hardman's description of him. "This man," he added, "gained his honours in the Redan business by disobeying orders, and afterwards lost us the only battle in which we were worsted in the Indian Mutiny." His military record apart, the General was a dubious protagonist in a lunacy inquiry: "The General refuses to enter the witness-box from a dread of having his foul practices exposed," wrote Hardman. "He was once accused of indecent exposure in Hyde Park, and was got off by his counsel on the plea of insanity." His nephew, on the other hand, appeared at the Commission several times, and conducted himself "with the utmost propriety and decorum". *The Times* reporter described him as of "middle height, with a full habit of body, inclining to corpulency, dark complexion and hair parted down the middle". He wore a moustache, which covered the congenital defect in his upper lip.

How Many Eggs for Breakfast? One hundred and forty witnesses were heard—fifty for the petitioners and ninety for "Mad Windham". The Master in Lunacy, who was an undistinguished novelist as well as an undistinguished lawyer, exercised almost no control over the proceedings which often degenerated into a bedlam of irrelevancies. Much of the evidence was absurdly trivial. Men and women were brought great distances to swear that young Windham ate like a hog, or did not, or to affirm or deny that he liked blacking his face and playing on a banjo. Many of these witnesses were tutors who had wrestled with him in his adolescence. The Rev. H. J. Cheales told how at a party Windham had "suddenly seized a strange gentleman by the whiskers and ran him up against a wall, screeching and howling all the time". To refute this, the strange gentleman was produced in person. He was an Italian music-teacher and he testified that Windham had only pulled him gently by the whiskers as a joke, *"pour s'amuser"*, and had not run him against a wall. Another tutor, Mr. Peatfield, was imported from St. Petersburg to tell the Commission that Windham used to imitate cocks and cats and jump about violently. "All this," said Mr. Peatfield "would be mixed up with snatches of negro songs such as:

> *I'm off to Charlestown*
> *So early in the morning*

and *"We're all off to Dixie Land"*. Mr. Peatfield also revealed that Windham liked to dance on billiards tables.

Colonel Bristol of the Guards told how he had been persuaded to take Windham on an educational tour of Europe, but had given up the job after three months. "I might as well have taken charge of a wild beast," he said. His attempts to interest his charge in the beauties of literature had been singularly ineffective. Windham had read nothing but two *Ingoldsby Legends*: of which he memorized two lines that he would often repeat. They were:

The modern monk
Got jollily drunk.

With this couplet on his lips, Windham moved to his lodgings in Duke Street. Here, said Mr. Montague Chambers, opening the case for the petitioners, "his gormandizing propensities were exhibited in many curious ways. Once as many as seventeen eggs were served up to his breakfast." Also, he would cut joints and throw the pieces round the room, and he had a habit of calling everybody "Old Bob Ridley" and frequently, while at dinner, would lay down his knife and fork to beat that tune upon the table. ("Old Bob Ridley" and "Dixie's Land" were Mr. Facey Romford's favourite airs on his flute.)

One of Windham's witnesses was a former Eton boarding-house keeper. She admitted that he was known as "Mad Windham" at school but added: "Many boys were called 'mad' at Eton. It was generally the more clever boys who were termed so."

Nourished on enormous quantities of such trivia, with expert witnesses contemptuously refuting expert witnesses, and grandiloquent advocates engaging in marathons of oratory, the inquiry crept on through a chill December into the New Year. "Be this man mad, or be he not," said *The Times* in a terse editorial during its third week, "could any madman make a madder waste of money than that which now made of it each day. . .?"

An Intellectual Study? Windham's exploits as an engine-driver were discussed and analysed at length. To the petitioners they were contributory proofs of his insanity. "I regard the driving of an engine by an amateur, though he may be competent, as an act of folly," said Dr. Forbes Winslow. "The driving of a private four-in-hand or a stage coach by an amateur is not an act of folly . . . In the one case the amateur endangers the lives of hundreds of unconscious passengers; in the other he is dealing with a few friends who have placed themselves at his mercy . . .

Another distinction is that the driving of a railway train is a more difficult and intricate performance . . ."

This distinction was interpreted in Windham's favour by another amateur engine-driver, Lord Claude Hamilton, M.P., a colonel in the Donegal Militia. "I do not consider a taste for driving railway engines a proof of insanity, and such is the opinion of many who hold a distinguished rank in society," he said. "Many years ago I joined with half a dozen others in studying the great motive power of modern times. We attended a course of lectures at the Polytechnic. After a time we were allowed, under proper supervision, to drive engines on railways. . . . I can assure you that it requires a good deal of skill, self-possession, coolness of head, and delicacy of touch. . . . It is decidedly an intellectual study." Lord Hamilton admitted, however, that he had not been permitted to experiment on passenger trains. A juryman who expressed some perturbation that Windham had been given this privilege was reminded by the Master in Lunacy that they were concerned not with the conduct of railway directors but only with Windham's sanity.

On the Power of Love: Towards the end of the inquiry, Mr. John Duke Coleridge addressed the jury on behalf of his client, Mrs. Windham. Coleridge, who was to become a peer and Lord Chief Justice of England, was then a 41-year-old Queen's Council, tall, handsome, and eloquent. During the long hearing he had come to the conclusion that the petitioners would succeed. "There are some low-Church Pharisees on the jury," he wrote to his father. Despite this, and despite the fact that Mrs. Windham had left her husband so soon after her marriage, he made no apologies for his client when he began his address. Instead, he boldly tried to invest the affair with a garland of romance. Mrs. Windham, he told the Commission, was not yet twenty-two; she was a very pretty and attractive person; she had lady-like manners; she was a celebrity in certain circles in London . . . Perhaps even in the lives of the jury themselves there was a time when they were capable of doing foolish things—of giving a great deal for a smile from a young, fascinating and beloved woman . . .

It was a bitterly cold January. The Sessions Room was bleak and draughty. Many of the jury sat huddled in heavy overcoats and skull-caps. Perhaps some warm glow of remembered desire thawed the hearts even of the low-church Pharisees as Coleridge in his musical voice reminded them of the power of love: "Where in the world would be all our poetry, half our novels, the function of some of the most celebrated writers of the present day—even the Master himself"—a bow towards Mr. Samuel Warren —"if there was to be an end to the passion of man for woman, and to the desire of the one sex to connect itself to the other?"

In his opening for the petitioners. Mr. Montague Chambers had described Miss Willoughby as a prostitute. "She was not the chastest of the chaste," he had said. "Her favours in love-affairs were not few." It was difficult to deny this, but Mr Coleridge offered the jury an apposite anecdote from history. Lord Chesterfield, he said, when told of a famous but frail beauty of his time—Mrs. Chudleigh—that the world was so censorious as to say that she had twins, made a profound bow and said he never believed more than half the world said. If the jury would apply that wholesome rule to the opening statement of Mr. Chamber's they would not be doing Mrs. Windham more than justice. There was not a tittle of evidence that she was a common prostitute. And, as to criticisms of her behaviour in marrying Mr. Windham: "A beautiful girl gives herself to an old earl or an old marquis for the sake of position. Why is that which is honourable, pure and right in Lady Mary or Lady Susan to be characterized as abominable, mercenary baseness in Agnes Willoughby?"

"*Himself, His Messuages: His Tenements*": The addresses were finished at last. On the thirty-fourth day of the inquiry, Windham was interrogated in private for nearly four hours, and acquitted himself in "a highly creditable manner". The jury retired. They had listened for more than thirty days. It took them only thirty minutes to return with the verdict: "Mr. Windham is a person of sound mind so as to be sufficient for the government of himself, his manors, his messuages, his land, his tenements, his goods and his chattels." Cries of "joy and exultation" spread quickly from the court-room to the corridors outside. "An attempt was made to restore order but in vain," wrote *The Times* reporter. "Cheers made the Westminster Sessions House ring like an ale-house."

The Times, which had devoted about 170,000 words to reporting the case, observed: "It has been our disagreeable duty to publish evidence of a very disgusting character, but the public may be assured that our reports have been purity itself compared with the horrible mass of nastiness laid before the jury."

Endorsing the jury's decision, it capped Mr. Coleridge's appeal to history with an anecdote about Viscount Bolingbroke: "When Henry St. John was made a Minister of State, the gossip ran that an elderly woman of evil-fame exclaimed in delight *Cinq milles lives de rente, mes enfants, et tout pour nous!*" This verdict will be received in many similar quarters with an equal joy. The sharks of society, the borrowers and the usurers, the toadies and the swaggerers, the procuresses and the courtesans . . . have their prey marked out to them." None the less, the verdict was "emphatically right". For "society cannot undertake to protect men against the consequences of their own vices".

This doctrine that men must not be prevented from compassing their own damnation so long as no one else is affected by the process, was still stoutly held by England's upper-classes, despite the efforts of the messiahs of Nonconformity to outlaw sin by Act of Parliament. It was expressed even more emphatically by the *Saturday Review:* "If you are to deprive a man of the conduct of his own affairs because he is, as in this instance, a profligate, a fool, and a spendthrift, and because he is certain to bring himself to ruin, of course you must prevent a man ruining himself by drink, by gambling, by harlotry, by extravagance, by buying rare books, or sumptuous pictures. There is no limit to the frightful consequences which follow from the argument that Windham ought to be coerced because he has ruined, is ruining, and will ruin himself."

The fate of "the poor fool Windham" was unimportant compared to the right of the individual to go to heaven or hell in his own fashion. "By giving Windham a verdict, you consign him to certain beggary. And why not? Why should not the certain and tremendous consequences of unbridled lust and egregious folly follow? Why should not the prodigal who wastes his substance on harlots and prodigal living be brought down to the husks and the swine-troughs in the end?"

Every Morning (Sundays Excepted): Before Windham was brought down to the swine-troughs, he climbed to the seat of his own public coach. Early in 1863, placards were distributed in Cromer and Norwich announcing a coach service between the towns. A coach would leave Cromer for Norwich every morning (Sundays excepted), "enabling passengers to catch the up mid-day train for London, while it will leave Norwich for Cromer every afternoon at 5 p.m. on the arrival of the afternoon day train". The announcement was signed "William Frederick Windham, proprietor". Reporting this, *The Times* commented: "Mr. Windham has thus far kept very good time . . . His self-imposed task must involve some labour, as he is $2\frac{1}{2}$ hours on the road, and must rise every morning at 7."

One of his passengers was another old Etonian, Sir Francis Burnand, who records in his reminiscences how Windham spoke a Norfolk dialect, intelligible only to the guard, ostlers, and local inhabitants. When Sir Francis recalled old days at Eton, Windham talked amiably to him in public-school English, "but suddenly threw care and refinement to the winds, exchanged some coarse chaff with the passers-by, laughed with the guard, used the most outlandish expressions, whipped up his team, and took us up to the inn in fine style." At the inn, he jumped from his seat, touched his hat, said "Good da-a-ay, Sir" in broad county accent, and accepted his two crowns as a tip.

Even to the master of Felbrigg Hall, ten shillings in the sixties was quite a handsome *pourboire*.

Journey's End: The last item in the issue of *The Times* for 3rd February, 1866, was a short paragraph at the bottom of column six that began: "The notorious Mr. W. F. Windham expired rather suddenly at the Norfolk Hotel, in this city . . . He had given up the coach with which he had latterly occupied his time, but still passed his life in more or less dissipated company . . ." The exact cause of death was "obstruction of the circulation by a clot of blood in the pulmonary artery".

Windham had squandered away his first fortune, *The Times* observed, and his estate at Felbrigg had passed into the hands of a Norwich merchant, but in 1869, he would have inherited the estate at Hanworth, Norfolk, with rents of £5,000 to £6,000 a year. His life was insured "to the extent of £12,000 in five different companies" the policies being held by Mrs. Windham. "By Mr. Windham's death," said *The Times*, "the estate would revert to Mrs. Windham's infant child, but it is stated that questions of legitimacy are likely to be raised."

But young Windham inherited Hanworth, with its rents and a considerable amount of accumulated capital. "Though not particularly eccentric," says Mr. Ralph Neville, who claims to have known him well, he was "extravagant to a degree, losing large sums of money to sharpers of every description. The day he came of age, I remember, he lost £6,000 pigeon shooting in Hanworth Park. He died young, a comparatively poor man."

Neville is as unreliable as he is unscrupulous in filching his material. In another of his patchworks of plagiarism, he has Windham junior retaining "a comfortable income" all his life.

V. VIRTUE OUT OF A BROTHEL

Gentlemen Preferred Whores: Though few received as much public attention as "Mad Windham", many of his contemporaries, without the excuse of eccentricity, also married whores.

Sir Kenelm Digby, who wedded the beautiful Elizabethan courtesan, Mrs. Venetia Stanley, observed that "an honest lusty man who was discreet might make a vertuouse wife out of a brothell-house"; and the precept was followed by a surprising number of Victorians. The frequency and casualness with which these middle- or upper-class Englishmen married strumpets is one of the curiosities of the times. We have seen how middle-class snobbery led some young men to prefer a mistress to a wife; what made others marry a whore rather than a virtuous girl?

"Full many a simpleton has conceived a passion in the course of a night's debauch," wrote Dr. Acton, in his study of prostitution, "which . . . could not be assuaged except by marriage in hot haste." And considering "the immense concourse of marriageable males at the height of their passions, who, for various causes, seek female society more in the streets than in the boudoir," he did not marvel at "the occasional explosion of these flagrant cases".

The doctor's explanation is inadequate. It was not only simpletons who married whores, and many of these marriages were made in cool deliberation. Nor was there a shortage of respectable women. In 1857, 40 per cent. of the women in London over twenty were unmarried. At the end of the 'sixties, there were 700,000 more women than men in England, more than half belonging to the "educated and semi-educated classes". A woman who was not married by the age of twenty-five, says a contemporary writer, "was left out in the race".

Yet in spite of social sanctions, "gentlemen of wealth and noblemen of position", to quote from *Vanity Fair*, continued to marry pretty horsebreakers, and "the most distinguished men in the country, Cabinet Ministers, Commanders-in-Chief, and the Bishops of the Church not excepted . . . dined at their houses."

These gentlemen of wealth and position, it seems, sought more liberal sexual partners than they could find in the drawing-rooms of the respectable.

VI. IMPORTANCE OF THE BROUGHAM

Verdict for Mrs. Brookes: When John Hollingshead was proprietor of the Gaiety he put up a notice on the stage-door:

LADIES DRAWING LESS THAN 20/- A WEEK ARE POLITELY REQUESTED
NOT TO ARRIVE IN THE THEATRE IN BROUGHAMS

A similar thought was expressed by a poet in *Beeton's Christmas Annual:*

> *Vice has its brougham: Virtue its foul alley*
> *That is the reason why girls join the ballet*

The brougham, a light enclosed vehicle drawn by one or two horses, was as essential to the fashionable whore of the 'sixties as a telephone is to the Manhattan call-girl of to-day. Appropriately, it was designed by Lord Brougham, who, like Palmerston, brought a resonant echo of the Regency into Victorian life; before he became a peer and Lord Chancellor of the Realm Brougham had been the warm friend and perhaps client of Harriette Wilson.

The importance of the brougham as a tool of trade was the subject of an instructive argument conducted before Mr. Baron Bramwell in 1865. One summer day in 1864, Mrs. Rose Brookes a 22-year-old harlot from Pimlico, called at the Long Acre establishment of Messrs. Pearce and Countze, coach-builders, and ordered a miniature ornamental brougham. It was fitted with a card-basket, and a looking-glass that let down from the roof, and the initials R.B. were entwined in a decorative cipher on the door. The cash price was £135; Mrs. Brookes paid £50 on account, and promised to pay the balance at the end of twelve months, or forfeit an additional £15. Before the second payment was due, she returned the pretty vehicle to the makers, who sued her for £37, a sum which included the hire of some extras—a whip, a pair of mud-wings, and a silver-plated harness.

Mrs. Brookes, through her counsel, claimed that as Messrs. Pearce and Countze knew the brougham was to be used in the pursuit of her profession, the law could not recognize the contract. The partners were keenly examined on this vital point. Mr. Countze stoutly denied that he had known Mrs. Brookes was a "woman of the town", but Mr. Pearce admitted that he had often seen her, rather conspicuously dressed, at Cremorne Gardens, though he had never spoken to her. Mrs. Brookes, who explained that as she could neither read nor write, she was unaware of the nature of the hire-purchase agreement, contradicted Mr. Pearce. He had often spoken to her, she swore, sometimes as late as midnight and when she was drinking champagne.

The plaintiffs argued that it was impossible to say that the sale of the brougham was for the express purpose of prostitution, because Mrs. Brookes might have used it to go shopping or to visit the theatre. Mr. Baron Bramwell's sympathies were obviously with the defendant. Addressing the jury, he pointed out that the two parties did not stand upon equal terms, for while the plaintiffs belonged to a highly respectable class of society, the defendant was one of a class truly termed "unfortunate". He did not make this observation to excite their sympathy but merely to impress upon them that she was entitled, if not to pity, at all events to justice. Having thus excited their sympathy, His Honour told the jurors that they would have to decide whether they considered a carriage was less necessary to Mrs. Brookes than a smart pair of shoes, or whether it must be classed with jewellery and smart dresses supplied for the purpose of attracting men, which had been held not to be a necessary.

After brooding on this delicate distinction, the jury declared that the brougham was not a necessary, but a luxury forming part of her display, which assisted her to attract and capture men. The verdict, therefore, was for the defendant. It was upheld on appeal by Chief Baron Pollock.

Chapter IV

A Theme of Fair Women

I. THE GIRL WITH THE SWANSDOWN SEAT

"And Who is 'Anonyma'?": Sir William Hardman, the indefatigable gossip and letter-writer, had a lively story for his friend in Melbourne, Edward Holroyd, when he sat down at the end of December, 1862, to compile his regular budget of London news: "A gossip anent 'Anonyma'," he began with relish, "And who is 'Anonyma'? Thereby hangs a tale":

"Anonyma" is "Skittles", or according to the name on her cards, Miss Walters, of equestrienne and pony-driving celebrity. "Anonyma" was the name given to her by *The Times:* "Skittles" was bestowed upon her by equally discreditable sponsors, as follows. The fair Walters was in liquor, as was her habit, and being chaffed by sundry guardsmen of the baser sort, she informed them in drunken but flowing periods, not unmixed with bad language, that "if they didn't hold their bloody row, she'd knock them down like a row of bloody skittles!" Thenceforth was she known as "Skittles". A whore, sir, much sought after by fast young swells. Well, my friend, she has bolted to that hot-bed of abomination, the City of the West, New York, to wit. Her luxuriously decorated house is in the hands of the auctioneer, her horses and carriages are sold; fair patricians, eager with curiosity to know how such a one lived, and if possible, to learn the secret of her attractions to the young men of their acquaintance, throng to the deserted halls of "Skittles", and admire

le cabinet with its seat padded with swansdown.... Skittles
has bolted with a married man of good family. His name is
Aubrey de Vere Beauclerk....

Moralists complained about the "prurient curiosity" of these
"fashionable women, mothers and daughters", who paraded
through the drawing-room, with its heavily gilded woodwork
and panels of vivid cerise silk, and the dining-room where gold
cupids congregated on crimson repp; who peeped nervously
at the virginal saxe-blue silk of Skittles' bedroom, and awedly
at her abandoned swansdown seat.

"By No Means Shy": Catherine Walters, "Skittles" to the
public, "Skitsie" to her intimates, and the self-crowned Queen
of mid-Victorian harlotry, was as representative of her age as
the little Queen who lived not far away in Buckingham Palace,
and whose eldest son, as one of Skittles' enduring friends, long
represented the Court of St. James's at her rival Court of Cytherea. But her life-story is more elusive than Victoria's. No
comets flared when she was born in Liverpool in 1839, the
daughter of a tide-waiter in the Liverpool Customs who took to
pub-keeping, and her history until her early twenties is largely
conjectural. According to one legend, perpetuated in a street
ballad, she worked for some time in the skittle-alley of the
Black Jack tavern:

> *In Liverpool in days gone by*
> *For ha'pence and her wittles,*
> *A little girl, by no means shy,*
> *Was settin' up the skittles.*

This is the more commonly accepted version of the origin of
her famous nickname. Another ascribes it to her proficiency
on a Parisian skittle-alley where, years later, she competed with
young men of the British diplomatic service. Equally ambiguous
are details of Skittles' life until her emergence as a public, almost
a national, figure in the early 'sixties. There is a shadowy

glimpse of her, as a young girl, following the Cheshire hounds when her father kept an inn in Cheshire. At seventeen, she is said to have launched herself in London whoredom. One chronicler has her selling oranges and water-cress at the top of Sloane Street; another detects her in the constellation of harlots that glittered nightly in the Haymarket. Here, in one of the flash nighthouses, she is supposed to have attracted a prominent livery stableman who engaged her to display his horses and phaetons in the Park.

In 1861, when a young lawyer called Alfred Austin was about to begin a poetic career that was to earn him the Laureateship and the execration of lovers of poetry, Skittles was sufficiently celebrated as a pretty horsebreaker to be included in his Juvenal-esque satire on the sins of London society, *The Season*. Describing Hyde Park in the afternoon, he wrote:

> *Gone the broad glare, save where with borrowed bays*
> *Some female Phaeton sets the Drive a-blaze:*
> *Or, more defiant, spurning frown and foe,*
> *With slackened rein swift Skittles rules the Row.*
> *Though scowling matrons champing steeds restrain,*
> *She flaunts Propriety with flapping mane.*

And addressing the virtuous maidens of the Park:

> *Answer me, all! belle, heiress, flirt and prue!*
> *Who has our notice? Skittles more or you?*
> *"The nasty wretch! Regard her saucy leer!"*
> *Well, own her conquest, and I'll own it queer.*

In a footnote, for the enlightenment of rural readers, Austin explains:

> Social celebrity travels slowly. Hence, fair readers who reside wholly in the Provinces may be puzzled by this passage; but to their Sisters of the Season, Skittles is as well known and as much an object of interest as the last shape of Madame Elisa

[a fashionable dressmaker]; and the skill with which in talk *à deux* they manoeuvre the conversation into speculations upon her origin, abode, and doings, fully supports their reputation for tact.

That year, too, Skittles had an even more remarkable triumph. She breached the forbidding walls of Burlington House. The Royal Academy "picture of the year" was an attractive portrait of her titled "The Taming of the Shrew" by the eminent academician, the faithful recorder of proud stags and pious people, Sir Edwin Landseer. For the Painter Laureate of the Victorian middle class to exhibit a picture of a well-known whore was an astonishingly bold gesture. As a concession to respectability, it was said that the subject of the portrait was a chaste horsewoman called Miss Gilbert, but as it bore no resemblance to Miss Gilbert and was a photographic likeness of Miss Walters, no one was deceived.

The *Annual Register* reported that Landseer's picture of the "jewelled and charming equestrienne" was one of the two most popular pictures in the show. It shared the distinction with a rather more sombre study, Faed's "From Dawn to Dusk", depicting a death-bed scene in a humble and over-populated Scotch cottage. Commenting on the portrait of Miss Walters, the *Annual Register* said: "Unfortunately the picture was suggestive of one of the social scandals of the hour, and the public was as much attracted by 'The Pretty Horsebreaker' as by the wonderful art of the painter."

The Birth of "Anonyma": Within a few months of her conquest of the Row, Skittles had also conquered the young Marquis of Hartington, later the eighth Duke of Devonshire. The legend says that having met him years before as the Cheshire innkeeper's daughter, she contrived a reunion in Hyde Park by colliding with him, and allowing herself to be thrown at his feet—an elaborate variant of the dropped-handkerchief gambit. Hartington set her up in a luxurious house in Mayfair, with carriages and servants and an annuity of £2,000, which she enjoyed for nearly sixty years. He was an unattractive, boorish fellow, as notorious for the gaucherie of his clothes as his behaviour, but he was also one of the wealthiest landowners in the kingdom, and for a while Skittles seems to have seen herself as the future Duchess of Devonshire. Their liaison was common gossip in 1862, when Hartington scandalized society by taking her to the Derby: here, with her noble escort, she was as great an object of public curiosity as the Japanese Ambassadors who in their enormous straw hats were mistaken by many for women. (It is strange to reflect that about this time Queen Victoria regarded Hartington as a future Prime Minister and a sobering influence on the young and wayward Prince of Wales.) In the same year, Skittles was christened "Anonyma" in Higgins' letter to *The Times*. It was the year of the South Kensington Exhibition, and Higgins, who enjoyed this sort of thing, solemnly pretended to be concerned with the traffic congestion in the approaches to the Exhibition that Skittles caused as she drove through the Park in her miniature phaeton, with its pair of tiny high-stepping chestnut ponies, souvenirs of a Russian prince.

Here, as a noteworthy document of the 'sixties, is the letter in full:

ANONYMA

TO THE EDITOR OF THE TIMES

Sir—Early in the season of 1861, a young lady whom I must call Anonyma, for I have never been able to learn her name, made her appearance in Hyde Park. She was a charming creature, beautifully dressed, and she drove with ease and spirit two of the handsomest brown ponies eye ever beheld. Nobody in society had seen her before; nobody in society knew her name, or to whom she belonged, but there she was, prettier, better dressed, and sitting more gracefully in her carriage than any of the fine ladies who envied her her looks, her skill, or her equipage.

A good many young gentlemen seemed to be acquainted with her, but their recognition was generally limited to a respectful bow as she passed by, or to a few friendly words slily interchanged on the step of her pony carriage when she drew up in some remote corner of the Park. Anonyma seemed at first to be rather a shy damsel. She is somewhat bolder now. Last year, she avoided crowds, and affected unfrequented roads, where she could more freely exhibit her ponies' marvellous action, and talk to her male acquaintances with becoming privacy. When all the fashionable world were sauntering on foot, on horseback, and in carriages along the Ladies Mile by the side of the Serpentine, Anonyma would betake herself to the deserted thoroughfare leading from Apsley House to Kensington.

But as the fame of her beauty and her equipage spread, this privacy became impossible to her. The fashionable world eagerly migrated in search of her from the Ladies Mile to Kensington Road. The highest ladies in the land enlisted themselves as her disciples. Driving became the rage. Three, four, five, six hundred guineas were given for a pair of ponies on the condition they should be as handsome as Anonyma's, that they should show as much breeding as Anonyma's, that they should step as high as Anonyma's. If she wore a pork pie hat, they wore pork pie hats; if her paletot was made by Poole, their paletots were made by Poole. If she reverted to more feminine attire, they reverted to it also. Where she drove, they followed; and I must confess that, as yet, Anonyma has fairly distanced her fair competitors. They can none of them sit, dress, drive, or look as well as she does; nor can any of them procure for money such ponies as Anonyma contrives to get—for love. But the result of all this pretty play causes a great public nuisance, and its on that account, and not at all on account of my admiration for Anonyma and her stepping ponies that I now address you.

I have said that up to the beginning of last year the fashionable world chiefly affected the Ladies Mile in the Park, and that the thoroughfare from Apsley House to Kensington was comparatively unfrequented, save by Anonyma. But this year, when that road is more specially required to be kept open for the convenience of visitors to the Exhibition, it is daily choked with fashionable carriages—from five to seven —all on account of Anonyma. Chairs are placed along it on either side; the best *partis* that England knows, the toadies who cling to them, the snobs who copy them—all sit there, watching for Anonyma. Expectation is raised to its highest pitch, a handsome woman drives rapidly by in a carriage drawn by thoroughbred ponies of surpassing shape and action, the driver is attired in the pork pie hat and the Poole paletot introduced by Anonyma, but, alas!, she causes no effect at all, for she is not Anonyma; she is only the Duchess of A—, the Marchioness of B—, the Countess of C—, or some other of Anonyma's many eager imitators. The crowd, disappointed reseat themselves and wait. At last their patience is rewarded. Anonyma and her ponies appear, and they are satisfied. She threads her way dexterously, with an unconscious air, through the throng, commented upon by hundreds who admire and hundreds who envy her. She pulls up her ponies to speak to an acquaintance, and her carriage is instantly surrounded by a multitude; she turns, and drives back again towards Apsley House, and then—away into the unknown world, nobody knows whither. Meanwhile, thousands returning from the Exhibition are intolerably delayed by the crowd collected to gaze on this pretty creature, and her pretty ponies, and the efforts of Sir Richard Mayne and his police to keep the thoroughfare open are utterly frustrated.

Could not you, sir, whose business it is to know everything and everybody, and who possibly, therefore, may know Anonyma herself, prevail on her to drive in some other portion of the Park as long as the Exhibition lasts? If she will but consent to do this, the fashionable world will certainly follow her, and the road to the Exhibition will be set free for the use of the public.

I am, sir, your obedient servant,

H.

A few weeks after this letter appeared, Skittles was at Ems, taking the waters with Europe's *élite*. As Hartington had also left London, it was thought that they had eloped. But the Marquis had gone to America to have a look at the Civil War, where he behaved characteristically, making no attempt to conceal his Southern sympathies in Northern society; a habit that caused Lincoln to christen him "Lord Partington". Skittles met de Vere Beauclerk at Ems. He was a young man of twenty-three, of Ardglass Castle, Co. Down, with an income of £4,000 a year and a wife and young children. According to his wife's evidence in a divorce action thirty years later, "Mr. Beauclerk became smitten" with Skittles, and travelled about with her for some months. They journeyed together to America, where Skittles is said to have called on Hartington, and been rebuffed. If this is true, it does not seem to have affected her much. She was soon back in Paris, and sleeping with Achille Fould, the wealthy banker who was Finance Minister to Napoleon III. Under his patronage, Skittles speedily took her place with the leaders of the Parisian *demi-monde*, the exquisites of *la garde*, that small group which constituted the aristocracy of the hundred or so top-ranking courtesans of France, and which included such immortals as Adele Courtois and Anna Deslions. It was, indeed, a proud day for England. Cora Pearl, another English girl, three years younger than Skittles, had also broached the inner citadel of Paris's *Haute Bicherie* and was commanding 5,000 francs—say £200—for twelve hours of her company; and Elizabeth Howard, then in her late thirties, said to be the daughter of a Sussex brewer, had retired from the public bed with the title of the Comtesse de Beauregard and five and a half million francs of Napoleon III's money.

At Longchamps, in the Bois, in the Champs Elysées, at the

Opera, and at the Italiens, Skittles and Miss Pearl openly challenged the lovely Empress Eugénie and her Court beauties. "Skittles' pony chase, with its pair of black cobs, and its two grooms on coal-black cattle behind," noted a first-hand observer, Albert Vandam, "beats everything from the Imperial stables; Cora Pearl's turn-out throws everything into the shade except Skittles." It is unlikely that Anglo-Saxon prestige, in the sphere of international erotics, will ever soar so high again.

The Dark Little Lady of the Sonnets: Skittles was a popular hostess. Her Paris house was crowded every night, and among her regular guests were the young men, diplomats and statesmen in the making, from the British legation. One of these *attachés* was a fair, handsome youth called Wilfrid Scawen Blunt, who was to develop into a brilliant amateur of life, one of those admirable Victorian individualists who brought a salty Elizabethan tang into the era of dundrearies, dividends, and elastic-sided boots. Blunt was an English gentleman who shamed his class by championing the lesser breeds in Egypt and India, a Christian squire who lived in Cairo as a Mahommedan sheik, a Sussex property-owner who was gaoled in Ireland as an agitator against landlords. He was also a poet, and if not a great one, at least one who loved greatly.

Skittles was the inspiration of much of his poetry. When they met at one of her receptions, Blunt was twenty-three, "a fair-faced, frightened boy", Skittles a year older. He has recorded how he sat shyly listening to her "fool's talk" and wondering "that she did not wear man's patience out" with it. But when the party was over, he wandered uneasily through the streets, unable to forget "that gay face" or "the torrent of her words". He drifted into a fair-ground and felt a touch on the arm. Skittles had followed him:

> *Who might describe the humours of that night,*
> *The mirth, the tragedy, the grave surprise,*
> *The treasures of fair folly infinite*
> *Learned as a lesson from those childlike eyes?*

Blunt subsequently re-created their love-affair, which lasted only a few weeks, in several sonnet-sequences. This verse from *Esther* has the suggestion of being a literal recollection. Esther, or Skittles, has taken him to her dressmaker's:

> Suddenly then my strange companion cried,
>   "Bring me the body". In a moment more
> She had thrown off her hat, her veil untied,
>   And motioning all the women to the door,
> While I sat speechless by who would have gone,
>   Undid her jacket and anon her dress,
> With the jet buttons of it one by one,
>   And stood but clothed the more in loveliness,
> A sight sublime, a dream, a miracle;
>   A little goddess from some luminous field
> Brought down unconscious on our earth to dwell,
>   And in an age of innocence revealed,
> Naked but not ashamed. Nay, wherefore shame?
>   And I ah, who shall blame me, who shall blame?

Skittles emerges recognizably, in such passages as:

> She was a little woman dressed in black
>   Who stood on tiptoe with a childish air.
> Her face and figure hidden in a sacque,
>   All but her eyes and forehead and dark hair.
> Her brow was pale, but it was lit with light,
>   And mirth flashed out of it, it seemed in rays,
> A childish face, but wise with woman's wit,
>   And something, too, pathetic in its gaze.

And:

> She went on talking like a running stream,
>   Without more reason or more pause or stay
> Than to gather breath and then pursue her whim,
>   Just where it led her, tender, sad or gay.

Skittles:
The girl with the
swansdown seat

Agnes Willoughby

Kate Hamilton's Night House (From *Mayhew's London Labour and London Poor*, 1862)

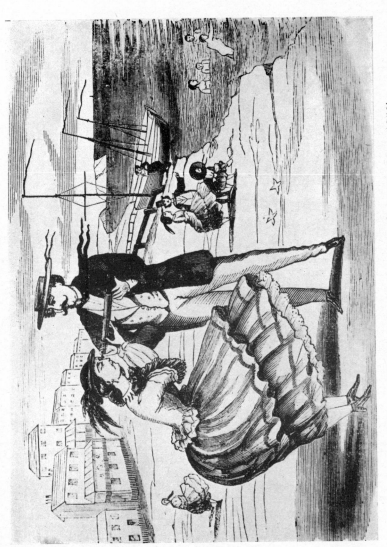

London on the beach: A Stereoscopic Gem (From *Paul Pry*, 1858)

Mabel Gray

Cora Pearl

Beauty and Billingsgate: Historians who are undecided about the beauty of Skittles' face are unanimous about the beauty of her slender body. Sir Willoughby Maycock describes her in "a habit that fitted like a glove, with a bit of cherry ribbon at her neck", as "a perfect dream". She had a small head with bright chestnut hair, an oval face with big grey-blue eyes and an ingenuous mouth, and slim sensitive hands. She dressed in quiet good taste. In Paris, her sober costumes were in sharp contrast with the gaudy ensembles of her rivals; like Brummel, she had an instinct for achieving distinction by under-display. But there was nothing demure about her behaviour. Her zest for living bubbled up in her endless and untrammelled speech. She had, says one writer, "the face of an innocent child" yet she could "swear like a cabman". Another, while paying tribute to her "tender, timid eye" notes that "her language, should one tread on her dress, is a *caution*". Many of the stories about her refer to her ruggedly uninhibited speech. The most famous, of which there are several texts, is about an incident when she was hunting with the Quorn. Its Master, the Earl of Stamford, had married a gamekeeper's daughter who had been a show rider at Astley's Circus and Cremorne Gardens. Whether she had also been a prostitute, and an associate of Skittles', is not clear, but at the meet either she or her husband rashly complained about Skittles being there, and asked a whip to get rid of her as an objectionable person. Skittles at first refused to leave but when she heard that the hunt was to be cancelled if she remained, yielded. As she galloped away she called out—and I quote the most economical version of the valediction—"What the hell is the good of Lady Stamford giving herself airs? *She's* not the Queen of our profession, I am."

Another spirited remark attributed to her was used by Charles Reade in *A Terrible Temptation*, where the courtesan Rhoda Somerset, who Reade admitted was suggested by Skittles, exclaims: "Lucky for you beggars I am a lady, or I would break every damned window in the house!"

The unbridled tongue of the mid-Victorian courtesan seems to have been a deliberate part of her stock-in-trade; perhaps it was a refreshing symbol of the unbuttoned corset. But the stories which were widely circulated, and perhaps fabricated, of Skittles' resonant oaths have tended to obscure other facets of her personality. Thus Dr. Wingfield-Stratford writes: "The famous Anonyma, or Skittles . . . was a foul-mouthed and drunken termagant without a vestige of self-respect." Could such a person have retained the friendship and affection of worldly and intelligent men long after sexual transactions between them had ended, or of men with whom she had never been in bed? Blunt was happily married in 1869 to Byron's granddaughter, but his regard for Skittles lasted till the end of her life. Her Sunday afternoon parties in London were attended by the Prince of Wales, who, too, remained her life-long friend, and for whom she sometimes acted as an intermediary in passing on, unofficially, Blunt's political views; European royalty, diplomats, artists and sporting peers were her frequent guests; the Rothschilds visited her, and so, "to the delight of Blunt and Skittles herself", says Edith Finch, in her biography of Blunt, did Gladstone, who looked in at a Sunday party "having sent before-hand twelve pounds of Russian tea". And this time, Gladstone was not trying to redeem a harlot, "at the very top of the tree"; Skittles lived and died comfortably unrepentant. Nor was he interested in the baccarat that many of her visitors played. It is difficult, then, to imagine him visiting, simply to be sociable, a foul-mouthed drunken termagant. Miss Finch's estimate of Skittles seems more accurate: "She was interested in modern art, knew something about music, liked serious reading, even on religious subjects. Her comments were piercing as well as racy—and her letters, although illiterate and nearly illegible were highly entertaining."

"*Fair But Frail*": Skittles spent about ten years in Europe, following the sun of high society and the no less brilliant satellite of the half-world on their constant orbits of pleasure-seeking, but returning regularly to Leicestershire for the hunting season.

She rode with the Fitzwilliam and the Quorn, high-class subscription packs; she wore a scarlet jacket and black skirt. Her mount was a horse that had run second in a Grand National, and that no other woman was supposed to be capable of riding. Once she put it over the railings of Hyde Park for a bet of £100 and "the tale is famous of her larking over the 18 ft. water side jump at the National Hunt Steeplechase at Northamptonshire", after three riders had fallen in. Her reputation as "the greatest horsewoman of the age" was well founded.

Though London saw little of her during the latter years of the eighteen-sixties, her memory was kept green by three yellow-back biographies. Two of them *Skittles, the Biography of a Fascinating Woman,* and *Anonyma, or Fair but Frail* appeared simultaneously in January, 1864, and went through many editions in the year. These books, though they owed more to imagination than research, helped to amplify and consolidate the Skittles legend. They were reprinted often during the next thirty or forty years. Some commentators find a portrait of her in Zu-Zu, the hunting harlot of Ouida's *Under Two Flags*, which also appeared in 1864, but apart from the fact that "the Zu-Zu" rides superbly and loves expensively, the resemblance is slight; any of a dozen pretty and successful horsebreakers could have served as a model.

Skittles returned in 1872 to the London of the Marlborough House set, the Albert Memorial, less freedom in the streets and more freedom in the drawing-room. Her sister, who was ten years younger than Skittles, and much prettier, was with her. They had a house in South Street, Mayfair, and an apartment in Brown's Hotel.

Roller-skating was introduced in England in the mid-seventies, and despite some criticism ("the din set up by these little American machines is something indescribable") soon became fashionable. Skittles took to the new sport with enthusiasm, and was as well known on the rinks in London and Tunbridge Wells as she was in the Row. It was at Tunbridge Wells that she met a handsome Eton schoolboy, the Honourable Gerald Saumerez. When he came up to London as a young man of twenty, he called on her and they fell ineluctably in love. Skittles was then forty; her life was almost exactly half lived. For the rest of it, she and Saumerez remained in the only word our language has to define any relationship between a man and woman, lovers. Saumerez survived Skittles for nearly twenty years, but to the end of his life, he used to say that she was the only woman he could ever have married.

The Unconquerable Talker: Skittles' friend, Edward, Prince of Wales, came to the throne in 1901. Through the Indian summer of his brief reign, she was still a familiar figure in Hyde Park, but no longer driving her phaeton or riding a spirited hack. She now made her parade in a bath-chair, alongside which old and new friends walked in homage—Lord Kitchener, with his splendid mustachios, or the eccentric Marquis of Clanricarde, a multi-millionaire with 56,000 acres in Galway, who lived meanly in the Albany and dressed like a tramp. Clanricarde had been one of the young men of the British Embassy in Paris who with Blunt, had paid court to Skittles in the 'sixties. Did he and Skittles ever talk of Blunt now? It was for exhorting Clanricarde's tenants to resist eviction that Blunt had been sent to gaol in 1888.

Skittles had lived in Paris in the pinchbeck glory of the Second Empire, and seen it shattered in the war of 1870. In 1914, when German troops were again marching on Paris, she wrote to Blunt:

I knew the present Emperor well when he was Crown Prince and I have two letters he wrote me and he also gave me his photograph and a jewelled sunshade, the latter I have sold to get some money for the poor wounded troops. He was most charming to me, the Emperor, when I was a girl. ["N.B."— Blunt wrote in here: "She cannot have been less than forty."] And he went cracked over my riding. He couldn't ride a bit but he looked well on horseback, and had a very handsome face for a German, it had not got hard at that time. He was a short man, not so tall as myself, but most charming and nice and simple at that time.

She still visited Blunt occasionally, at Newbuildings, in Surrey, where he had his stud of Arab horses, and Blunt would receive her in sheik's robes and burnous. "Though deaf and partially blind," he noted in his diary in March, 1918, Skittles was "unconquered in talk". He gave her a bucket of butter and eggs "to eke out her London ration".

She lived through the war almost alone in her South Street house. Her sister was in France, and apart from doctor and priest, she had few visitors. But Saumerez still called every day when he was in London, and he was with her one afternoon in August, 1920, when she had a stroke, and two days later, when she died. Blunt arranged for her to be buried, as she had wished, in the churchyard of the Franciscan Monastery at Crawley which his brother Francis had built, and where Francis was buried. The initials C.W.B. are on her tombstone. In her later years she had been known as Mrs. Bailey.

The Poets Talk of Heaven: Wilfrid Blunt died two years after Skittles, and was buried, as he had wished, in the tall grass of the woods, wrapped in his travelling carpet and uncoffined. Once, during the war, he and Alfred Austin, then Poet Laureate, had exchanged their ideas of Heaven. Austin's was "to sit in a garden and where he sat to receive constant telegrams announcing alternately a British victory by sea and a British victory by land". It was a not surprising vision of eternity for a singer whose poem on the Jamieson raid had contained the couplet:

> They went across the veldt
> As hard as they could pelt.

Blunt preferred "to be laid out to sleep in a garden, with running water near, and so to sleep for a hundred thousand years, then to be woke by a bird singing, and to call out to the person one loved best 'Are you there?' and for her to answer 'Yes, are you?' and go to sleep again for another hundred thousand years".

It was more than half a hundred years since Austin had written of "swift Skittles" daunting propriety with "flapping mane"; more than half a hundred years since Blunt had loved her as "a little goddess from some luminous field".

II. PILLOW TO PULPIT

A Prince, a Ring, and a Girl: If Skittles were unchallengeably the most celebrated London harlot of the 'sixties, an equal pre-eminence in the 'fifties must be conceded to Laura Bell—though, unlike Skittles, she betrayed the code of the successful courtesan by a spectacular repentance. Laura Bell was born—exactly a decade before Skittles—in Antrim, Ireland, where her father was bailiff on the estates of the Marquis of Hertford. She became a shop-girl in Belfast, but soon moved to richer rewards. Before she was twenty, she was famous by the Liffey for her beauty and her barouche, with its pair of white horses. She came to London about the middle of the century. Sir Francis Burnand, who was born in 1836, recalls seeing her as "a boy about town" among the "notorious Hetaerae" of Hyde Park:

Clearly do I call to mind Laura Bell's pretty, doll-like face, her big eyes, and quick vivacious glances . . . as she sat in an open phaeton, vivaciously talking to a variety of men, all "swells" of the period . . . while her smart little "tiger" stood at the horses' heads. . . . What strange stories I used to hear of her recklessness, her prodigality, and her cleverness! Was not her *liaison* with the chief of the Nepalese princes, Jung Bahadoor, who alone was a temporary fortune to her, the theme of "songs of the period". . . .

Bahadoor was the Nepalese ambassador in London, the brother of the Maharajah of Nepal. A pleasant Arabian Nights' story survives of how, after leaving London and Laura, he sent her a magnificent ring, with a note saying that if ever she needed help she had only to send back the ring and he would do anything in his power for her. When the Indian Mutiny broke out in 1857, Laura, then a respectably married woman, is supposed to have related this to a friend, who passed the information on to the India Office. The ring and the prince's letter were then sent to India, with a request from Laura that the Government of Nepal should either side with the British or remain neutral. As a result, the tale tells, Nepal did not join the mutineers and its Ghurka regiments were faithful to the British Raj. In one version, the Prince of Wales is identified as the "friend" to whom Laura told the romantic story of the ring, but as "Bertie" was not sixteen at the time, and subject to formidable monastic discipline, this is rather implausible.

Two years after her début in London, Laura Bell was one of the sights of the town. One night in 1852, when she went to the Opera, the whole house is said to have stood to watch her depart. In the same year, she married an officer and a gentleman, Captain Augustus Frederick Thistlethwayte, whose mother, Tryphena, was a daughter of Bishop Bathurst of Norwich. The marriage was not very successful. The captain must have been a fairly difficult person to live with; he had a habit of firing a pistol through the ceiling of his room when he wanted to summon a servant. And his wife, whom he established in a mansion in Grosvenor Square, was so extravagant that on several occasions he advertised that he would not be responsible for her debts. There is a theory that it was his recalcitrance in these matters that led her into the path of religion. By the 'sixties, she had emerged as a fervent and eloquent preacher—"A sinner saved by grace through faith in the Lamb of God", she signed herself— taking all England as her pulpit. "Her intellectual capacity was almost phenomenal and to this was added a very poetical imagination," says the anonymous author of *Fifty Years of London Society*. "Her appearance on the platform of the Polytechnic was a realization of beauty and art. Mrs. Thistlethwayte was not much inferior to Spurgeon. . . ."

Mr. T. H. Escott, the historian of London clubs, describes her as "the greatest beauty of the age", and Lady St. Helier, who attended some of her revivalist meetings in Scotland says:

> She was a very striking-looking woman, and the large black mantilla which covered her masses of golden hair, the magnificent jewels she wore round her neck, and the flashing rings on the hands with which she gesticulated, added to the soft tones of a beautiful voice, made a great impression upon those who listened to her.

In her unregenerate days, she had also been famous for the beauty of her shoulders. She was the model for a popular picture called "The Nun", and was painted by Buckner and by Girard, whose portrait of her may be inspected at the Wallace Collection.

"Is it not strange," wrote Hardman to Holroyd in 1862, reporting on Mrs. Thistlethwayte's mission to the north, "to recall the time when she was the Queen of London whoredom and had the Nepalese ambassador in her meshes. . . . But I have lived almost long enough to cease to wonder at anything, save great scientific discoveries."

Twelve years later, she was still an impressive figure. Sir Willoughby Maycock, who heard her preach at the Polytechnic in 1874, noted "the lustre of her beautiful eyes . . . only surpassed by the sparkling of an array of large diamond rings, which adorned her fingers, as she raised them in eloquent exhortation to follow the path that alone leads to salvation". Some of her more sceptical listeners may have wondered by what path she had been led to these large diamond rings.

Mr. Gladstone Calls Again: The headquarters of Mrs. Thistlethwayte's mission was her home in Grosvenor Square. To her evangelical tea-parties came many godly men and women, including the ubiquitous Mr. Gladstone and his wife. Gladstone was on very confidential terms with Mrs. Thistlethwayte; when he resigned the premiership in 1892, she was told of his decision before the Queen, and after her death a large collection of his letters to her were found.

Captain Thistlethwayte died mysteriously in 1887. He was found shot by the revolver that he kept near his bed. Mrs. Thistlethwayte then moved to a cottage in Hampstead, where she continued her pious works, and her association with the Gladstones, till her death, in 1894. She was buried in her husband's family vault at Paddington Cemetery, beside her mother-in-law, the Bishop's daughter.

III. "LA LUNE ROUSSE"

"*Une Femme Toute Nue*": Mr. Sacheverell Sitwell, in *La Vie Parisienne*, tells an agreeable story of two small boys in Paris who, one Sunday morning in the 'sixties, were taken for a walk by Prince Paul Murat. In their pretty sailor-suits they followed the Prince into a big house in the Bois, where they found Cora Pearl relaxing on a sofa—

> the focus of a hemicycle of diplomats, senators, and academicians, all seated with their chins leaning on gold-knobbed walking-sticks, their yellow gloves placed in the "cylinders" at their side, upon the floor. The Prince presented his *jeunes amis*, and they joined the hemicycle. When they returned home their mother asked if the Bois had been nice and whether they had seen any animals, to which their reply was "*Mais non, Mamam, beaucoup plus que ça; une femme toute nue!*"

Though Cora Pearl achieved her greatest glory outside of England she must be included among the distinguished English whores of her day. She shares with Harriette Wilson the honour of recognition in the *Dictionary of National Biography*, and her repute in the richly competitive *demi-monde* of the Second Empire should be a matter of pride to her countrymen, many of whom seem to have accepted uncritically Villon's chauvinistic thesis: *Il n'est bon bec que de Paris.* Dr. Wingfield-Stratford, for example, though the author of a massive *History of English Patriotism*, has only contempt for the harlotry of mid-Victorian England. "They did these things better, because more openly, at the court of Napoleon III," he writes. "It was better to gaze on the Countess Castiglione's lovely body than to listen to the damns and bloodys of Anonyma." But the courtiers of Napoleon III were pleased to gaze on Cora Pearl's lovely body, in spite of her damns and bloodys, and her pre-eminence in her particular sphere has been attested by many European authorities. A journalist of her day, no doubt after checking his facts, wrote of her "almost superhuman knowledge of the art of love". M. Kracauer, in his biography of Offenbach, says "She was able to keep in the front rank . . . because of her inordinate talent for voluptuous eccentricities," and he quotes the testimony of Prince Gortchakoff who described her as "the acme of sensual delights". This is high praise indeed, for the vulgar stupid daughter of a humble London music-master.

The Man With the Watch-Chain: She was born at East Stoneham, near Plymouth, in 1836, one of the elder of sixteen children, and christened Eliza Elizabeth Crouch. Her father taught and composed music—*Kathleen Mavourneen* and *Dermot Ashore* were two of his successes—and her mother, when she was not child-bearing, did a little concert-singing. When her father ran off to America with a mistress, Emma Elizabeth, at the age of five, was sent to a convent at Boulogne. There is a story that she left it in her teens with a barber. Her own account, in her often unreliable *Mémoires*, written with an eye to blackmail in the last years of her life, has her returning to London at the age of thirteen to live with her grandmother near Covent Garden. Here, one fine Sunday morning, as she was hurrying home from church, she was accosted by a diamond-merchant called Saunders who asked her if she liked cakes. He took her to a low-ceilinged, crowded, smoke-filled room behind the markets and gave her, not cakes, but gin-and-water that was drugged. "The next morning," she says in the *Mémoires*, "I woke up to find myself beside the gentleman in his bed . . . *flétri*." Mr. Saunders dressed himself, folded his arms over his watch-chain, twiddled his thumbs, lit a cigar, and told Emma that if she liked to stay with him he would give her a good time. When she declined, he handed her five pounds, put on his hat, and left with a laugh, saying—"Just as you like, my dear. . . I never forced anyone. . . . Goodbye." This story, absurdly like a piece of vintage melodrama, may have been literally true. Reports of similar cases are to be found in the newspapers of the time, when the seduction of children was a recognized sport among certain men with watch-chains and cigars.

Emma, who was fourteen when she met Mr. Saunders, did not go back to her grandmother. She moved into a room of her own, and within a year or so became the mistress of an amiable young man called William Buckle, who ran the Albert Rooms, a Covent Garden dancing establishment. They lived happily together for about two years, and only parted because Emma, who had gone with Buckle for a holiday in Paris, decided she wanted to stay there. It was a city to be conquered and, at seventeen, with very little equipment, she began her historic campaign. Her only weapon was her body. Her skin and teeth were good, and her red hair attractive, but her face, with its small eyes and high cheek-bones, was not beautiful. Many thought it ugly—"a clown's head on a body worthy of Diane de Poitiers", a Paris critic wrote of her in her prime. She spoke "the French of an illiterate stable boy"—with a Cockney accent; she had no charm, no taste, no elegant clothes.

Her first manoeuvre was to christen herself Cora Pearl, thus eliminating the unpleasant ambiguities of Crouch in its French pronunciation. Her second, though it may not have been a conscious decision, was deliberately to exaggerate her coarseness, her loudness, her vulgarity. Instead of trying to compete in elegance with the established leaders of the profession—the gentle Courtois, a gifted conversationalist, with a talent for clothes, or the witty and cultivated Leblanc, who owned the Hope diamond, and was patronized by Duleep Singh, Clemenceau and the Duc d'Aumale—Cora Pearl created a new cult of the hoyden. The anonymous author of *Uncensored Recollections* recalls a lunch at her house when she "put her hand in a dish of cutlets or something and put a large dripping piece of whatever it was on the head of Ferdinand Bischoffscheim".

The banker Bischoffscheim smiled meekly through the veil of thick sauce but the Duke of Hamilton, seeing her dip into the dish again, cried: "Damn you, Cora, if you put that on my head I'll strangle you." The hostess shrieked with laughter. "That was her idea of fun."

"Good-night, Sweet Prince": With a keen sense of advertising, and something worth while to sell, Cora climbed rapidly from bed to bed—an unnamed sailor, a businessman, a duke, and ultimately, a glittering galaxy of princes: Achille Murat, followed by his father Joachim; the Prince of Orange, who disliked being called Citron: and then Plon Plon, Prince Jerome Bonaparte, cousin of the reigning Emperor; in her own words, "a golden chain of lovers".

Money from vaults that seemed inexhaustible showered on her bed; she was burdened with jewels; her apartments were crammed with a muddle of treasures and rubbish, Boule, ormulu, gilt, tapestries, mirrors, bronzes, such as one encounters in a stall at the Flea Market; she danced a cancan on a carpet of orchids and bathed before her guests in a silver bath-tub filled with champagne. She was a spectacle and a legend. Her horses, which cost £1,000 a pair, and her carriages, were the finest in Paris. M. Worth, whose house now dressed her, describes how, when she wore lemon-coloured hair, it was exactly matched by the yellow-satin trimmings of her blue carriage and the yellow liveries of her jockeys. For her red hair, she had a canary barouche with red upholstery. She would spend £500 on a dinner for twenty men, and sometimes, the chroniclers say, offer herself as the *plat du jour*, naked, on a silver platter in a large pie.

Many gourmets claim to have encountered this unusual dish. The Marquis de Vellavieja described it to his cousin the Baroness de Stoeckel, wife of a Russian Minister to Washington. He was dining *chez* Cora, when—

> the door flew open and four footmen in her livery brought in a life-size dish with a cover. They placed this in the middle of the long table and on taking off the cover there lay Cora Pearl nude. . . . She had such a wonderful figure. . . . that all the guests gasped with admiration.

Gastronomic Footnote: The story of the eminent courtesan being dished up *au naturel* is as persistent as the story of the Indian Rope Trick. La Belle Otero claims in her autobiography that she was served thus at a banquet at St. Petersburg, for the diversion of some Russian officers who fell on their knees before the beauty of the spectacle, and the American cotton king McFadden is reported to have ordered a similar *bonne bouche* at Maxim's, with the refinement of having the naked girl served in a delicate pink sauce. It would be interesting to know how many restaurants in the nineteenth century were equipped with the silverware necessary for this service.

"Avec Madame Cora, Tra la la": Cora Pearl reached the peak of her career about 1867, when Prince Napoleon installed her in a mansion in the rue de Chaillot, opposite St. Pierre de Chaillot; it was known as Les Petites Tuileries and according to Cora, cost her lover £80,000. Of its namesake, she observed stridently: "Why, the Tweeleries is my lumber-room." Her pearls at this time were said to be worth £40,000 and her annual expenditure about £25,000. To maintain this budget, without unduly embarrassing her royal patron, she was not averse to an occasional descent to the bed of a commoner; a handsome Irishman called James Whelpley was supposed to have spent £80,000 on her in a few months.

There is a characteristic glimpse of her at Baden-Baden, just before the Franco-Prussian war, with an entourage of princes and harlots, invading the casino and scattering toy explosives to the accompaniments of wild shrieks; while the terrified croupiers huddled over the heaps of gold and notes, the visitors danced the cancan and two German princes, one the brother-in-law of the Emperor of Austria, joining hands, cavorted round her singing:

> Nous donnerons, tout, même l'Allemagne
> Pour aller ce soir boire du champagne,
> Avec Madame Cora,
> Tra la la.

It was at Baden-Baden, a few years earlier, that the young Henry Adams had austerely watched the Duke of Hamilton, surrounded by fashionable Europe and America, "improving his social advantages by the conversation of Cora Pearl."

Her liaison with Prince Jerome, who, though he snored, was a very desirable protector—royal, rich, handsome and clever—lasted about seven years. His devotion to her was profound. When she made her calamitous stage début at the Théâtre des Bouffes, playing, Cupidon in Offenbach's *Orphée Aux Enfers* as a rival attraction to Adah Menken's triumphant Mazeppa at the Gaité, he installed her in a flat next to the theatre from which he had built a private staircase giving swift access to the stage door. Despite her almost nude costume of blue feathers and diamonds—there were diamonds even on the soles of her yellow-striped sandals—she was not a success. Her professional friends acclaimed the opening performance, but after twelve appearances she was hissed off the stage. She farewelled her audience with the immemorial gesture of the thumbed nose and the wiggling fingers and returned to the boudoir where her talents were less in doubt.

The Red Moon Wanes: "La lune rousse", as Cora Pearl was called for her red hair and round face, had risen with the Second Empire and reflected its tinselled corruption. M. Kracauer observes that the extravagant crinolines and cosmetics that she and her colleagues displayed were symbolical of the politics of the day, "for they sought to smother physical realities as effectively as the régime of Napoleon III sought to smother social realities". Her decline, appropriately, coincided with that of his toy Empire. In the first year of the war that drove him for the third time into exile, she went to London to meet Prince Jerome and was refused admission to the Grosvenor Hotel. She returned to Paris, broke out the Union Jack over her house in the rue de Chaillot, and turned it into a hospital for wounded officers. For some strange reason, her neighbours, who had never objected to her using the house as a lupanar, were scandalized by this use of the moral British flag, and asked the British ambassador, Lord Lyon, to have it pulled down. When there was an attempt to have her deported as an undesirable alien, she called on him and pointed out that she was a considerable landowner in France, as well as a British subject. But the moon was setting fast. Next year, when still technically under the protection of Prince Jerome, she had her last grandiose *affaire*. The Empire had fallen and the Prince, though faithful, was no longer rich. Conveniently, young Alexandre Duval, son of the founder of the famous Duval restaurants, fell ardently in love with her. He had inherited a fortune of about £400,000 which he spent on her so freely—he paid £28,000 for one string of pearls—that it lasted less than a year. Too late, his mother applied for a "judicial council" to restrain him. At the end of 1872, Duval was worse than penniless, for he owed jewellers vast sums, and Cora Pearl, who was busy pawning the jewellery he had not paid for, instructed her servants not to admit him to her house. His passion for her was undimmed, and after several attempts, he forced his way into her drawing-room, confronted her despairingly, and shot himself. Cora Pearl had left the room before he pulled the trigger; when she saw what had happened, she is reported to have said: "Sale cochon, il a foutu mon beau tapis." Duval did not die; when his mother called to see him in Cora Pearl's house, his first words were: "Have you brought me money? I must have some. . . . I owe Cora for three months." Next day *Figaro* announced: "We are informed that Mlle Pearl is to be ordered to leave Paris immediately."

From Kerbstone to Garret: She was in London briefly, and returned to Europe to be expelled in turn from Monte Carlo, Milan, Rome, Nice and Baden-Baden. Prince Jerome, also an *expulsé*, was still fond of her. But in 1874, he wrote her an affectionate letter of farewell: "Faced with my duty, I must not hesitate. . . . You have always been charming, and you please me very much. . . . I will not see you again for a while, but later I will shake hands with you with much pleasure, if you wish it, my dear Cora."

Cora Pearl was thirty-two when she lost her last grand lover. For the remaining thirteen years of her life, she wandered through Europe, taking such lovers as she could find, and living on her dwindling store of treasures. She was allowed back in Paris on a special permit in 1873 to sell her house, which *Figaro* valued at £10,000. Four years later, some of her silver and *objets d'art* were auctioned at Drouots. How, with these assets, she finished in abject poverty is hard to understand.

In appearance she aged rapidly, though the beauty of her body remained. Julian Arnold, son of Sir Edwin Arnold, tells of a strange meeting at Monte Carlo in the 'eighties. Near the steps of the Casino he saw a woman sitting on the kerbstone, weeping. "She appeared to be about fifty years of age, handsome, fair-haired, and well-complexioned but much bedraggled." She told him she was hungry, homeless and penniless.

"Your English accent is so good, madame, that I would venture to ask your name?" "I am Cora Pearl."

Mr. Arnold called a cab and drove her to the villa he was sharing with two gentlemen friends. One, a tall Scotchman, bowed low to her saying: "Higher heads than mine have bent to Cora Pearl." The other, a short Irishman, courteously thanked providence for ordaining that dinner-tables should accommodate four. Over a good meal, Cora Pearl told her hosts stories of her fabulous life. Late that night, as Mr. Arnold was reading alone in his library, someone came in softly, and Cora Pearl's voice said: "Forgive my disturbing you."

> Glancing up from my book, I discovered that the lady of the voice was standing directly in front of me. She was wearing a man's dressing gown much too long for her. . . . Hastening to rise from my chair, I found my embarrassment not lessened when she incontinently let fall to her feet the dressing-gown, which fell in crumpled folds around her ankles, leaving her as unencumbered as Venus arisen from the foam!
>
> "A woman's vanity," she remarked demurely, "should be my sufficient excuse. I found it difficult to rest until I had shown you that, if Cora Pearl has lost all things else, she still retains that which made her famous—a form of loveliness."

She came back to Paris, no longer proscribed, a shoddy woman with a rivelled face and ugly voice, and lived, the last months, in a third floor apartment at No. 8 rue de Bassano. Here, in 1886, she died of cancer. A curious collection was discovered in her room; asparagus tongs, napkin rings, a fish slice, silk underwear, silver cruets, a plaster model of her breasts.

"It must make Paris feel that the Empire is receding very fast into history when she hears that Cora Pearl is no more," said the London *Daily News*. "The most severe moralist who shall undertake to draw a faithful picture of that epoch can never leave this figure out."

"On summer afternoons, when the Emperor passed in one carriage and Cora Pearl in another, one might have asked which was the equipage of the Chief of State. There was as much gold on the liveries of one as on the other, as much satin on the cushions, and quite as much dust. . . ."

Curious Myopia of the Historians: Cora Pearl died in a garret. Elizabeth Howard, who also had a Bonaparte for a lover, died in an eighteenth-century château, with the title of Countess of Beauregard, and a 450-acre estate near Versailles. For an English girl who has been called the Ninon de l'Enclos of her day, who played an important part in the creation of the Second Empire, and who, for a time, was its unconsecrated Empress, she has been curiously neglected by historians. Blanche Jerrold, in his ponderous four-volume biography of Napoleon III, does not even mention her. Nor have later writers done her justice. Mr. F. A. Simpson, perhaps the greatest contemporary English authority on Louis Napoleon and his Empire, dismisses her in a few unsatisfying sentences, and Philip Guedalla's study of *The Second Empire* is similarly reticent.

Accounts of her origin are vague and contradictory. An unreliable Holywell Street chap-book of the late 'sixties, *History of Lizzie Howard,* refers to her as "the low-born cobbler's daughter". She has also been described as the daughter of a Thames boatman, the daughter of a waiter, as an oyster girl, and as a barmaid at Wapping or Lambeth. "In spite of all that has been said," Albert Vandam gallantly observes, "Miss Howard was never born in a garret or bred in a kitchen. She may not have been a gentlewoman by birth and breeding . . . but she was by no means the utterly vulgar, ignorant and debased creature people have tried to make out." Hector Fleischmann, a student of Napoleon III's rather complex love-life, who says, "Nothing has been revealed about her in spite of attentive researches," claims to have discovered her birth-certificate which sets out that she was born in Preston, Sussex, in 1822, the daughter of a brewer called Herriott, and christened Elizabeth Herriott. But she has also been identified with a girl whose baptism is registered at the parish church, Brighton, in 1823, and whose parents' names are given as Joseph Gawen and Elizabeth Haryett.

In either case, she provides a link in the history of English whore-dom between Harriette Wilson, who was born in 1786, and Skittles, who was born in 1839. Her early history is as obscure as Skittles'. There is some agreement that after a few probationary years she became the mistress, in turn, of a well-known London gambler and cardsharp called Jack FitzRoy, who used her in a secondary role of decoy, of a gentleman-rider called Howard, whose name she adopted, and of a military gentleman, Major, later, Colonel, Francis Martyn. It is certain that by the 'forties, she had become one of London's most desired whores, counting among her friends and patrons the Duke of Beaufort, the Earl of Chesterfield, the Earl of Malmesbury, and Count d'Orsay.

Strong-Box and Heart: Miss Howard met Louis Napoleon, whose father was the ex-King of Holland and whose mother was the daughter of Josephine by General Beauharnais, at a reception at Gore House given by d'Orsay's mistress, Lady Blessington. (There is a story that Louis picked her up in the streets and accompanied her home for a fee of three shillings, but though the approach is not inconsistent with his known habits, it is hard to believe that Miss Howard, one of the costliest whores in the kingdom, would have made so great a concession, even out of sympathy for an exiled prince.) The meeting took place in 1839. Louis, an adventurer whose life was cast in roles from *opera bouffe* to Greek tragedy, was then consoling himself in London with harlots, hostesses, gamblers and conspirators, after his first humiliating essay in insurrection at Strassburg; and Miss Howard, though only about seventeen, was already a wealthy girl—so wealthy that she was able to lay at the exile's feet, as a French writer puts it, her strong-box as well as her heart. Both were well filled. The fact that this humbly born girl, while still in her early 'teens, had been able to amass a considerable fortune is not surprising if one accepts the contemporary report that Lord Clebden paid £1,000 for a single demonstration of her skill. Such a fee is not implausible, according to the inflated tariffs of the time. The wicked Lord Hertford is said to have paid the Countess Castiglione £40,000 for one night's entertainment, and to have demanded so exacting a return for his investment that the Countess spent the three following days in bed.

A Cargo of Carriages, Wines and Muskets . . . : In 1840, Louis hired the paddle-wheeled pleasure-boat *Edinburgh Castle* and steamed down the Thames with fifty-five assorted followers to seize the throne of France from Louis Philippe. Their *matériel* included second-hand French uniforms with new British buttons, elegant evening clothes, muskets from Birmingham, proclamations, bags of money, nine horses and two carriages, cases of wines and liqueurs, and a tame eagle that some said was a vulture. Whether Miss Howard opened her strong-box on this occasion is uncertain. The intimate friend of Louis Napoleon who published his memoirs under the pseudonym of Baron d'Ambes describes her embracing the prince tenderly just before the *Edinburgh Castle* sailed, and many writers take it for granted that she helped to buy the muskets and fill the money-bags. Others, including M. Fleischmann, are emphatic that her assistance was limited to the bedroom until Louis made his third and successful attempt to seize power. But all agree that she had a genuine passion for him. Alexandre Dumas said she loved the "awkward, sallow-faced, lank-haired adventurer . . . as ardently as Desdemona loved Othello". It was about this time that she rejected on his account the historian A. W. Kinglake, author of the popular *Eothen;* Kinglake never forgot the rebuff and avenged it by presenting a very malevolent picture of his successful rival when he wrote the history of the Crimean War.

The invasion of Boulogne was another absurd fiasco. The eagle, or vulture, escaped, but the prince was arrested and sentenced to life imprisonment in a fortress where he remained for six years; wrote theses on gunnery, sugar-beet and a Nicaraguan canal, talked to visitors, begat two bastards, and continued his plotting. He escaped in 1846, with the aid of his personal physician and a bottle of castor-oil, and returned to London where Miss

Howard was waiting for him. He had inherited some money from his father, out of which he bought her a house in Berkeley Street, and the liaison was continued. But for this attachment, he might have married an English heiress. Dickens' philanthropic friend Miss Burdett Coutts was one name mentioned by the gossips; the wealthy and beautiful Miss Seymour was another; and Miss Emily Rowles, whose family owned Camden House, Chislehurst—where twenty-seven years later the broken Emperor Napoleon III was to die—would certainly have married him, it was said, but for the open scandal of Berkeley Street.

The Exile Becomes President: It is hard to get a clear understanding of Louis Napoleon's finances during this period. After his father's death he is supposed to have had £120,000 deposited at Farquhar's and a smaller sum at Baring's; but he lived extravagantly, maintaining a costly little court of followers, and gambled. When the Revolution of 1848 drove pear-headed Louis Philippe, with his umbrella, from France, and Louis Napoleon crossed the Channel to stand for the Presidency, he was short of money for propaganda, bribery, and other electioneering necessities. How much, in this crisis, was provided by Miss Howard is again uncertain. The often-repeated figure of £320,000 is obviously absurd, even for a girl of Miss Howard's admitted potentialities. Albert Vandam computes it at £40,000; other estimates vary from £30,000 to Baron d'Ambes' more probable £13,000. Whatever the amount, it was to be repaid munificently.

The prince, by a great majority, was elected President of the Second Republic, and Miss Howard joined him in Paris, where she was soon recognized as his unofficial consort. She was established in a house in the rue de Cirque, communicating through a door in the garden wall with her lover's official residence in the Elysée; after a brief exercise of discretion, they were often seen together in public, and Miss Howard's Angora cat, with green ribbons in its tail, and a personal attendant in a matching green livery, attracted some attention. She accompanied the President on a formal tour of the provinces in 1849, to the scandal of the Receiver-General, M. Andre, in whose unoccupied house in Tours she was billeted. M. Andre wrote to the Prime Minister, inquiring whether France had gone back to the days when the King's mistresses were flaunted through the land, and Louis Napoleon, to whom the letter was shown, pleaded guilty, with curious humility, "to having looked to illicit ties for the affection of which my heart is in need".

Princes Prefer Red-heads: There is no adequate picture of Miss Howard at this triumphant stage in her progress. She is vaguely described as "blonde and beautiful", though Lady St. Helier, who saw her in Scotland some twelve years later, and thought her still a "very beautiful woman" was then struck by her "magnificent masses of deep red hair, in those days a very unusual adornment". Perhaps the colour of her hair, like Cora Pearl's, was influenced by her mood. "She was the courtesan", says the enthusiastic Albert Vandam, "*de grande facture et de grande allure* . . . with a natural charm that made up for the lack of education." But the *facture* and the *allure* are left undefined. The Countess of Cardigan, honeymooning in Paris in 1858 with the hero of the Light Brigade, had a less flattering impression. Miss Howard was then, according to the Countess, "a very fat woman" and at some unspecified time later "her embonpoint increased to such an extent that the doors of her carriage had to be enlarged".

The President Becomes Emperor: In 1851, to the clatter of printing-presses and the clank of artillery, by manifesto and massacre, Louis Napoleon made himself dictator of France, and in the following year, its Emperor Napoleon the Third. The next move was to establish a dynasty. He was still attached to Miss Howard, who, according to Vandam, was then being consulted by "great statesmen" and their emissaries as an authority very close to the Throne, but even by the relaxed standards of the Second Empire she was scarcely eligible to

158

found a royal line. Her dismissal, however much the Emperor may have regretted it, was a necessary prelude to an Imperial marriage; in 1852, the British Ambassador in Paris reported discreetly: "Mrs. H. [she then called herself Mrs. Howard] is, I believe, at last *congédiée*."

The Emperor looked round Europe for a wife; Queen Victoria, though admiring his *coup d'état*, would not sanction his marriage to her niece, Princess Adelaide of Hohenlohe-Langenburg, and in 1853 he announced that, following the dictates of his heart, he had chosen Eugénie de Montijo, a Spanish girl of twenty-six, who though not rich also had red-gold hair. The English red-head was angry: "Sire," she wrote to the Emperor, "if you were to marry a Princess I could readily sacrifice myself to a political necessity, but I cannot pardon you for immolating me to a mere caprice." Less formally, she remarked: "He is always very capricious but he is subject to indigestion and I know he will come back to me." If capricious, the Emperor was not ungenerous, and Mrs. Howard's immolation had some consolations. A week before his marriage, she was created Countess of Beauregard. Her son by a Cambridge livery-stable keeper was made Count of Bechevet; and her loans were repaid with interest. According to some accounts she received as well as the château and the estate, a pension of £20,000 a year. The Countess of Cardigan says the Emperor gave her £250,000; and M. Fleischmann quotes a figure close to this, based on a memorandum found among Napoleon's papers that lists payments made to her up till the end of 1854 that total £220,000. She was also given the concession to build the Palais d'Industrie in the Champs Elysées, a privilege said to have been worth £80,000.

Thunderbolt in Ross-shire: The Countess was obviously well dowered when, in 1854, she married a commoner called Clarence Trelawney, a Cornishman who held a commission in the Austrian Hussars. There are few records of their married life, which does not seem to have been harmonious. When the

Countess of Cardigan saw them in Paris in 1858, Mrs. Trelawney was still displeased with the Emperor:

> Mrs. Trelawney annoyed the Emperor and Empress as much as she dared by sitting opposite the Royal box at the Opera, and driving almost immediately behind the Empress's carriage in the Bois de Boulogne.

Lady St. Helier met the Trelawneys in Scotland about the beginning of the 'sixties when they had a shooting near Brahan. They lived there for two years but returned none of their neighbours' calls. "A thunderbolt fell", says Lady St. Helier, "when the news spread that Mrs. Trelawney was none other than Madame de Beauregard ... the religious and moral sentiment of Ross-shire was so strong that tradespeople began to doubt whether they were justified in supplying anybody with so stormy a past." Mr. Trelawney was a good shot. Mrs. Trelawney must have been a little bored. Not long after they were divorced; she returned to the château in the district where Madame de Pompadour had lived, and died there in 1865, at the age of forty-three. Her name is given in the official register as Elizabeth Ann Haryett. She was buried in England.

Mr. Trelawney married an American woman, got involved in debt, and shot himself. The Count of Bechevet died in 1907, leaving property in England worth £49.

V. KEEPING THE HOME FIRES BURNING

They Also Served: Of the many contemporaries of Skittles and Cora Pearl who adorned the Cytherean cavalcade of the Row, of the grottoes of Cremorne, while their more adventurous sisters were tooling through the Bois or high-kicking at the Mabille, there is little reliable record. Some, like Agnes Willoughby, married wealth; others, like Kate Cooke, who became the Countess of Euston, wealth and rank. What happened to such popular trulls as Baby Jordan and Nelly Fowler and Nelly

Clifton is obscure. Mabel Gray, whose real name was Annie King and who had been a shopgirl in Jay's mourning establishment in Regent Street, died in childbirth in Brussels, after some dealings with a young man in the Russian Embassy. Harry Vane Milbank as a youth in the Blues was restrained from marrying her only by the robust intervention of his father and the Duke of Cleveland. She was described by Emily Soldene as "the most notorious, extravagant, vampirish demi-mondaine of her day." At the end of the 'sixties, when she was one of the most photographed harlots in London, *Vanity Fair* published this elaborately ingenuous paragraph:

WHO?

Who on earth is Mabel Gray? Is she a Rumanian princess, or a distinguished advocate of women's rights, or a burlesque actress or a female missionary, or what? ... Her name does not appear in any play-bill, and I don't see that Lord Shaftesbury said anything about her in his last highly Christian speech on the coming conversion of Spain. But it is clear that she must be somebody very remarkable for her photograph meets me in every shop window in every variety of pose. It is so funny, too, that she has got no sort of handle to her name. Plain "Mabel Gray", as if she were one's sister, or one's aunt, or a new poem by Tennyson. It is really very puzzling altogether.

When her name did appear in a play-bill, as a principal boy in a Drury Lane pantomime, a London theatrical paper complained that it was a gross insult to the public. But she was more often seen at the other side of the footlights. Miss Soldene, who seems to have confused her with Skittles, recalls her as a regular patron of the Alhambra in the 'seventies:

a beautiful creature, who accompanied by her maid, and half-concealed by the hangings of her box, sat every night and received her courtiers. She was tall, slender, elegant, refined and wore outrageously costly but perfect toilettes and some of the best diamonds in London.

Like Skittles and Agnes Willoughby, she was the subject of a yellow-back "biography", *Mabel Gray, or Cast on the Tide*, published in 1869.

Dr. Hinton Among the Whores: It was in the Alhambra, about the time when Mabel Gray was holding court in her box, that Dr. James Hinton, whose work profoundly influenced Havelock Ellis, carried out a strange mission. It is described by his great friend, Dr. Berry:

> Late one evening James Hinton took me for a walk in the Strand. He led me into the Alhambra; we were soon surrounded by women of loose character. He took no notice of them but held me by the coat with both hands and looked me in the face, and began quietly talking about "unconscious sacrifice". Soon his gentle speech attracted the notice of the women, who grouped themselves round him, with the policemen who attend to keep order (the acting was all the time going on on the stage), and all were spellbound while he sweetly discoursed on Christ's hatred of sin and pity for the sinner; and finished a most touching address of some ten minutes by saying: "If our Saviour were on earth, where would he be? Why here." and then we left, and my dear friend wiped tears from his eyes.

Hinton, who said that "the happy Christian homes are the dark places of the world", advocated polygamy to save women from prostitution.

The Fragrance of Miss Fowler: Of "Sweet Nelly Fowler", a tender legend survives. It was currently believed, says a chronicler of the 'sixties, that:

> This beautiful girl had a natural perfume, so delicate, so universally admitted, that love-sick swains paid large sums for the privilege of having their handkerchiefs placed under

their Goddess's pillow, and sweet Nelly pervaded—in spirit if not in flesh—half the clubs and drawing-rooms of London.

It is pleasing to think of these sentimental young men pressing their fragrant tokens between the leaves of a brass-bound Family Bible, or a large-paper edition of *Idylls of the King*, carapaced in rich morocco; there is an echo of Sir Kenelm Digby, in an age that sometimes preferred lyrics to ledgers, as he looks upon the naked body of the sleeping Venetia Stanley, and observes how . . . "out of that darkness did glisten a few drops of sweat like diamond sparks, and had a more fragrant odour than the violets or primroses."

Miss Stanley and Miss Fowler, of course, both lived before the necromancers of Manhattan had transmogrified sweat into B.O.

"Hi, Say, Mareenee!" Marini, sometime mistress of the Maharajah Duleep Singh Bahador—the name seems to have been playfully derived from Mahareenee—began her professional career as a chambermaid in the Knightsbridge Hotel and even in her fairy-tale life as the lady of the lakhs, never outgrew her tangy Whitechapel accent, or her fondness for brandy-and-soda at breakfast. "Mrs. Marini", as her portrait was chastely captioned in all the photographers' windows, was a beautiful creature, very tall, fair and elegant, the archetype, until she spoke, of English patrician loveliness.

As a chorus-girl at the Alhambra in the late 'seventies she earned 25s. a week, wore sealskin, sable and exquisite diamonds, was driven to work in her own carriage and pair, and met at the stage-door afterwards by her footman carrying her cloak. Miss Emily Soldene, who was a star at the Alhambra when Marini was the rich little poor girl of the chorus, records that she was "charming, splendid and goodnatured. The girls used to coax her and say 'Hi, say, Mareenee, send us hup a bottle of fiz, will yer, Mareenee?'" And Marini always did.

Duleep Singh was so much in love with her that when he was

at Elvedon, his seat in Surrey, she had to telegraph him twice a day an assurance of her well-being. Perhaps it was her excellent taste in jewels that led the Prince to protest that the British Government's allowance to him of £25,000 a year was inadequate, and *The Times* to comment on what "if he were only an English country gentleman, we should be compelled to call extravagance, though, as he is an Eastern prince, it is more generous, perhaps, to describe it as magnificence."

Duleep published a pamphlet in which Britain's parsimony towards him was catalogued in detail, although in addition to his yearly dole of £25,000, he had received £198,000 from Her Majesty's Government to provide a roof for his head. But he claimed that when as a boy he was deposed from the throne of the Punjab, his personal property included about 150 villages, and a salt-mine worth £450,000 a year. These knick-knacks, he argued, should be restored to him, as well as the Koh-I-Noor diamond, which had belonged to his father and was now an ornament in the Crown of England. Because of this, Duleep used to refer to Queen Victoria as "Mrs. Fagin, a receiver of stolen property". But despite his comparative poverty in exile, he used to send a courier to Russia to buy his caviare, and he was seldom without the consolation of charming and expensive bedmates. One who probably made him sigh for his salt-mine even more urgently than Marini, was the dazzling Leonide Leblanc.

The Demi-monde Recalled in Tranquillity: A gentleman in Tom Brown's *London Amusements*, published in 1700, explaining why he would rather be seen with a well-known whore than a well-behaved wife, says: "You may rail at vanity as long as you please, but I would not give a farthing for a woman whom all the town does not desire to lie with. . . . This sets an edge upon a man's inclination." In our own time, the Baroness de Stoeckl has offered a similar explanation of the vogue of the fashionable nineteenth-century harlot. "The men who lavished huge sums on these darlings of fortune did it partly to *afficher* the fact before the public," she says. "It was a form of snobbishness." And she attributes the disappearance of the demi-mondaine at the beginning of this century to the appearance of the automobile. In the panting de Dions and Panhards of the 1900s, according to the Baroness, "these fashionable cocottes could no longer show off their beautiful gowns and wonderful jewels. ... With this their public *raison d'être* vanished." It is a dubious corollary, but the Baroness's summing-up is suggestive: "What madness when one thinks of these women, sometimes not even good-looking, but considered *chic* for merely having ruined several young men."

The specifications of the successful demi-mondaine provide, indeed, an interesting field for research. It is obvious that good looks, though useful, were not essential. Cora Pearl was ugly, and so, in varying degrees, were many equally distinguished *artistes*. Lord Pembroke, who was said to have spent nearly a quarter of a million pounds on a London ballet girl named Schaeffer, was once asked the reason for his costly devotion:

"Do you think her beautiful?"

"Certainly not."

"Clever?"

"No, she's a fool."

"Voluptuous?"

"Good heavens, no!"

"Well made?"

"No, flat as a pancake and hands and feet like a stable boy."

"What then?"

Lord Pembroke pondered the question carefully. "Well," he said. "I think it must be because she has rather nice shoulders."

VI. REPARTEE OF A LOVELY ROMAN

The Merry Prince of Marlborough House: It is a pity that no sympathetic history has been written of Edward VII's adventures as a man of pleasure during his long probation for the throne.

Rochester's description of Charles II, in the lines for which "he was banished the Court and turned Mountebank", might have been applied to the young Edward:

> The easiest Prince and best bred man alive

nor, in his French salad days, at least, was this couplet wholly inapposite:

> Restless he rolls about from whore to whore
> A merry Monarch, scandalous and poor.

Edward was just out of his teens when Hardman wrote of the rumours that his conduct was becoming loose, and a few years later Lord Clarendon reported from London to the British ambassador in Paris: "The Prince of Wales is leading a very dissolute life here, and so far from concealing it, his wish seems to be to earn for himself the reputation of a *roué*." But the glimpses of his unofficial life in England that emerge from the memoir-writers show him more as a sportsman and playboy than as an amorist. He is presiding knowledgeably at prize-fights; chasing London fires in shabby clothes; watching a well-backed dog kill 500 rats in an hour; coming down to dinner dressed as a white-faced clown; presenting tie-pins to *lions comiques*; joining Jolly John Nash, who was privileged to keep his hat on in the Royal presence, in a lusty chorus:

> Hi! Hi! Here stop!
> Waiter, waiter, Fizz pop!
> I'm rackety Jack
> No money I lack
> And I'm the boy for a spree.

A softer glow illumes the Prince in Paris, where the clamour of the prize-ring gives way to the *frou-frou* of frilled petticoats; we find him, night after night, with plump little Hortense Schneider in her dressing-room; chatting with the girls in the

Foyer de Danse of the Opera House as they exercise their legs on the high pedestals; entertaining—or being entertained by —La Belle Otero in the red-and-gold Grand Seize room of the Café Anglais; buying fizz for La Goulue as she arrests her *chahut*, one black-stockinged leg in the air, to cry: "Allo, Wales! est-ce-que tu vas payer mon champagne?" holding hands at Maxim's with Lilian Langtry—who, as an actress, Meredith said, made love "with all her arms and breasts".

Among the pilots of Edward's Parisian pleasure-barque were two of the most indomitable debauchees of the century—the Duc de Gramont-Caderousse, "le duc Darling", who once bribed the gendarmes not to look while Rigolle Boche, the can-can dancer, to satisfy his whim, walked naked from the Maison Doree, across the Boulevard, to the Café Anglais; and the Duc de Mouchy, "the youthful Heliogabalus", who, also to satisfy a whim, danced before the soldiers of the Pepiniere barracks, wearing only a pair of castanets. It was Gramont-Caderousse who contrived the memorable meeting, charmingly described in M. Frederic Loliée's history of *La Fête Impériale*, between the Prince of Wales and the lovely Roman, Giulia Barucci.

Edward had expressed a polite desire to meet the most eminent of the Parisian harlotry and Barucci, who called herself the greatest *putain*—she preferred this word—in all Paris, was selected by the Prince's advisers, among them Gramont-Caderousse, who fastidiously arranged every detail of the presentation. the place, the time, the food, the wine. He even coached Barucci in the refinements of behaviour at a Command Performance. "Be amiable always" he said. "And if you can also, be decent." Particularly, knowing Barucci's contempt for punctuality, he impressed on her not to be late.

But three-quarters of an hour after the appointed time, she had not arrived, and despite the spirited conversational essays of his host the duke, Edward began to show signs of impatience. Then Barucci swept in, splendid and serene; her hair was plaited in two bands behind her head and she wore a very low-cut gown of stuff so transparent that "she seemed to be enveloped in an imponderable veil".

"Monseigneur," said Gramont-Caderousse, "I present to you the most unpunctual woman in France."

Barucci turned round swiftly, and with a dazzling gesture pulled up her dress, disclosing to her noble host and his royal guest "the white rotundities of her callipygian charms." To the duke's scandalized reproaches, she replied ingenuously: "Didn't you tell me to be amiable to the prince? I show him the best part of me and it costs him nothing."

The eldest son of Queen Victoria and the pupil of the inflexible Baron Stockmar, contemplating the spectacle "with the eyes of a connoisseur", laughed heartily, and the party continued to everyone's satisfaction.

Chapter IV

London Amuses Itself

T*HE Goddess of Winking Feet:* An invention that, like the gas-lamp, helped to change the pattern of London prostitution, was the polka, that lively Bohemian dance that was as epochal in the eighteen-forties as New Orleans jazz was to be in the nineteen-twenties. It came to London in 1844, after seizing the "volatile and light-hearted" people of Paris "universally by the heels". Introduced first in fashionable assemblies —"as danced at Almack's and the balls of the nobility", said the *Illustrated London News* in March, 1844, when it published a polka dance specially written by Offenbach—it rapidly became the rage:

> *Why don't you dance the Polka?*
> *Won't you dance the Polka?*
> *Joys of earth are little worth,*
> *If you don't dance the Polka.*

There were polka hats, polka jackets, polka boots, polka ties, even pubs rechristened "The Polka Arms". Addicts were called polkists or polkers. The epidemic spread through the burgeoning middle classes, and created a demand for popular dance-halls, which the more discriminating whores soon found congenial to their trade.

> *First cock up your right leg—so,*
> *Balance on your left great toe,*
> *Stamp your heels and off you go,*
> *To the Original Polka, oh!*

In the days before the polka, the assembly room catered only for people of fashion—whether a highly exclusive institution such as Almack's in King Street, later called Willis's Rooms, to which the Duke of Wellington was once refused admission because he arrived seven minutes after the mandatory hour of 11 p.m., or a less fastidious rendezvous such as the Clipstone Street hop, where lords, bloods and trulls danced the hay quadrille to a violin and a harp. Writing in 1860 of this place, Baron Nicholson observed:

> The frequenters of magnificent casinos now flourishing in London would smile if they could see that small, but flash and aristocratic assembly room. It was down a timber-yard in Clipstone Street, Fitzroy Square, in a loft, which was reached by a ladder. By means of that ... the fashionable and frail, after the opera and theatre, were wont to assemble.

The first popular casino in London seems to have been the Adelaide Gallery which M. Laurent opened in 1846 on the site in Adelaide Street that later housed the Marionette Theatre, and then Gatti's restaurant. The gallery had formerly been a gloomy sort of fun-parlour that like its modern equivalents offered some rather bizarre entertainment: a steam-gun, a living electrical eel, air-pumps, devices for giving galvanic shocks, and microscopes that revealed the horrors lurking in drinking-water. M. Laurent, inspired by "bright news of Terpsichore's palaces" in Paris, particularly of the "glittering Bal Mabille, with its palm-tree lights and trellises of bronze vines", cleared out the didactic engines, instruments and jars, and dedicated the rooms "entirely to the goddess of 'winking feet'." These phrases are from an essay by Albert Smith, written in 1848. Mr. Smith recorded also that the innovatory sherry-cobbler, sipped through long straws, was the favoured drink of the polkers:

> The polka finished, refreshments are eagerly sought after, and of these the "sherry-cobbler" is the one in greatest request.

. . . . It is not strong, to be sure, but this is an advantage, in addition to that of the corresponding modesty of price. It is amusing to drink, combining pneumatic and hydraulic principles taught in a far more pleasing manner than was once the case with the air-pumps. . . . It is the most social refreshment known, as two straws may be employed in its absorption—straws that show clearly which way the wind blows; and when eyes are so closely opposed to one another, no one knows what may result. . . .

Dr. Acton, in his study of prostitution, first published in 1857, noted the "great improvement in the manners and appearance" of London's harlotry since "pre-polka days", which he attributed to the substitution of dancing and music for sedentary drinking:

> The graceful, and indeed, unnaturally slight forms now prevalent, contrast no more strongly with the Rubensesque development which was the horror of former days, than the decorum of the Argyll Rooms with the traditional intoxication and bruising of our father's time.

Fast and Furious Revelry: For many years, the Argyll Rooms was the most celebrated casino, and whore-market, in London. It was situated in Great Windmill Street, next to St. Peter's Church that Lord Derby caused to be erected, probably as a counter-attraction, in the early 'sixties. Admission to the ground-floor dance-hall was one shilling, but an extra charge was made for *entrée* to the gallery, with its "bedizened and brazen-faced harlots" and alcoves with plush-covered benches. There was an excellent orchestra—in 1862 it was under the direction of M. Boulcourt, "of *cornet à piston* celebrity, the greatest player in Europe"—and for the studious, French, German and English newspapers were available.

Dr. Acton was impressed by the decorum of the Argyll Rooms. M. Taine, coming from the city of the Mabille, the

Chaumiere, the Montagnes Russes and the Château Rouge, seems to have been depressed by it:

> There is no brilliancy, dash and liveliness ... as in France; when a gentleman wishes to dance, a master of the ceremonies, with a badge and a white tie, goes to find a partner for him; the two often dance without exchanging a word. The poor girls are often beautiful, many have a sweet and honest look; all dance very properly, smile a little, and do not gesticulate; they are in low dresses, but when dancing keep their cloaks on,

The men, whose appearance suggested to M. Taine that they were "leading merchants, wharfingers, middle-class manufacturers or their sons, and their foremen", liked the gaudy show of coloured lights and women in gay dresses and "white shawls embroidered with red flowers and exotic birds". With champagne at 12s. a bottle, M. Taine estimated that an evening's amusement, inclusive of love, of course, might cost £6.

Another observer, writing in the *Queen's Messenger* in 1869, gives a more sombre picture of the Argyll's patrons:

> Every third face has the vacant, silly eyes, the blubber lips, the long gums and short teeth, above which the infirm lips cannot close, and the unmistakable aspect of a born dunce. ... Towards midnight an electric light is lit; the revel races fast and furious, and the darkened hall in the lurid and ghastly glare might seem to a fanciful person like an entrance into the abode of Evil.

But there was general agreement that the Argyll was an admirably conducted place. When the Middlesex magistrates closed it in 1857, it was said that five or six hundred "noblemen or gentlemen" had offered to testify to this effect, and the *Saturday Review* observed that it was better that "some hundred females of loose life should be entertained for a few hours in a single room than that they should be encouraged to prowl about the streets". This view probably influenced the magistrates when, a year later, they allowed the Argyll Rooms to reopen.

In *Mr. Sponge's Sporting Tour*, written in the early 'fifties, Sir Harry Scattercash, Captain Seedybuck, and Miss Glitters have a scholarly after-dinner discussion "upon the elegance and lighting of the Casinos in the Adelaide Gallery, and Windmill Street, and the relative merits of those establishments over the Casino de Venise in High Holborn". This dance-hall, sometimes known as the Holborn Casino, was the Argyll's only serious rival. It also charged one shilling admission. When Dr. Acton visited it, "the brilliant ballroom, glittering with a myriad prisms ... was given over to a troop of dancing dervishes. The frenzy of these fanatics was stimulated not by poisonous champagne and spirits, but by the act itself of dancing, glasses of bitter beer, and bottles of soda water." The dance was, of course, what Dr. Acton called "the levelling polka". The doctor found that the women ("all prostitutes") were "for the most part pretty and quietly though expensively dressed". They were not kept mistresses, though their dress and deportment suggested this status. There was little observable solicitation, and the "outward proprieties of demeanour and gesture" were strictly observed:

One woman merits a passing note. . . . In the casino to which she has given pre-eminence over its rivals, she holds a mimic court ... surrounded by a crowd of admirers, idlers, and would-be imitators. It is said that the diamonds worn by this woman are worth £5,000. She is supplied daily from a florist in Covent Garden with a bouquet of the choicest flowers, amid which are interspersed specimens of most beautifully coloured beetles, the cost being about 30*s*., and her habit on entering the room is to present this really splendid trifle to the female attendant at the wine-bar, as a mark of her condescension and favour.

On permission to visit her being requested, she would probably, like another celebrated "fille de joie", take out her pocket-book, and after a careless glance at it, reply that she was full of engagements, but if the petitioner would call at her house at a given hour that day week, she would, perhaps, spare him some twenty minutes of her society, for which favour she might expect the modest sum of £25.

Mott's, or the Portland Rooms, in Foley Street, was an old-established place, dating back to the end of the eighteenth century. For many years, it had a more selective policy than the Argyll or the Holborn. Its ordinary admission charge of 2s. 6d. was increased to 5s. ladies, and 7s. 6d. gentlemen, when a Bal Masque was held, and its proprietor, Mr. H. C. Frere, rigidly excluded those of whose social standing he disapproved. He had a well-bred aversion to people in trade, though harlots, as professionals, escaped this sanction; there is a story of him denying admission to a wealthy London hatter, whose protest and proffered card he coldly rejected, saying: "Not necessary, I assure you, sir, not necessary at all. Your name has been in the lining of my hat for many a year." It was in Mott's octagonal ballroom that the young Marquis of Hastings caused some confusion by having a crony release from a sack, just after the Marquis had turned off the lights, two hundred famished sewer-rats.

Mr. Frere's successor, Charles Mann, was less exacting. "Formerly only men in evening dress were admitted," Mr. Mayhew noted in 1861. "Now this distinction is abolished, and everyone indiscriminately admitted. This is beginning to have its effect, and in all likelihood Mott's will in a short time have lost its prestige. It is always so with places of this description." Three years later, when Mr. Mann was fined £5 on a charge of harbouring prostitutes, his counsel said that the women who patronized the rooms "were of the same class as found their way to Willis's and the Hanover Square Rooms", and no complaints of disorderly conduct had ever been made against Mott's "subscribers" in the seventy years of its existence.

Next in size to the Argyll Rooms, but serving a humbler

clientèle, was Caldwell's dance saloon in Dean Street, Soho. Here admission was only sixpence, with an extra twopence for looking after hats and bonnets. "Dancing is becoming very popular with the lower classes of people," Mr. Caldwell told a parliamentary committee in 1854, and though he claimed that his customers included "some of the first noblemen", and "very respectable tradesmen", as well as an occasional tipsy medical student, the majority were working men; these, however, wore black, not corduroy, trousers. Most of the dancers wanted a glass of wine or negus or brandy-and-water, which was procured from a nearby tavern. "Do you find that the ladies drink brandy-and-water?" asked the chairman. "Yes," replied Mr. Caldwell. "And no inconvenience results from it?" "No."

Concern Among the Methodists: The popularity of these dance-rooms caused great perturbation to the men of God who claimed an exclusive knowledge of His views on the polka and other Satanic inventions. Late in 1857, the Wesleyan Methodists discussed with feeling at their annual conference, "the growing custom of dancing and other worldly amusements closely allied to it". Mr. Keely proposed that the rule of the Church prohibiting dancing should be made clearer and more stringent. Dr. Bunting reported that in London there were dancing parties even in the houses of some of their members. He recalled how, twenty years before, in Manchester, they had had to exercise discipline on dancing Methodists, and, as a consequence, lost some of them—but such members, who practised dancing, he pronounced solemnly, were better lost than found. The Rev. T. Pugh lamented the fact that the evil was a growing one. Card playing, too, he declared, as well as dancing, was practised in some Methodist families. The Rev. P. M'owan, said sharply that no discussion was necessary—they were all of one mind—the practice of dancing was not in harmony with religion. More cautiously, the Rev. J. Scott said that as the evil was chiefly among the younger members of Methodist families, he hoped they would enforce their rule with great affection as well as firmness, so as not to lose their hold on young people.

After the Ball was Over: Saloons like the Argyll and the Holborn, which were licensed for drinking and dancing, had to close at midnight. The focus of London revelry then shifted to the unlicensed nighthouses, cigar-divans, oyster-rooms, and cafés of the Haymarket and its tributaries, which "literally blazed with light" till dawn. The Piccadilly Saloon, on the site now occupied by the Criterion, was one of the most esteemed, though not the most decorous. It was a small room, with a discreet upstairs gallery, as at the Argyll. A guard stood at the outer door, and half-way up the passage that led to the dancing-floor was another door with a custodian who took the entrance money. On one side of the room was a fully equipped bar and at the end a three-piece orchestra of piano, harp and violin. Police were supposed to inspect these establishments every night. When they approached the outer door a message was passed inside, and two or three minutes would elapse before the inspector and his men were allowed into the main room. "The interval of time," says Mr. Montague Williams, Q.C., whose briefs brought him into close contact with this trade, "had been sufficient to enable all the bottles and glasses to be whipped off the counter, and placed on the shelves underneath, innocent coffee-cups being substituted". As "the Pic" had neither a dancing nor a liquor licence, the orchestra, too, had to be disposed of:

> Sufficient time had also been given to enable the three musicians to vanish through a doorway. This doorway was at the back of the room, and opened into a sort of cupboard, large enough to conceal the three delinquents. Here they remained until the police, having gone through the usual sham of walking round the room, had taken their departure.

The police seem to have been well rewarded for their quiescence. Mr. Mayhew, though reluctant to believe rumours that "large sums of money are paid...to insure their silence and compliance" remarks that "circumstances do occur that seem strongly to corroborate such suspicions", and Mr. Montague Williams quotes a current report that Inspector Silverton, who had charge of these operations, retired with "a very smug competence".

Other all-night resorts in the Haymarket were the Café Riche, next door to the Piccadilly Saloon; Bob Croft's, whose daughter married a baronet; Barnes's; Barron's Oyster Rooms; The Burmese, where, in the absence of a bar, brandied cherries were served with the coffee; and the Blue Posts, not to be confused with a place of the same name in Cork Street—"the wildest of wild houses", where the *flaneurs* from the Burlington Arcade took caviare and champagne before dinner. Panton Street, was another candid carnival of sex, with Rose Burton's, Jack Percival's, Sam's and Sally's, as well as some dubious bathing establishments and unequivocal brothels, competing for the custom of the antelucan pleasure-seeker.

A "Corpse-Reviver" with Kate: The acknowledged Queen of London night-life in the eighteen-fifties, the Kate Meyrick or Tex Guinan of her day was Kate Hamilton; neither the Forty-three nor the 300 Club in the fatuous nineteen-twenties enjoyed a greater celebrity than her luxurious saloon in Princes Street, Leicester Square, in its heyday. The entrance was flanked by two splendid commissionaires, and you were admitted, after a scrutiny through eye-holes, only if you were known to the establishment, or were sponsored by someone acceptable. You walked down a long tunnel-like passage, and up a short flight of stairs into a large, brilliantly lit saloon. At one end was an American bar dispensing mixed drinks under such names as "gum-ticklers", "eye-openers" and "corpse-revivers"; at the other, was a dais with a velvet-canopied throne on which, attended by attractive young ladies-in-waiting, the hostess sat, sipping champagne and issuing commands in a fearful booming voice. Gas-lit lustres played upon her jewels, and mirrors multiplied her porcine bulk. She was an enormous and hideous woman; in her low-cut evening-dress, says a contemporary writer, she shook like a blancmange when she laughed. She had climbed the ladder of strumpetry from *poses plastiques*—the strip-tease of the day—to fashionable procuring. Her nighthouse was one of the sights of London, and her patrons included aristocratic idlers, officers of both Services, professional men, university students, young squires, provincial magnates up in Town on business, and legislators relaxing after a dull debate in the House. Men-about-town were proud to be summoned to a seat beside her, a privilege which carried the obligation to buy large quantities of champagne.

Mr. Mayhew testifies to the high standing of the whores who visited Kate's—"not only to dissipate ennui, but with a view to replenishing an exhausted exchequer":

> for as Kate is careful as to whom she admits to her rooms—men who are able to spend, and come with the avowed intention of spending, five or six pounds, or perhaps more, if necessary—these supper rooms are frequented by a better set of men and women than perhaps any other in London. Although these [women] are seen at Kate's, they would shrink from appearing at any of the cafés in the Haymarket, or at the supper rooms with which the adjacent streets abound, nor would they go to any other casino than Mott's.

Dark Men and Light Women: Kate Hamilton's hospitality was sometimes invoked to assist in the entertainment of very important persons, as when the dual Kings of Siam, in 1857, dispatched three ambassadors, with their retinues, to pay tribute to the Great White Queen. They carried out their mission by crawling towards Her Majesty, pushing before them as they advanced, a crown of gold set with diamonds and rubies, a heavily jewelled gold collar, a state palanquin, a metal drum, a throne, gold-embroidered umbrellas, a rare shell, and other useful pieces.

The British Government installed them at Claridge's and showed them places of historic and architectural interest in the metropolis, but the inquiring plenipotentiaries expressed a desire for more robust entertainment. They were therefore conducted, with suitable escorts, to Kate Hamilton's, where one of the senior envoys, Phya Mantry Suriywanse, glittering in golden robes, and displaying a belt encrusted with rubies, made a profound impression on the whores who had just swept in from Mott's and the Argyll. With the aid of the Royal Interpreter, Mom Rajoday, who was also picturesquely accoutred, the amiable diplomat ordered unlimited champagne for all. He continued to dip liberally into the Treasures of the two Kingdoms until daybreak, when he was respectfully hauled into a waiting cab, and on to his hotel bed.

The Shah of Persia, Nasr-ed-Din, was another foreign dignitary who was said to have patronized Kate Hamilton's during his first visit to London in 1872. The Shah was an embarrassing guest at Buckingham Palace because of the spontaneity with which he performed some of his natural functions. Equally unconventional by English standards was his order that a member of his staff who had displeased him should be executed with a bow string. This, it is said, was done, and the body buried by night in the Palace grounds. When the King of Kings next visited England, in 1889, he brought with him a young Circassian girl and a small and very ugly boy.

Kate Hamilton died at the beginning of the 'sixties but the saloon was carried on under her name for some time. In 1862, her successor, William Barton was summoned for permitting prostitutes to assemble. Inspector Draper, who seems to have lacked Inspector Silverton's tolerance, told the Court that he had found ninety men and ninety-five prostitutes on Mr. Barton's premises, of whom five or six were sipping lemonade. He said: "You have more than seventy prostitutes here," to which Barton replied: "It does not matter if there are 150, if they conduct themselves in an orderly fashion." The inspector said he had never seen a poorly-dressed prostitute there. There were eight other houses of the same class in the neighbourhood. Mr. Archibald Smith, who resided opposite, complained that women came at all hours of the night with men in cabs and broughams.

As many as 300, he said, were let in nightly. The magistrate fined Barton 60s., but advised him to take the case to a higher court.

When Kate Hamilton's was again prosecuted in 1869, the police said that "most of the frequenters were young men from the universities and Aldershot".

The Assault on Mr. Sala's Nose: The Hamilton saloon, like the Argyll Rooms, was conducted with decorum, but there were many places where the more riotous mood of the Regency night-house prevailed. It was in one of these, in Panton Street, that George Augustus Sala, one of Dickens' young men and one of London's young men-about-town, had the contours of his already notable nose remodelled. Sala, belligerent in liquor, hotly disputed the price of a bottle of champagne, and offered some provocative comments on the proprietor's race, legitimacy and ethics. The dispute soon became a duel of fisticuffs, in which Sala was obviously outclassed. He crashed to the floor, and his opponent, taking up a position astride his chest, rained a series of heavy blows upon his nose with a fist heavily fortified with diamond rings. The hardness of the diamond is well known to men of science, and Sala's nose, which at the beginning of the combat had resembled a rubified potato, was split "throughout its entire length" and now resembled a bifurcated radish. Sala, half-insensible, was rolled into the street, and lay on the footpath till he was rescued by Mr. Coney, the proprietor of an adjacent nighthouse, who had him delivered to Charing Cross Hospital, where his nose was reintegrated.

This incident occurred towards the end of the 'fifties, a period according to police returns, of considerable drunkenness in London. In 1857, the arrest of disorderly prostitutes reached the record figure of 5,178. By 1870, it had fallen to 1,391.

II. BARON NICHOLSON ON THE BENCH

The Satyr of the Strand: Heaven and Hell in mid-Victorian London were sometimes only a few yards apart. Piety had its

General Headquarters in Exeter Hall, destroyed during World War II: in the Great Hall, holding 3,000 people, and in the two smaller halls, the shock-brigades of Nonconformity, evangelicism, and sabbatarianism, held their missionary rallies, their sacred concerts, their temperance clinics, their Messianic conventions and their tactical classes. Its purity was guarded so zealously that *Sally in our Alley* was once struck from a programme, not because of the last verse in which the singer promises that he and his Sally will wed and then bed, though not in their alley—for this verse was never sung by the polite—but because of the allusion to the enjoyment of Sunday in the verse:

> *Of all the days that's in the week*
> *There's none I love like one day;*
> *And that's the day that comes between*
> *The Saturday and Monday.*

But just across the Strand, off Fountain Court, was the Coal Hole Tavern, for many years a stronghold of Victorian bawdry and booze. Here the notorious Baron Nicholson, whom the *Saturday Review* called "that huge Satyr", presided over his obscene Judge and Jury Show, and his Poses Plastiques, proudly advertising his address as "Opposite Exeter Hall".

"The Judge and Jury . . . is a peculiarly English institution," said the *Daily News* in 1869. "No other country, no other capital in Europe, would permit an exhibition of this kind." Perhaps it is because the English are a law-abiding people that they enjoyed these bawdy burlesques of the law. Judge and Jury societies were a fashionable and then a popular entertainment in London for more than three-quarters of a century. The first was established in Old Compton Street, Soho, in 1788, with the ambiguous Chevalier d'Eton, who spent forty-nine years of his life as a man and thirty-four as a woman, participating; the question before the court was one on which London gamesters wagered hundreds of thousands of pounds—was the Chevalier male or female? Similar courts were started in many London public houses, but it was not till Baron Nicholson opened his assizes at the Garrick's Head, Bow Street, in the early 'forties, that the Judge and Jury Society became celebrated.

Renton Nicholson was born in the Hackney Road a few years before Waterloo. He served his apprenticeship with a pawnbroker and then set up the golden balls in the Quadrant. His debaucheries soon bankrupted him and he spent much of his life, before and after his elevation to the bench of bawdry, in debtors' prisons. When he was not lodging in the King's Bench, Southwark, which had also accommodated Chatterton, Morland, Haydon and Lord Cochrane, or in Whitecross Street, Cripplegate, he was sleeping on the doorstep of the Bishop of London's house in St. James's Square or in a gambling hell or brothel and living by the manipulation of roulette-wheels, cards, dice and billiards-cues. He was a character out of Pierce Egan, a Cockney Corinthian of the age of railroads and respectability, a burly rogue with a robust humour and a huge appetite for life. For a few years he edited *The Town*, a scandal sheet that promised its readers reliable news of "Metropolitan Gaming Houses—Free and Easies—The Prisons—The Swell Mob—Licensed Victuallers—Pawnbrokers and Their Assistants—Cigar Shops—Pretty Women—Bow Street Officers—The Doings of Courtesans and Demireps of Quality—etc. etc." *The Town* redeemed this promise faithfully, and was not too proud, it seems, to practise a little blackmail as well. Among its contributors were "bright broken" Dr. Maginn and Blanchard Jerrold, who years later wrote of Nicholson as a man of excessive kindness and generosity—"a Falstaff with Bardolph and Nym at every corner". While Nicholson was editing, and largely writing, *The Town*, for a salary of £3 a week, he was also conducting a "high-priced and high-church" organ called *The Crown*, in which he attacked the immoralities of his own writings in *The Town*, replying in *The Town* to his onslaughts in *The Crown*.

From his two editorial desks, Nicholson moved in 1841 to the Garrick's Head and Town Hotel, opposite Covent Garden

Theatre, to begin his long career as Chief Baron. His first court was in a low narrow room, lit with tallow-candles and furnished with benches for the public, a railed-off space for the jury, a table for the bar, and a raised desk for the judge. Outside was a big oil painting of celebrities from the Duke of Wellington and Count d'Orsay to pugilist Owen Swift, all of whom, it was implied, were patrons. Certainly, very many eminent citizens were—"members of both Houses of Parliament, statesmen, poets and actors of high repute", says Nicholson in his autobiography. The jury was chosen from the audience, and, according to Nicholson, was often entirely composed of "noble lords and M.P.s". Greville attended a session in 1842, but found it disgusting. "It is difficult to imagine anything more low and blackguard than this imitation of and parody on a court of justice," he recorded in his diary:

> Here they try such notorious cases as have been brought . . . under public notice, and last night we had "Chesterfield *v.* Batthyany", the names being slightly changed . . . *Maidstone*, for example, was examined as a witness under the title of Lord Virgin Rock . . . the jury are sworn upon *The Town*. . . . They deal in very gross indecencies, and this seems to amuse the audience.

Greville was told that the address of the judge was generally the best part of the proceedings, but he did not wait to hear it. He was slightly amused by a counsel who caricatured Lord Brougham. This was Henry Pellat, a former dissenting minister, who had some resemblance to Brougham and traded on it in Baron Nicholson's court for many years.

The admission fee was one shilling which entitled you to a glass of grog—rum or gin and water—or beer, and the jury was rewarded with unlimited free drinks. Women were not admitted. Everyone smoked cigars, including the Chief Baron, whose burly form, red face, framed in whiskers, and leering eye, loomed through a pungent blue haze. "Ushers, get me a cigar and a little brandy-and-water," uttered with tremendous dignity, in a rich and mellow voice, was the unvarying formula with which the court opened. The humour was as bawdy as Shakespeare's, and Nicholson's contempt for the respectabilities gave him, in a perverse way, the stature of a national figure. *The Dictionary of National Biography* describes his wide renown as "one of the sternest realities of eccentric history". Attorneys suing him addressed him deferentially as "my lord"; sheriff's officers, executing a writ, apologized for the disagreeable duty they had to perform "on the court". On one of his appearances in the bankruptcy court, he had a poem of his own read in which he compared himself with Prometheus:

> *His fate hath no terrors for me on the brain*
> *At the fury of Jove I don't shiver,*
> *For years have the lawyers again and again*
> *Like vultures, been gnawing my liver.*

The Chief Commissioner listened to it sympathetically, and in granting Nicholson his discharge, said: "Mr. Nicholson, however you may shine in your own court, don't bring yourself into mine again."

Even a man of the cloth, the Rev. R. H. Barham, was not afraid to pay tribute to his wit. In one of the *Ingoldsby Legends* he writes of Bow street:

> *. . . though there are ones who deem that same a low street*
> *Yet I'm assured, for frolicsome debate,*
> *And genuine humour, it's surpassed by no street,*
> *When the "Chief Baron" enters and assumes*
> *To "rule" o'er mimic "Thesigers" and "Broughams".*

"The trials were humorous", says the *Dictionary of National Biography,* "and gave occasion for much real eloquence, brilliant repartee, fluent satire, and not infrequently, for indecent witticism." The Rabelaisian guffaws, of course, clashed harshly with the hosannahs of Exeter Hall, and evoked some criticism— "Every remark of the mock judge was a grave and deliberate piece of obscenity," said a writer in *Temple Bar* in 1862. "A more

184

deliberate scene of wickedness was probably never enacted and countenanced since the world began." And he deplored the fact that it was promoted and fostered by "gentlemen", and that most of the illustrious men of the day patronized it.

Sometimes the Chief Baron went on circuit, and held his court in provincial towns. As a result of this, perhaps, "persons coming from the country sought out the Judge and Jury Society as the first and choicest resort of the metropolis". In 1846, the Baron added to its attraction by introducing *Tableaux Vivants*, in which buxom women in skin-tight pink silk coverings, were displayed on a hand-cranked revolving stage. In the year of the Great Exhibition, 1851, he moved the whole entertainment to the Coal Hole, Fountain Court, which had been a place of glees, madrigals and smutty songs. The tradition of the songs was maintained; Mr. J. Balfour, a Vespucci of London's uncharted vice, heard some of them one night in 1854, "and certainly," he told a parliamentary committee, "the singing I heard there I should have expected to have heard, if I had been accustomed to go to such places, in a common brothel. . . . It was no double meaning but plain out."

The Chief Baron's handbills now offered "his best friends, the Public", his "Mimic Court of Law at half-past nine, *Poses Plastiques* at half-past seven and after the theatres, an Ordinary daily at 6 o'clock, chops, steaks, etc., dressed in the Coffee-room, Private Rooms for Dinner and Supper Parties, and beds, 1s. 6d." *Paul Pry* counselled "those who admire nature slightly adorned" to visit the Coal Hole, "where their love of the real will be amply satisfied, and their rude notions of the ideal somewhat improved". Country cousins were advised to spend "a most delightful evening . . . by dropping their 'bob' to the Judge and Jury, with its rich, racy and witty trials, and winding up with a peep at the slightly-veiled daughters of Venus".

The Chief Baron presided over his dubious pleasure-dome, untroubled by the constabulary, till his death in 1861. His wig and his wickedness were inherited by an associate, Henry George

Brookes, who did his best to maintain the standards of his predecessor. But the Society's clientèle had now changed. The "scum and outscourings of society"—to quote again from *Temple Bar*—had replaced the Peers, the Members of Parliament, the university men, and the exquisites of Rotten Row. In accordance with the Anglo-Saxon tenet that the less money you have, the more stringently you must be protected from corruption, the police in 1869 charged Mr. Brookes with "keeping a refreshment house where he permitted disorderly conduct". They described the clinging attire of the women in the *Tableaux Vivants,* and the "ribaldry and obscenity" of the members of the mock court. The real court, presided over by Mr. Knox, said it was nothing less than "disgusting bestiality", and fined Chief Baron Brookes 40s. Knox who had been a leader-writer on *The Times,* was one of London's most distinguished magistrates, but his attitude towards its night-life was unsympathetic.

Within a fortnight, Brookes was before Mr. Knox again, and six of his court staff, charged with "unlawfully representing an indecent performance". Mr. Knox said that as a man of the world he was not readily startled by what he heard, but he had never listened to such a mass of disgusting indecency. But he thought there was one thing in the defendant's favour—the fact that the police had allowed this thing to go on for years. He agreed to let the summons stand over if Mr. Brookes would promise, not to stop his performances altogether, but to "give up the disgusting obscenities of some part of them". Mr. Brookes promised.

The long immunity enjoyed by Chief Baron Nicholson may be compared with the experience of a brother in an inferior jurisdiction, Mr. William Clark, licensee of the "Jew's Harp" in Edward Street, Hampstead Road, who was charged at Mary-le-bone police court in 1853 with having allowed a Judge and Jury Club at his house on Sunday evenings.

A policeman stated that at eight in the evening of Sunday, 26th December, he went in plain clothes to defendant's house, paid 2d. for admission to a Judge and Jury Club, which was held upstairs. He there found about 200 persons, men, women, and children, and in the centre of the room was a raised platform, so as to give a good idea of a court of law. Upon the bench was a person with a big wig, who was sitting as judge, and just beneath him were three others who were in attendance as counsel, they had also on wigs and gowns. When he went in, a case was going on in which a man was charged with the offence of stealing a goose from the "Cow", in Tottenham Court Road, the bird in question being in an unfit state for human food. Numerous witnesses were examined in the case, one of whom was a wild Irishman, named O'Connor, who flourished his shillelagh in a most awful manner; he was the principal witness, and had been tutored to simulate intoxication; the answers which he gave to questions put to him by the learned judge and counsel elicited great applause, but as he went beyond the bounds of propriety the judge ordered him out. A regular row then ensued, the judge and counsel took off their wigs and gowns, and the utmost confusion and disorder prevailed. The judge used bad language and, in fact, swore, awfully. Two other policemen confirmed this evidence. The magistrate considered that the exhibition itself was calculated to bring the administration of justice into contempt, but apart from all considerations of that nature, the holdings of such meetings on a Sabbath evening was highly reprehensible. He therefore inflicted a fine of 40s. and costs.

III. WHO NOW REMEMBERS GAY CREMORNE?

Desire Under the Elms: In the spring, when a livelier iris changed on the burnished dove and a young man's fancy lewdly turned to thoughts of love, or in the summer, when a similar mood settled on him, he could abandon the airless pavements of the Haymarket and pay homage to Priapus in the more appropriate setting of one of London's pleasure gardens. A steamboat would take him to Cremorne or Rosherville, a cab to the Highbury Barn or the Pavilion Gardens, places with flowers and trees, lights and drinks, open-air dancing and open-hearted girls. The suppression of these pleasant places, linked by an unbroken tradition with the Paris Garden of Elizabeth's day, was another triumph of late-Victorian Nonconformity in its zealous campaign to stop people enjoying themselves.

The Tree that Puritanism Clipped: "Cremorne", said the *Saturday Review* in 1861, "is a point of attraction not only to all London but to all England. The provincial farmer who comes to the capital on business, and seasons his business with pleasure, would scarcely think he had his full measure of enjoyment if he did not visit the famous Chelsea Gardens. In the country, he is perhaps a strict Puritan . . . but he feels that when in Rome he must do as Romans do."

For nearly half a century, these twelve acres of lawns, groves, flower-beds, dance-floors, refreshment-rooms, kiosks, and sideshows were London's best-known playground—as the Spring Gardens had been when Pepys noted young gallants, "almost forcing" women in the arbours, or when, as Vauxhall Gardens, Horace Walpole and Johnson and Goldsmith patronized them. Cremorne Gardens were at their peak of popularity when Vauxhall closed down in 1859. They ran along the Thames at Chelsea, just west of Battersea Bridge. One entrance was in the King's Road, but the more attractive approach was through the ornate ironwork river-gate. There was a huge open dance-floor, with a pagoda-like orchestra in the middle, and a tent covering several acres for dancing under in bad weather.

Dante Gabriel Rossetti, says his brother William, went to Cremorne Gardens every now and then, "partly for mere relaxation, partly to find a model". Thousands visited Cremorne in the afternoon and early evening "for mere relaxation"; they found it in the Ballet Theatre, the Oriental Circus, the American Bowling Saloon, the Stereorama, the Fernery, the Menagerie, the Shooting-galleries, the female Blondin, the Man Frog, and the fireworks—which were painted by Whistler in a way that puzzled Ruskin. For 10*s*., you could take a ride in a captive balloon; once, before the police intervened, you could have seen a lady soar aloft on the back of a heifer; and for half a crown you could have an excellent supper and sample a sherry "free from acidity and recommended to invalids". But as the evening wore on, the character of the Gardens changed, and more worldly relaxations were pursued. "None but an idiot", said the *Saturday Review,* "could shut his eyes to the fact that at 10 o'clock . . . the female population of Cremorne is increased by a large accession of fallen characters, whose fall, by the way, has generally consisted in a transition from a state of vicious squalid poverty to a state of vicious brilliant opulence."

Dr. Acton becomes almost lyrical as he describes this metamorphosis:

> On a pleasant July evening . . . as calico and merry respectability tailed off eastward by penny steamers, the setting sun brought westward hansoms freighted with demure immorality in silk and fine linen. By about 10 o'clock, age and innocence had seemingly all retired . . . leaving the massive elms, the grass-plots and the geranium beds, the kiosks, temples, "monster platforms" and "crystal circles" of Cremorne to flicker in the thousand gas-lights . . . on and around that platform waltzed, strolled and fed some thousand souls—perhaps 700 of them men of the upper and middle class, the remainder prostitutes, more or less *prononcés*.

"A sort of Bal Mabille, where the folly of the day is continued throughout the night," was Taine's description of the Gardens, which he visited about 11 o'clock at night:

> All the men are well or properly dressed; the women are harlots, but of a higher class than those of the Strand; they wear bright shawls, white stuffs of gauze or tulle, red cloaks, new bonnets; there is a dress which has cost £12, but the faces are

rather faded, and sometimes, in the crowd, they raise terrible cries—the cries of a screech owl. What is most comical, and proves their state of excitement, is their notion of pinching people, particularly foreigners.

One of his party, a man of forty, "being sharply pinched and otherwise scandalized" left, but the philosophic Taine remained to reflect on the gay scene, which helped him understand "the joyous rustic festivals of the sixteenth century, Shakespeare's 'Merry England' ". He divined in the laughing, dancing—and screeching—crowds, "the abounding primitive sap of the tree" which Puritanism had clipped and pruned.

The pruning shears of Puritanism hovered over Cremorne for many years. They were wielded most zealously by Canon Cromwell, of St. Mark's Training College nearby. In 1871, when he succeeded in having the Gardens lose their licences for music and dancing, many London papers deplored the passing of "the trim parterre, the crystal platform, the music-hall, the bowling-alley". *The Observer* said that despite "a certain amount of noisy and somewhat vulgar hilarity", the abolition of the Gardens was a serious deprivation for seekers of cheap out-door amusement. Next year, when the Middlesex magistrates again refused the licences, *Reynold's* described them as a set of "drivelling Dogberries" and the *Saturday Review* pointed out that "even the unfortunate class of persons who are habitual frequenters of Cremorne have got to go somewhere". Their winter resorts, such as the Argyll and the Holborn Rooms were licensed; why not their summer ones? In making his application for licences, the proprietor of the Gardens, John Baum, said he paid £3,000 a year for the lease, and during the season, employed from 400 to 500 people. A police inspector said that on gala nights, there were 3,000 people at Cremorne, and 300 cabs in attendance.

Cremorne regained its licences in 1874, and remained open till 1877. Its end was hastened by a Baptist minister and tailor named

Alf Brandon, a man skilled in the use of shears. He published some verses on "the Horrors of Cr-m-ne", and Baum sued him for libel. In court, Brandon described the Gardens as "a nursery of every kind of vice", and proved what everyone knew, that "large numbers of improper characters assembled in them". Baum was awarded one farthing damages, but no costs. He was in debt and ill, and it was obvious that the corrosion of Puritanism, the assault of the latter-day Cromwell, was irresistible. He did not apply again for licences, and in 1878 the Gardens were demolished. A more moral age has established in their place the squalid and joyless amusement arcades of the West End.

> *Who now remembers gay Cremorne*
> *And all its jaunty jills,*
> *And those wild whirling figures born*
> *Of Jullien's grand quadrilles?*

Goldfish and Tittle-cum-tortars: In its heyday, Cremorne's closest rival was Highbury Barn, which grew out of an eighteenth-century cakes-and-ale house into an elaborate pleasure-grounds. At the beginning of Victoria's reign it was noted for its huge dining-rooms, seating 1,000 people, and its four acres of gardens offered "resting places for the weary—secluded haunts for the studious—marquees for bacchanals—umbrageous bowers and Arcadian groves for lovers—ambrosial and salubrious promenades for the valetudinarian—and gymnastic areas for the youthful and vigorous".

To these enticements, a "monster dancing platform" was added when Highbury Barn got a licence in 1856, and the proprietor, Mr. Archibald Hinton, was able to describe his domain to readers of *The Times* thus:

HIGHBURY BARN—The château des Fleurs de Londres— This suburban paradise opens every day at 4. Dancing commences at 7, with Grattan Cooke's military band. The new

monster platform is pronounced by 100,000 visitors to be unrivalled in Europe. Ball rooms, club rooms, banquetting
halls, cosy private rooms, panorama of Constantinople, swings
and tittle-cum-tortars, battledore and shuttlecock, trap-ball,
football and other rural sports. The beauty of the pleasure
grounds, the freshness and purity of the air, the brilliantly
illuminated walks, the banks of flowers, the fountains and
goldfish, the noble chestnut and lime trees, under whose
branches hundreds can be seated and refreshed, the spacious
meadows, the winding avenues, the numberless embowered
recesses, besides a hundred other attractions render this old
and renowned place of harmless pleasure unequalled by any
other. N.B.—There will be moonlight for parties who prefer
walking home. Coffee as at Paris.

The rural sport with the provocative name of tittle-cum-
tortars was the innocent see-saw, also known in dialect English
as titter-cum-totter and tittem-a-tauter. It was not to play these
folksy games, however, that the young men came in their
hansom-cabs all the way to Islington, and when, in 1870, Highbury Barn lost its dancing licence, it was finished. It struggled
along, hopelessly, for a while. In 1871, it was in the hands of the
sub-dividers.

Rosherville, the creation of Mr. Jeremiah Rosher, occupied
the site of a Gravesend chalk quarry, allowing "a miniature combination of mountain and plain which was at once picturesque
and unique": Like the Pavilion Gardens at North Woolwich,
it had more local customers than Londoners; neither place
attracted the type of high-class whore which patronized Cremorne. Nor did the Eagle Tavern, with its Grecian Saloon and
gas-lit gardens, in the City Road, which after fifty-eight years of
existence came to a symbolic end in 1882, when it was bought
by the Salvation Army.

"*First Catch Your Whore:*" Mr. Beeton, as well as being Mrs.
Beeton's husband, was an enterprising publisher and an enthusiastic Radical. For many years he produced a Christmas Annual
which began in the conventional style as a collection of innocent
tales, games, and puzzles, and was transformed in the early
'seventies into a long satire on the abuses of the day. Beeton's
favourite subjects were the parsimony of Queen Victoria and the
profligacy of the Prince of Wales, and as Republican sentiments
were then popular, the Annuals were a great success; one, which
W. H. Smith banned from his bookstalls, sold 250,000 copies in
three weeks. The Annual for 1873, a parody called *The Siliad,*
contained a tour in verse of London vice. Despite some anach-
ronism, it gives a good picture of London when the era of
laissez-faire night-life was almost ended.

The Homeric heroes, Peelides and Bersites, look in at a West
End nighthouse and find

> *. . . a bravery of gilt, a mass*
> *And wealth of waving hair, and glittering glass;*
> *A hundred rainbows cross and intertwine,*
> *A thousand wicked eyes enchanting shine.*
> *Lips, full of sin, yet plump and ripe withal,*
> *Shape naughty kisses, and for liquids call.*
> *Hands, gloved divinely, creep beneath men's arms;*
> *Whilst shapely ankles tell of hidden charms;*
> *Toilettes, too ravishing for mortal pen*
> *Flit everywhere, and prey on helpless men.*
> *Houris in eau de Nile, and salmon pink,*
> *And peacock blue, distract, and daze, and drink.*
> *The utter stranger greet they with a smile,*
> *So artless seeming, yet so versatile:*
> *As some in distant corners toy and sport,*
> *Others lap deeply lemonade and port.*

> *While shop-boys, trying tip-top swells to be,*
> *Have robbed the till, and call for S. & B.*

Here, they encounter Liobed, a handsome rake who has been expelled from Eton, sent down from Trinity, gambled and debauched away his fortune, and is now a card-sharper, bludger, and public-relations man for prize-fights, cock-fights, rat-and-terrier conflicts, and expensive brothels. They set up sherry-cobblers, and invite Liobed to show them the town:

> *"Now," said the Blacklegged, "whither shall we go?*
> *The Judge and Jury? No, that's awful slow.*
> *Cremorne? The poses plastiques are not so bad;*
> *But then the drive there drives a fellow mad.*
> *The 'Gyle'? for that we're just an hour too soon;*
> *What say you to a Grassmarket saloon?"*

Things are lively in Windmill Street, where they dance the London gas-lights to sleep. . . .

> *The final galop comes, with rush and roar*
> *The giddy throng whirls madly round the floor;*
> *Frilled skirts eclipse no longer, rounded charms,*
> *And wicked waists are clipp'd by clasping arms;*
> *Cheeks rouged and chalked, not wisely and not well*
> *Leave smudges on the shoulders of the swell;*
> *And here and there excited demireps*
> *Delight old roués with the cancan steps;*
> *Sounds the last chord, and through the swinging doors,*
> *Terpsichore her rapt adorers pours.*
> *Now sounds of revelry the ears disturb,*
> *And carriages and hansoms line the curb.*
> *Delicious burdens, fashionable and frail,*
> *Big swells, immaculate in tie and tail,*
> *Dive into shady brough'ms, and swearing tryst,*
> *Drive to the Groves of the Evangelist.*

Liobed and his protégés have picked up three "sirens" at the Argyll. There is a unanimous move towards supper, but where? "Scotts", Verey, the Café Regence, the "Globe", "The Cremorne Branch" are nominated, but Liobed dismisses them. All shut at 12 o'clock. He will take them to a place that is "under no such law". They make their way down the crowded Haymarket, "the main artery of vice", and turn into a side street. While they are presenting their credentials to the "burly bully" at the door of the all-night nighthouse, Mr. Beeton moralizes on the Haymarket:

> O England, quick to note another's sin
>   Canst thou not clean this ugly spot within
> The greatest city of thy mighty land;
>   Nor waste thy warnings on a foreign strand?
> Or can thy nostrils only sniff the stench
>   Of immorality, when it is French?
> Look thou at home, survey the nightly scene,
>   Close to the palaces of thy pure queen.
> (Altho' the walls of Buckingham the Chaste
>   Have lately blushed to see the Shah's vile taste.)

It is after midnight, but a café in the Haymarket is still open. In it, a midnight mission for fallen women is being held. Many kneel and sing, but one girl sweeps out, laughing defiantly, her hazel eyes flashing contempt, to where her brougham is waiting to take her to the Wood. It is Golden Nell, the Siren of the West. She has laughed aloud at the preacher's invitation to repent:

> Repent? Of what? Of fortune and renown?
> Repent and abdicate? Throw riches down?
> Go to a Refuge? Be a household drudge?
> Or work a "Singer", or a mangle?—Fudge!

By now, Liobed and his companions have been admitted to Kate Hamilton's. Liobed addresses his hostess:

> *O, buxom woman! handsome in thy day,*
> *Whose gay career th' police courts cannot stay;*

> *   *   *

> *Thou source of liquor after licensed hours!*
> *Thou brave defier of the legal powers!*

and commands a splendid supper.

The party moves upstairs to Kate's "Secret chamber". On the way, Liobed opens the wrong door, and breaks in upon the Shah:

> *. . . the wily potentate*
> *Was studying the secrets of our State,*
> *Which three fat actresses, with might and main*
> *Had been in turn endeavouring to explain.*

Liobed and his companions make themselves comfortable in Kate's room—

> *And, till the advent of the supper tray,*
> *They worshipped Venus in a quiet way.*

> *   *   *

> *And yet the room the visitor invites*
> *To thorough worship and elaborate rites:*
> *The ceiling glass, tall mirrors line the walls,*
> *Beneath, the footsteps on pile velvet falls,*
> *Three satin-covered couches—one sky blue,*
> *And one coal-black, and one rich crimson's hue.*

The pictures echo a single theme, "female loveliness unmarred by dress", a fountain bubbles with rich perfume, soft wax tapers, "soothe while they illume" and "celestial music" (from an undisclosed source) "fills the sensuous air".

> *Such are the joys, and such the transports great,*
> *Of those who win the confidence of Kate.*

Two of Kate's handmaidens now appear with supper: plump sweet oysters, an ethereal lobster salad, a capon with Béchamel sauce, croquettes, potatoes *à la maître d'hôtel*, an ox-tongue rolled, fowl *à la mayonnaise*, a *vol-au-vent*, tomatoes cooked two ways, a fricassée of chickens, lamb and peas and devilled kidneys, followed by a "surplusage of sweets"; a snowy trifle, ice-creams, meringues, tipsy cake, charlotte-aux-pommes, and stewed pippins in cream and Crème de Noyeau; accompanying this is a nectar—a cunning compound of champagne, curacoa, herbs, soda-water, sugar and powdered ice—served in a mighty four-handled gold goblet, with erotic motifs in bas-relief. This golden bowl is refilled many times. There follows a line of asterisks, and, not surprisingly:

> *At length repletion follows appetite*
> *And surfeit emanates from great delight.*

The three complaisant girls are liberally dowered, and dismissed, Peelides pays the bill ("O, muse be dumb!") and the jaded revellers take a final glass with Kate. More Hebes, "this time in lowly disarray", bring in the mocha, cigarettes are deftly rolled, and "dreamy ecstasy comes down on all".

They fall asleep, and are rudely wakened by the noise of trampling feet. It is a police raid. Twenty of Kate's patrons are hastily mobilized, and decide to fight their way out.

> *Let each one, then, his nerve and courage brace,*
> *To save himself from night-cell and disgrace!*
> *Blows we shall get; but better blows to-night*
> *Than Knox to-morrow. On, then to the fight!*

A truly Homeric struggle follows, but Liobed and his friends, despite the sherry cobblers, the lobster, the tipsy cake, the nectar and the ardours of the coloured couches, break through the cordon. Bersites claims a truncheon and a peeler's helmet as spoils of battle. Other trophies exhibited at the club where the swells restore themselves with arnica, sal-volatile and "glad libations" include a bull's-eye lantern and three pairs of policeman's Berlin gloves.

V. BAWDRY IN THE BEST CIRCLES

Coarseness and Kidneys: The full-blooded bawdries of the Judge and Jury were a survival from the days before the Crimean War, when music-halls were unknown and song and supper rooms, serving men only, flourished. Most of them were in stuffy basements and some, like the Cyder Cellars in Maiden Lane, which for a time housed the Chief Baron's court, dated back to the eighteenth century; it was as famous for its smutty songs as its devilled kidneys. Thackeray writes of it in *Pendennis* as the Back Kitchen, and in *The Newcomes,* he describes as the Cave of Harmony, the most celebrated of the subterranean supper-rooms, Evan's *late* Joys, where food and fun were equally robust. Half the great men of London—Thackeray and Dickens and Landseer among them—would descend the worn stone steps from the Covent Garden Piazza, to applaud its bawdy choruses, and perhaps join in them. "In those days, Sam Hall and Billy Barlow were the popular melodies," said the *Spectator* in 1866, "and the only thing to be said in their favour was that their coarseness was partially redeemed by a rough licentious wit." The supper that accompanied them called for strong stomachs, too. George Augustua Sala dips his pen in sauce and catsup to describe it:

See the pyramids of dishes arrive; the steaming succession of red-hot chops, with their brown, frizzling caudal appendages sobbing hot tears of passionate fat. See the serene kidneys, unsubdued though grilled, smiling though cooked, weltering proudly in their noble gravy, like warriors who have fallen upon the field of honour. See the hot yellow lava of the Welsh rabbit stream over and engulf the timid toast. Sniff the fragrant vapour of the corpulent sausage. Mark how the russet leathern-coated baked potato at first defies the knife, then gracefully cedes, and through a lengthened gash yields its farinaceous effervescence to the influence of butter and catsup.

Idol of the Queen: It is difficult, because of the reticences and falsifications of biographers, adequately to map the rich stream of bawdiness that flowed under the polite macadam of Victorian life. Not only the spreeing lords, the downy swells, and the bowsy Bohemians, enjoyed a dirty joke. Victoria's favourite poet, Tennyson, and one of her most respected magistrates, Sir William Hardman, had their Rabelaisian moods. Tennyson, who liked broad Lincolnshire anecdotes and rude limericks, and late in life, was interested in de Sade, surprised the Archbishop of Canterbury, on the occasion of their last walk together, by suddenly asking: "Shall I tell a bawdy story?" Dr. Benson who related this to Edmund Gosse, said he replied: "Certainly not." "I feel sure your Grace heard that story," said Gosse. "Well," said the Archbishop, "it wasn't so bad after all."

The Case of the Two Large Widows: "No one is fonder of good sound bawdry than I (or you)", wrote Sir William Hardman to his old friend in Melbourne, Edward Holroyd (later to become Acting-Chief Justice of Victoria)—though the Marquis de Sade, Hardman admitted, completely bowled him over. Hardman's letters to Holroyd over two decades record the kind of talk that circulated with the port when the ladies had withdrawn. Although his editor, S. M. Ellis, often exhibits an irritating squeamishness ("It is expedient to omit. . . ." "It is impossible to print . . . ." etc.) sufficient examples survive the Bowdler shears to show what "good sound bawdry" meant to a prosperous Tory magistrate, host, and literary man of the 'sixties.

One of Hardman's "best jokes" was an advertisement that appeared in *The Times* on Saturday, February 28, 1863, a few days before Princess Alexandra drove through London on the eve of her wedding with the Prince of Wales. For days before, the front page of *The Times* had carried announcements from benevolent landlords who were prepared to let rooms along the route of the royal procession, preferably to noblemen or gentlemen, for sums varying from twelve to twenty-five guineas. In the midst of these dignified offers, appeared this piece of calculated whimsy:

> ROYAL PROCESSION—FIRST FLOOR, with two large widows, to be LET, in the best part of Cockspur street, with entrance accessible behind. For cards apply to Mr. Lindley No. 19 Catherine Street, Strand, W.C.

"*The Times* people thought there was something more than carelessness," Hardman wrote, "and discharged whoever was responsible for dropping the N out of window—at least, one of *The Times* staff told me so. . . . A copy of *The Times* of 28th February has since fetched 7/6." Hardman later reported that *The Times* was in "an unapproachable rage" about the hoax that had been played on it. No. 19 Catherine Street, it transpired, was a brothel.

In another issue, *The Times* "nearly extinguished" Hardman with laughter by telling, in its report of the Sheffield reservoir disaster, how a small boy had jumped out of bed as the water poured in, and was "drowned in the chamber". "Poor little fellow—that I should have to laugh at his death," was Hardman's sentimental afterthought. He was also amused by an "awkward misprint" in the Court Circular of the *Standard* that read: "The Queen drove out accompanied by Princess Christian, Lord Alfred Paget being in attendance on horeback." Contemporary collectors of newspaper "bulls"—and most newspaper offices have a few discerning amateurs—would appreciate these specimens as much as Hardman did. But sometimes his humour is less attuned to mature modern ears. There is a schoolboy *naïveté* about many of the stories that he thought worth transmitting over 12,000 slow miles of sea to Australia—such as that of the obtuse bible student who was asked how Samson killed the lion, and misinterpreting a prompter's whisper, "Jawbone of an ass," shouted out triumphantly, "Jobbed him in the arse, sir." Equally juvenile is the story of the bashful Mr. Kettle, who is chaffingly asked by a forward young lady "if he has any little Kettles", and replies that he has four, "two with spouts and two without"; at which, according to Hardman "the chaffy young lady is utterly extinguished".

The Merry Mr. Meredith: Even the dignity of the House of Lords did not inhibit Hardman's appreciation of a rugged jest. He was sitting in the gallery with his friend George Meredith—who shared his taste for good sound bawdry— and noticed a restlessness on the Episcopal Bench, the occupants constantly going out and returning. "There goes another Bishop to pump-ship", he remarked. "I wonder if they sit down," replied Meredith, speculatively. "This notion convulsed me and others within earshot," writes Hardman.

Over his dinner-table one night they were discussing Swinburne. One of the guests suggested that Galen's phrase "omne animal post coitum triste est" might be applied to the young poet. Thomas Hinchcliffe said: "By the bye, that reminds me of a firm that used to be in St. Paul's Churchyard, whose names translate that passage perfectly, —Mann, Rogers and Greaves." The company, which included Meredith, "yelled out approval in shrieks of laughter". Hardman thought it was one of the best things of the kind he had ever heard. He also liked the story of the lady who complained to the Bishop of Oxford ("Soapy Sam" Wilberforce) that her clergyman was making himself very disagreeable by reason of his ritualist practices. "How so?" inquired S. Oxon, "What does he do?" "Well, for one thing he always reads the lessons from the rectum." "Indeed," said the Bishop, "then I am not surprised if he is offensive to his congregation."

A Garrulous Guardsman: A story that Thackeray used to tell "with great unction" was also included in Hardman's antipodean budget. "I like those Guardsmen," Thackeray would say, "their conversation is so interesting. I met one once in the smoking-room of the Club; we never spoke a word, but he was civil to me—he rang the bell for me, or he didn't ring the bell for me, I forget which—no matter. When I left, he left too, and we found we were both going in the same direction along Pall Mall. Silently we walked side by side—you must know that I had not been *introduced* to him. At last we met a woman. I said, 'That's a nice-looking girl.' After a pause, he replied, 'Haw yes, I have had her.' After a longer pause, 'Haw, yes, my brother has had her.' After a still longer pause, 'Haw, haw, in fact, we've both had her.' No more was said, and shortly afterwards we parted. I *do* like these Guardsmen."

A Time for Everything: When Hardman visited Brussels with his wife, sister and female cousin, they went together to see the Manneken Pis—"event never to be forgotten", Hardman wrote enthusiastically: "A small and well-executed, bronze naked figure of a little boy pisses vigorously night and day a copious but not inordinate stream . . . we all four burst into inextinguishable fits of laughter." Next morning Hardman bought photographs of the Manneken for the whole party but his "British ire was roused", he reports, when a Belgian boy tried hard, in spite of the ladies' presence, to sell him some indecent books, "for there is a time for everything and this seemed very inappropriate".

Les Amours de la Reine: Swinburne, when he was not writing lovely lyrics or dreary drama, or acute criticism, or childish odes about flagellation, sometimes amused himself and his friends with brilliant excursions into ribaldry. One, a bawdy French novel called *La Fille du Policeman*, delighted Meredith: "the funniest rampingest satire on French novelists dealing with English themes that you can imagine," he wrote, after Swinburne had read it to him, and he thought the chapter "Ce Que Peut Passer dans un Cab Safety" in which Lord Whitestick, Bishop of Londres, ravishes the heroine, "quite marvellous". Swinburne himself said its "mildest ingredients" were "rape, perjury, murder, opium, suicide, treason, Jesuitry".

In this, and in another piece of uninhibited whimsy, *La Soeur de la Reine*, Queen Victoria appears in irreverent and unhistorical roles. *La Soer de la Reine* was a French verse drama in the manner of Victor Hugo. W. M. Rossetti described it as a "very amusing performance . . . a rollicking skit, over some detached pages of which we used to laugh heartily, purporting to deal with the early life of Queen Victoria. Lord John Russell, of all men in the world, figures as her ardent and I fear overmuch favoured lover." From a fragment which survives, it seems that Russell had taken over this privilege from Wordsworth. W. H. Mallock, who heard Swinburne acclaim his drama to under-graduates at Oxford, recalled that the first act showed England on the verge of a revolution, because of the frightful orgies of the Queen at "Buckingham Palace":

The Queen, with unblushing effrontery, had taken herself a lover, in the person of Lord John Russell, who had for his rival "Sir Peel". Sir Peel was represented as pleading his own cause in a passionate scene which wound up as follows: "Why do you love Lord John Russell, and why do you not love me? I know why you love Lord John Russell. . . . He is young, he is beautiful, he is profligate. I cannot be young. I cannot be beautiful, but I will be profligate." Then followed the stage directions: *Exit for ze Haymarket.* In a later act, it appeared that the Queen and Lord John Russell had between them given the world a daughter, who, having been left to her own devices, or in other words, the streets, reappears as "Miss Kitty" and is accorded some respectable rank. Under these conditions she becomes the object of much princely devotion; but the moral hypocrisy of England has branded her a public scandal. With regard to her so-called depravities, nobody entertains a doubt, but one princely admirer, of broader mind than the rest, declares that in spite of these she is really the embodiment of everything that is divine in woman. "She may", he says, "have done everything which might have made a

Messalina blush, but whenever she looked at the sky, she murmured 'God' and whenever she looked at a flower, she murmured 'mother'."

The anonymous author of *Things I Shouldn't Tell* has a slightly different recollection of the drama, according to which "Princess Katy", a barmaid, is the legitimate Queen of England:

The last act is in Queen Victoria's bedroom. She has been confined of the Heir Apparent and Sir Locock is with her. Her Majesty dismisses him. She is agitated; she has heard of Princess Katy and knows she is the rightful Queen. What is to be done? Obviously destroy Katy. So she sends for the Public Hangman and tells him he must do away with this dangerous young lady. He refuses to do so vile a deed. . . . Then says Victoria: "*Levez-vous, Sir Calcraft, Pair d'Angl-e terre.*" But the glorious fellow rises proudly and puts aside the tempting honour. "*Pardon, Madame, je ne suis que le bourreau de Londres.*"

There was also a scene in which Sir Peel, the rival of Sir Russell, serenades the Queen at Windsor:

> *Ce qu'il faut chercher sur la terre*
> *Nuit et jour.*
> *Ce n'est pas la vertu severe,*
> *C'est l'Amour!*

Like Tennyson and Dante Gabriel Rossetti, Swinburne enjoyed improper limericks, but when he came under the moral guardianship of Watts-Dunton, his smutty Pegasus was often snaffled. "Shall I tell our visitor about the man of Peru?" he asked one day. "I think that one goes a little too far, Algernon," said Watts-Dunton coldly.

VI. THIS FREEDOM

The Nonconformist campaign to prevent Englishmen from drinking and dancing when they pleased, and to force whores from the comfort of nighthouses and pleasure-grounds to the gutters, continued through the 'seventies; because it was accompanied by a contradictory process at the top level of society, it has often been overlooked by historians, who see the decade as one of expanding social and sexual freedom. In the drawing-rooms of Belgravia, the influence of the pleasure-loving Prince of Wales and his Marlborough House set was helping to break up what Mr. A. C. Benson calls "the mid-Victorian tradition of frozen pompous dignity, and all its repressions and reticences". But while this superficial emancipation was taking place in a small sphere, English life over a much broader area was becoming more and not less repressed.

These two processes are easily illustrated. It was in the early 'seventies that a deputation of noblewomen invoked the help of the Archbishop of Canterbury to stop what they regarded as a breakdown in the moral standards of society, particularly of its young women. These women, partly because of the spread of education, partly because of the example of Marlborough House, were slowly emerging from their traditional obscurantism. They were taking up sport, discussing what Queen Victoria denounced as the "mad wicked folly of Women's Rights", even entering the professions. About this time, the *Saturday Review,* perhaps a little hyperbolically, said: "The English world seems to be given up at this moment to a race of moral Maenads"; and on another occasion:

> We are sensible of a distinct moral relaxation among women, and of a sort of unwomanly recklessness in the presence of man. We complain of a prevalent coarseness even among the virtuous, not only of manner, but of imagination in pursuits, and we are sometimes tempted to prefer the age of Nell Gwynne or Madame Pompadour to the actual confusion of daredevil women and unabashed spinsters.

Yet while this familiar lament of lost innocence was being chanted, Puritanism was making its fiercest assault on the freedom of the nineteenth-century Englishman. "I have long associated the Liberal Party with every form of social repression," said John Hollingshead. "If I want pure social liberty I should seek it in St. Petersburg or Moscow, rather than London." It is another of the ironies of history that the men who fought to free the factory slaves fought no less ardently to shackle everyone with their snivelling morality.

Honourable Members cried "Oh! Oh!": The continuing assault on English freedom was often bitterly resisted, as the pages of *Hansard* testify. Parliament still had men who believed that morals were a matter for the conscience, not the constabulary. In 1872, for example, when Parliament fixed the closing hour for places selling alcohol at 12.30 a.m.—Hollingshead called it the "slap-you-and-put-you-to-bed-act"—there was spirited opposition.

The Marquis of Salisbury, whom Disraeli once described as a great master of jibes and flouts and jeers, used these noble talents to condemn the "fanaticism" of the Bill. One of its provisions was for public houses to remain closed till 7 a.m., instead of 6 a.m. Lord Salisbury said this was apparently designed to make working-men drink tea or coffee with breakfast instead of beer, on the grounds that beer was less wholesome. "This is to apply an utterly false principle," he said. "In the same sense, pork is much less wholesome than mutton, yet Parliament would never legislate to force working-men to eat mutton and not pork. ... There will be great difficulty in convincing me that there is anything wrong in drinking beer, or that it is the business of Parliament to take care that the labouring man does not drink too much. Our business is only to take care that the public houses are properly conducted."

Another clause in the Bill, designed to prevent prostitutes from entering a public house even to get refreshments, was attacked by Mr. Vernon Harcourt, who said that, as always, the penalties were proclaimed in the name of humanity and liberty: "There is nothing in the world so cruel as the tender mercies of a real philanthropist," he said. "There is no barbarity which he is not prepared to commit in pursuit of his crotchet. . . . We must seek some protection against that form of legislation which in the name of liberty, puts everybody into prison, and in the name of humanity, treats everyone with cruelty." From the House came a chorus of "Oh! Oh!".

A similar concern for personal freedom inspired the memorable remark of the Bishop of Peterborough: "I would rather see England free than England compulsorily sober," and led Sir William Bodkin to quash convictions against a number of nighthouse keepers charged with harbouring prostitutes, because no "overt act" of prostitution had been proved. This judgment displeased the *Saturday Review* which said that notorious prostitutes found at Kate Hamilton's might have gone there, in Sir William's view, to discuss the Irish Church Bill and the Spanish Revolution.

Melancholy Homecoming of the Colonel: Two comments on London life, separated by only seven years, show how swiftly the tide of repression swept in. Writing in 1874, Disraeli noted how much brighter London had become in the thirty-seven years of Victoria's reign. Describing the London he knew as a dandy of the 'thirties, he said:

> At that time London was a very dull city, instead of being as it is now, a very amusing one. Probably there never was a city in the world with so vast a population which was so melancholy. . . . There were no Alhambras then and no Cremorne, no palaces of crystal in terraced gardens, no casinos, no music-halls, no aquaria, no promenade concerts. Evan's existed, but not in the fullness of its modern development; and the most popular place of resort was the barbarous conviviality of the Cider Cellar.

But in 1881, when Sir Francis Burnand's play *The Colonel* was the success of the year, this exchange between Forrester and the Colonel was good topical dialogue. The Colonel has been absent in India and proposes an old-fashioned "night-out" round town.

Colonel: "We'll begin at Evan's."

Forrester: "It's closed."

Colonel: "Surrey Gardens."

Forrester: "Closed."

Colonel: "Highbury Barn—Coal Hole—Cider Cellars."

Forrester: "Closed—closed—closed."

Colonel: "Well, then, we'll just look in at the Arg—"

Forrester: "The Arg—"

Another character, Streyke, breaks in: "The 'Gyle's closed. No 'Gyle. Everything's closed."

A Deed That Won the Empire: With the closing of these nighthouses and casinos, the whores congregated in the music-halls, as they had done, before there were casinos and music-halls, in the theatres. "It is inevitable that this should be so," said the *Spectator:*

> These poor creatures are rigidly excluded from every place where they would naturally take shelter. The recognized and regular haunts of vice have been suppressed by the energetic action—to quote the stereotyped phrase—of parochial authorities, and as the demand for prostitution still exists . . . the women who supply that demand are driven to frequent these places of entertainment.

The most popular of these whore-markets was the Empire music-hall in Leicester Square, which by the 'nineties had acquired the status, appropriate to a decade of Kiplingesque imperialism, of a national institution. Young empire builders, grappling with a survey peg in Canada, or a chota peg in Kandahar, cherished wistful memories of its glittering lounge, with its "scented-sachet" beauties, the pride of their profession, splendid, haughty creatures, who, according to Sir Seymour Hicks, "only considered granting their favours to a friend of a friend".

208

In 1894, when an assault, inspired by two American visitors, was launched against this institution, London made perhaps its last resolute stand against the impertinence of Puritanism. Newspapers published columns of protesting letters, of which this, headed "Prudes on the Prowl", was typical:

> How long is this great London of ours, so proud and yet so patient, to wait for the strong and inevitable voice of public disapprobation, that mighty roar of disgust which is heard to-day in private in every assemblage of common-sense men and women protesting against and execrating the tyranny of the self-satisfied minority? . . .
>
> How much longer must we listen to the impudent piety of these provincial pedlars in social purity who come red-hot from their Chicago platforms and tinpot tabernacles to tell this London of ours how she is to amuse herself and how she is to disperse and harass and drive from pillar to post those unfortunate outcasts whom we have always had and always shall have amongst us?

The licence of the Empire was cancelled, and after some hullabaloo, renewed on condition that the lounge be abolished. To carry out this edict, the bars were cut off from the promenade by flimsy canvas barriers. When the Empire reopened with its castrated lounge, a force of indignant young men stormed the barricades and tore them down. One of the leaders was a twenty-year-old Sandhurst cadet named Winston Churchill, who adorned the victory with an oration. Mounted on the debris, he exhorted the crowd: "You have seen us tear down these barricades to-night," he said. "See that you pull down those who are responsible for them at the coming election!" This was four years before the cavalry charge at Omdurman, six years before his maiden speech in the House. In his account of the action, Churchill says that after "the temples of Venus and Bacchus" were once more united, "we all sallied out into the square brandishing fragments of wood and canvas as trophies or symbols. It reminded me of the death of Julius Caesar, when the conspirators rushed forth into the street waving the bloody daggers with which they had slain the tyrant. I thought also of the taking of the Bastille. . . ."

Perils of a Pedestrian: The Empire lounge was reprieved till another wave of repression, during World War I, swept away all music-hall lounges. Meanwhile, the Englishman's right to do as he pleased as long as he did not deny the same right to his neighbour, was becoming more and more circumscribed. In 1895, the *Law Journal* was deploring "the very limited right of the public to use the streets. Disobedience to, or a slow compliance with, an arbitrary order to move on, seems enough to turn a citizen into a criminal."

This comment was evoked by two cases, both involving well-known people, that occurred within a few days of one another. Professor Ray Lankaster, a distinguished anatomist, a Fellow of the Royal Society, and later a knight, was walking home from the Savile Club just after midnight when he saw in Piccadilly a woman, apparently a prostitute, arrested with "cruelty and violence". A group of prostitutes was discussing the arrest, and he stopped to ask them what had happened. Before he got a reply a policeman told him brusquely to move on. "My good man," said the professor. "Don't speak to me that way. Surely there is no obstruction." He was seized by both arms and taken to a police-station, charged with resisting the police in the execution of their duty. An accused person could not then give evidence on his own behalf, but Lankaster sent *The Times* from the Athenaeum Club a full account of the affair: "I need hardly say that an Oxford professor does not 'laugh and talk', [as the police had alleged] in the public thoroughfare with groups of prostitutes," he wrote. But no policeman in the 'sixties would have challenged the right of an Oxford professor or a pious stockbroker or a tipsy bishop to laugh and talk in the street, even with prostitutes. The magistrate was so obviously prejudiced in favour of the police that Lankaster's solicitor, Sir

George Lewis, withdrew from the case. Lankaster was convicted and bound over to keep the peace.

In the same week, George Alexander, London's best-known actor-manager, was accosted a few yards from his home by a "poor, miserable, starved and ill-clad" whore. He gave her half a crown and was continuing on his way when they were both arrested by a constable and charged with misconduct. The constable said that because he had india-rubber on his boots, he was able to approach quietly enough to see that Alexander was "having connection" with the woman. Alexander, too, wrote a full account of this preposterous business to *The Times*. He was grudgingly given the benefit of the doubt and discharged. Two days later, when he appeared on the stage of his St. James's Theatre, the audience cheered him enthusiastically. By a happy chance, the play was *Liberty Hall*.

But liberty was a fading concept in England. The orbit of personal freedom had contracted sharply since the time, a generation or so before, when a Windham could act the policeman among the whores of the Haymarket, or a Waterford could lead a procession of half a dozen cabs at full gallop down Piccadilly each with a musician on the roof playing as loudly as he was able. Certainly, the antics of these boisterous buffoons enjoyed the special licence of rank. True reform would have extended the licence to all, subject only to the preservation of public peace and order, and not allowed these ends to become confused with the mumbo-jumbo of bethel-house morality. I would rather see a Waterford go his silly raffish way, unmolested, if it meant that a Lankaster could talk to a Piccadilly whore without being dragged to the lock-up.

Chapter V

Dress and Undress

I. THE INDECENCY OF CRINOLINE

*A*LLUREMENT *and Enticement:* The mid-Victorian age was dominated by crinoline; to-day this enormous billowing tent seems like the symbol of an imprisoned and impregnable virtue, instinct with a fragrant sentimentality and romance. But as Mr. James Laver, that intrepid speleologist of our grandmothers' petticoats, reminds us, "the crinoline was certainly not a moral garment".

> The crinoline was in a constant state of agitation, swaying from side to side. . . . Any pressure on one side of the steel hoops was communicated by their elasticity to the other side, and resulted in a sudden upward shooting of the skirt. It was probably this upward shooting which gave mid-Victorian men their complex about ankles, and it certainly resulted in a new fashion in boots. . . . Without wishing in any way to accuse the entire mid-Victorian world of shoe-fetishism one can hardly resist the conclusion that the erotic significance of boots and shoes received partial encouragement from the invention of the crinoline.

"No fashion is ever successful unless it can be used as an instrument of seduction," says Mr. Laver, "and seductive the crinoline certainly was." The Victorian would have agreed with both these propositions. In 1866, a rather fearsome American woman came to London on a lecture tour; Dr. Mary Walker, of Oswego, was a surgeon, a feminist, a temperance advocate, and a dress-reformer. In the last role, and undeterred by the failure of a similar mission undertaken by her country-woman, Mrs. Amelia Jenks Bloomer, in 1851, Dr. Walker appeared before a large London audience dressed in a long frock-coat and black trousers. *The Spectator*, while urbanely conceding a woman the right to wear anything she pleased, criticized the *ensemble* on the grounds that it was "false to the ethical theory of a woman's dress, which should always be faintly enticing or fascinating":

> Woman's first function is to be mothers, and in any sound system of ethics, even the dress of the Second Empire which ... passes the narrow line between enticement and allurement, is a better dress than a mannish variety of the Bloomer costume.

Though the line between enticement and allurement is too fine for my coarse perceptions, I find much good sense in this paragraph, and the trousered and steatopygous young hoyden of to-day, even if motherhood be not her immediate function, might well perpend it.

They all showed their —— on occasion: At the Kensington Petty Sessions in 1853, Mrs. Lowe, of Victoria Grove, Kensington, was charged with permitting her female servant "to stand on the sill of an upstairs window, in order to clean it, whereby the life of the servant was endangered and the public decency shocked". The charge was laid under 14th and 15th Vict. c.116, and the informer, Mr. Henson, said he was desirous of stopping the dangerous and indelicate practice of allowing female servants to clean windows.

The indelicacy of such displays was greatly increased by the invention of the steel-framed crinoline which enabled a woman to discard the innumerable petticoats she had hitherto worn; and for the next fourteen or fifteen years, as crinolines expanded monstrously, shrank, and finally disappeared, this indelicacy was to be commented on in sermon, editorial, and smoke-room jest.

When a meeting was held in 1862 for the purpose of abolishing crinoline, William Hardman wrote to Holroyd: "Crinoline will never be extinguished by public meeting or female combination. The girls of our time like to show their legs.... I don't see why they should be interfered with; it pleases them and does no harm to us." Next year, Hardman asked if the crinoline had reached its climax: "Women getting into omnibuses, servant girls cleaning door-steps, and virgins at windy seaside watering places," he wrote, "all show their—— on occasion." What they showed, I am afraid, remains undisclosed, whether because of Hardman's reticence, or his editor's, I cannot say, though I have my suspicions. About this time *Punch* rejected a joke, which Hardman thought "decidedly good and effective" but which "was not quite so free from 'double entendre' as to warrant insertion in that scrupulously moral periodical":

"Why may crinoline be justly regarded as a social invention?"
"Because it enables us to see more of our friends than we used to."

Mr. J. Robertson Scott confirms this. When he was an "observant child"—he was born in 1866—women, he says, still wore a "bifurcated white garment" that was open at the back:

As long as the old garment survived, women were, indoors, in trepidation on staircases and outdoors, were equally in fear of the wind and of stumbling, and they dared not go up the steps to the tops of buses.

One of these garments, worn by Queen Victoria, is to be inspected at the South Kensington Museum.

The *Saturday Review* was not sure that the crinoline was "quite decent". "Do fine ladies", it asked, "ever happen to hear the criticism of their own footmen on the exposure which the use of crinoline makes almost normal?" And Miss Florence Nightingale was naturally concerned with the revelations of crinoline when worn by nurses. "I wish," she wrote, "that people who wear crinoline could see the indecency of their own dress as other people see it.":

> A respectable elderly woman, stooping forward, invested in crinoline, exposes quite as much of her own person to the patient lying in the room as an opera dancer does on the stage. But no one will ever tell her the unpleasant truth.

Britannia Rules the Waves: The resources of an inventive age were geared to the problem of reconciling crinoline with decency, and an advertiser in 1864 promised one solution:

> *CRINOLINES:* The Patent Oninda, or Waved Jupon, does away with the unsightly results of the ordinary hoops, and so perfect are the wave-like bands that a lady may ascend a steep stair, lean against a table, throw herself into an arm-chair, pass to her stall at the Opera, or occupy a fourth seat in a carriage, without inconvenience to herself or others, or provoking the rude remarks of the observers, besides removing or modifying in an important degree all those peculiarities tending to destroy the modesty of Englishwomen; and lastly, allows the dress to fall into graceful folds.

"Naked to the Visible Eye": That the modesty of an Englishwoman of this period was imperilled by the accidental exposure of her legs but not affected by the deliberate exposure of her breasts, is a good example of the preposterous and protean forms that decency assumes. For the age of crinoline was also the age of what has recently been called the "plunging neckline" —as though it remained for an indurated atom age to take the plunge. But in 1933, when legs had ceased to be news, chorus girls at the Adelphi Theatre struck when asked to wear a costume that was mildly *décolleté*—"Certainly no lower", says Mr. Laver, "than would have been worn without any embarrassment by an *ingénue* of the 'eighties."

Even for the "scrupulously moral" pages of *Punch*, Leech had no qualms about drawing women in evening-dresses with the division between the breasts clearly shown, and Elizabeth Barrett Browning's description of the wicked Lady Waldemar in *Aurora Leigh* is a good fashion note of the late 'fifties:

> *The woman looked immortal. How they told,*
> *Those alabaster shoulders and bare breasts,*
> *On which the pearls, drowned out of sight in milk,*
> *Were lost, excepting for the ruby-clasp!*
> *They split the amaranth velvet-bodice down*
> *To the waist or nearly, with the audacious press*
> *Of full-breathed beauty. If the heart within*
> *Were half as white!—but, if it were, perhaps,*
> *The breast were closer covered, and the sight*
> *Less aspectable, by half, too.*

Mr. Alfred Austin, when he wrote *The Season*, a few years later, had a similar thought. Lashing at the "nude parade" of London society women, as "o'er the box their beauteous busts they bend", he asked, in lines of characteristic felicity:

> *What can be Man's, while Woman deems her part,*
> *To bare her bosom, but to hide her heart?*

"Nothing is so chaste as nudity," says George du Maurier in *Trilby*, but the semi-nudity of women's evening wear shocked him. After dining *à la russe* with the Earl and Countess Somers one night in 1862, he wrote to his mother: "Miladi very handsome woman; but she and all the women were *décolletées* in a beastly fashion—damn the aristocratic standard of fashion; nothing will ever make me think it right or decent that I should see a lady's armpit flesh-folds when I am speaking to her . . . about thirty or forty upstairs nearly all in the same state of partial nudity as per diagram."

And, of course, Hardman told a story about the fashion for the Melbourne mail. It concerned Bernal Osborne, M.P., a tolerated buffoon who had the reputation of being the rudest man in England, and a lady who entered the drawing-room "very much *décolletée*":

She wore a rose in the centre [Hardman wrote] between certain hills of snow which were naked to the visible eye— I mean visible to the naked eye, and the said rose was encircled by many leaves. Bernal Osborne advanced . . . and looking at the rose and its leaves, said: "Pardon me, madam, but don't you think you wear your fig-leaf rather high?"

II. A BELLY FOR THE BELLE

Le Ventre de Madame la Princesse: Towards the end of the 'sixties, as the crinoline shrank, and became looped up behind in a bunch that foreshadowed the bustle, couturiers, with what Mr. Laver calls "that infallible instinct for seductiveness", found that "the fullness of the skirts at the back enabled them to be drawn with extreme tightness over the hips in the front, so outlining the figure".

The vogue of tight pleatless gowns focused attention on the belly and made a "certain rotundity of form", such as develops during the early months of pregnancy, fashionable. To comfort those women who were neither pregnant nor normally rotund, the artifices of invention were again invoked. *London Society*, in 1867, reported rather awedly on this development: "A *ventre* of gutta-percha is the remedy for these natural defects," it said, "and ladies are persuaded to wear it under their dresses which are made *sans plies*". The dresses were "duly strained" over this "artificial protuberance". *London Society* thought it "almost incredible that any ladies can be found to submit to such an indignity, but what will they not submit to that they may be in the fashion?"

A story is told [it said] of an English lady who desired to be dressed in the height of fashion, and who, therefore, applied to the most eminent dressmaker in Paris, who happens to be a man, and whose fiat is irreversible. The lady ordered her dress, her measure was taken, and a day fixed for trying it on. She repaired at the proper hour to this man's house and tried on the gown. The dressmaker lifted his hands with horror, exclaiming at the same time, "Mais, Madame, vous n'avez pas de ventre!" "What?" inquired the astonished lady. She could not believe her ears. But it was fully explained to her that no gown would fit unless this want were supplied. The lady had never been aware till then of such a want. She had always been satisfied with the supply which nature had given her, and could not see any necessity for the intervention of art. But the dressmaker was inexorable. "Il faut absolument," was his ceaseless reply to her protests; and when he called to one of his attendants, "Apportez-moi le ventre de Madame la Princesse de —, et de Madame la Marquise de —", she was overwhelmed and silenced. The contrivance was fitted on, the dress strained over it, and she walked forth a plump and comely dame, and the rotundity of her form almost put her to shame.

"It is further asserted," said *London Society*, "that as everything, even modesty itself, is to be sacrificed to dress . . . art has other inventions to supply other defects. These are *seins-palpitants*, and ears, all made of gutta-percha."

A French fashion-writer noted "magasins speciaux de petits matelas pour la poitrine", where, apparently, the visiting Englishwoman acquired these deceitful devices, to which the refrain of a popular song applied:

> *Il y en a pour tous les gouts*
> *En fils de fer, en caoutchouc.*

But I can find no evidence of them being on sale in England.

"These freaks of fancy make us burn with shame for our countrywomen," said *London Society*. "They savour too much of the *demi-monde* and are suggestive of all that is coarse and sensual and of those enticements which ought to be unknown amongst gentlewomen. . . ."

Imagine a woman of any modesty submitting to such indignity, consenting to go forth as an imposter; her form rounded by art; her bosom heaving, not with emotion, her delicate ear, pink like a shell, and of exquisite form, purchased in the Boulevard.

The function of gutta-percha in improving the proportions of a reluctant bosom is explicit even to a layman; I find it less easy to understand how a rubber device could transform a sow's ear into a dainty little pink shell, suitable for whispering sweet nothings into.

Lasciviousness in the 'Seventies: With the burgeoning of the bustle in the 'seventies, woman made no bones about harnessing Dame Fashion to the chariot of Eros. As Dr. Wingfield-Stratford says, she began to use her increasing freedom "as a tight-fitting cloak of lasciviousness".

Attention was now solicited for the buttocks. . . . Hence the false buttock, the pullback or bustle, with which women did not hesitate to cumber themselves in the cause of sexual selection. The curves of the figure were seductively exaggerated in front as well as behind. If the bustle was used to swell out the hinder parts, the same office could be performed for the breast by suitable paddings, and it is quite obvious . . . that this expedient was freely employed.

"The belly", notes the doctor, "was advertised with a frankness . . . that left nothing except colour to the imagination" and he quotes a statement from Fischel and Boehn's work on costume that the Empress of Austria, to achieve the desirable tightness, had her riding-habit sewed on over her naked skin.

His Royal Highness approved: At about the same time as the Englishwoman was putting on her tight-fitting coat of lasciviousness, a Frenchwoman was introducing England to a dance that was to become a permanent item in the repertoire of sex stimulation. The cancan was first danced on an English stage on Boxing Day, 1867, by a Creole known as Finette, who had been Whistler's mistress and whose real name was Josephine Durwend. Mr. W. S. Gilbert, not yet linked in acrimonious collaboration with Mr. Arthur Sullivan, provided the setting for this epochal début; a pantomine at the Lyceum Theatre entitled *Harlequin Cock Robin and Jenny Wren, or Fortunatus! The Three Bears; The Three Gifts; The Three Wishes and the Little Man Who Wooed the Little Maid.* It was a lush and glittering production, typical of the Great Age of Pantomime, with three transformation scenes and a ballet of 100. In the seventh scene, following a grand ballet of gold and silver fish, "a very handsome gipsy-like woman", dressed more like a dancer than a danseuse, performed a cancan which was enthusiastically encored. "It is right to say", said *The Times,* "that the lady's style of dress ... was different from that in which the dance is done in Paris ... and therefore, much of the objection which an English audience would have to the French dance was removed." Among those who applauded Finette was the Prince of Wales, who had already studied the subtleties of the cancan at the Jardin Mabille, where 5,000 gas-lamps blazed on the blazing executants, and had watched his friend—some said lover—Hortense Schneider, perform it in the current Parisian success, Offenbach's *Grand Duchess of Gerolstein.* Satisfied with the propriety of Finette's pioneering work at the Lyceum, Edward a few nights later brought Princess Alexandra to see her.

Significance of a Kick: Though the cancan was not known in Paris before the eighteen-thirties, savants tell me that its most characteristic movement, the high kick, is an old fertility motif, common to many traditional dances; the Aurrescu of the Basques, the Sardana of the Catalonians, and the Triori of the Bretons. Panurge describes women lifting their dresses in front and kicking their legs up to the ceiling as they dance the Triori.

In 1832, there was a scandal in Paris when the cancan was danced at the Théâtre des Varietes, and for some years it was threatened with suppression by the police. "The cancan, just like a new religion, did not spread without persecution," says Count d'Alton-Shee, one of its early apostles.

M. Kracauer, the biographer of Offenbach, finds political as well as erotic significance in its popularity in Paris during the 'forties. "Revolutionary-minded romantics used the dance to express their derision and contempt for the sanctimonious social conventions of the new régime, and for Louis Philippe and his dynastic ambitions," he says, "while the young scions of the Legitimist aristocracy used it to show their disdain for the court balls and the bankers who attended them." It must have been a fairly exhausting form of political criticism, if the description of a German visitor to Paris about this time is to be accepted:

The beat of the music is hastened, the dancers' movements become more rapid, more animated, more aggressive; and finally the *contredanse* evolves into a great gallop. . . . Though at this stage individual indecent movements are no longer seen, the dancers' behaviour and facial expression bear witness to a more intense voluptuousness. . . . For the music gets quicker and quicker, until one finally sees masked women, like ecstatic maenads, with flushed cheeks, breathless heaving breasts, parched lips, and half-undone, flying hair, careering round the room, less on their feet than being dragged along bodily. . . .

A more distinguished German, Heinrich Heine, also saw the cancan as a symptom of social disillusion. The dancers, he thought, had seen their high ideals betrayed and were pouring scorn, through the wild gestures of the cancan, on things once held noble and holy. If this is so, the mood of disillusion must have survived the disappearance of the bourgeois Louis Philippe and the rise and fall of his flamboyant successor, Louis Napoleon, for the popularity of the cancan in Paris remained undiminished till it was given fresh erotic, if not political significance, in the 'nineties.

The Prince de Joinville, Greville noted in 1848, had "acquired some popularity by wearing a beard, smoking a short pipe, dancing the cancan, and hating England", rather a curious formula for winning friends and influencing people. A few years later, the cancan was being danced in London. Mr. John Caldwell, of Dean Street, Soho, told a parliamentary committee in 1854 that he was at times obliged to confront his customers and "tell them they were dancing improper". "Sometimes young men do not care how they dance," he said. "They have a nasty manner of dancing in the French style, called cancan." Whether any criticism of Queen Victoria was involved in the dance, Mr. Caldwell did not say.

The music to which the cancan is danced to-day was written by Offenbach in 1858, for *Orpheus in the Underworld,* which M. Kracauer calls "a token, a portent of the times". It had 228 performances, and conferred on Offenbach and the cancan a joint immortality.

Offenbach repeated his triumph in 1867, the year of the World Exhibition, with *The Grand Duchess,* a satire on little German courts and big French ambitions. Bismarck, the Tsar Alexander, the Kings of Prussia and Portugal, Bavaria and Sweden and the Prince of Wales, all paid court to Hortense Schneider at the *Varietés.* "Schneider is fair; she understands the best manner in which 'the wink' should be given" wrote the dramatic critic of the London *Tomahawk,* "but after all one gets bored of low-necked dresses and *cancans.*" A few months later, when *The Grand Duchess* was produced at the Theatre Royal, Covent Garden, with an Australian actress, Julia Mathews, in La Schneider's part, the *Tomahawk* critic noted that the London production had been weakened by the elimination of the "highly-prized" cancan. But "we must not be understood to advocate the importation of this dance to our saint-like shores, even if there were anybody in England who could dance it", he wrote. Mr. G. F. Hollingshead, then the director of the Alhambra in Leicester Square, took the hint and went to Paris, where at the Café du Helder he encountered Finette, "the somewhat up-roarious belle of the evening". He engaged her to appear in London, but, he knew "that in England—the country with a dozen licensing systems and only one fish-sauce—where names excite more horror than things, the cancan was not a welcome sound to the licensing authorities". So he thought "it would be prudent to get the Lord Chamberlain's stamp on Finette" at the Lyceum before taking her to "the debatable ground of Leicester Square". This strategy, incomprehensible to anyone who has not tried to plumb the bottomless idiocies of English stage censorship, was successful, and "Finette, duly stamped with the legitimate stamp, after the Lyceum pantomine was over, appeared at the Alhambra and made a success".

It was at the Lyceum that William Hardman, following the Prince of Wales' example, first saw the cancan. He made no comment. But Mark Twain, innocently abroad in Paris in 1867, said the idea of it was to dance "as wildly, as noisily, as furiously as you can; expose yourself as much as possible if you are a woman; and kick as high as you can, no matter which sex you belong to".

Sundry Mysteries of Anglo-Saxon Morality: Despite the success of Mr. Hollingshead's original manoeuvre, and the approval of *The Times* and the Prince of Wales, the cancan and the English licensing authorities were engaged in intermittent conflict for some years. In 1869, *The Times* had to warn its readers that at the end of the French production of Offenbach's *Orpheus* at the St. James's Theatre, "the most outrageous cancan ever seen on any London stage is danced by the whole of the company and rapturously encored". *The Times* strongly advised its readers to leave the theatre at the end of the third tableau though "perfectly aware that by this very advice we are only recommending a large majority of the audience to remain. . . ." Next year, while the "outrageous" cancan was again being danced at the St. James's, the Middlesex magistrates refused to relicense the Alhambra, because Colonna and a troupe were performing a cancan in it, the inference being that a high kick was indecent only when accompanied by English dialogue. Colonna moved her girls to the Globe Theatre, where by some other caprice of licensing, they kicked away without interference.

The cancan, surviving these occasional irritations, spread into more theatres in the 'seventies. Correspondents discussed it in *Notes and Queries*, and pointed out that though *cancaner* in French meant to gossip maliciously, and *cancanier* was an ill-natured gossip, only in England was the word *cancan* known. In 1871, a French dancer named Mlle la Ferte sued Mr. Botham, proprietor of the Oxford Music Hall, Brighton, for breach of contract, complaining that he had dismissed her because her cancan was "too respectable" and her dresses "not indecent enough". In 1872, the *Saturday Review* said Astraea herself might not unreasonably resent the imputation of having trodden the stage more loosely than the "hundreds of half-naked ballet-girls who now dance the cancan nightly at the most fashionable theatres". And in 1874, *The Times* said, "Anybody can now talk about a cancan as freely as about a quadrille." The tide of indecency, it decided, could be traced to the great popularity of *The Grand Duchess* seven years before. But this year the tide was to be turned back.

In June 1874, another Offenbach comic opera, *Vert Vert*, opened at the St. James's Theatre. The critic of *Vanity Fair* did not like the show and said it introduced "some of the worst orchestra, some of the flattest singing, and one of the most indecent dances in London". This dance, performed by the Orpheon troupe, was a ripirelle, and when Thomas Gibson Bowles, proprietor of *Vanity Fair*, was sued for libel, he told the court that the ripirelle was "simply a cancan with all the indecency and none of the art of the original". He then described the "details, intention and meaning" of the dance in a way which *The Times* found unfit for publication. Among the witnesses Bowles called was the Lord Chamberlain, the Marquis of Hertford, who said he had attended the theatre and thought the dance "decidedly and professedly indecent". The jury immediately gave a verdict for the defendant and the Lord Chamberlain gave instructions that "all dances of a cancan character" were to be banned for evermore.

The *Saturday Review,* recalling that until recently this vicious and profligate French dance could have been seen any night in half a dozen London theatres, said: "It is satisfactory to know that the Censor has . . . cleared the stage of this pollution. That it should ever have been introduced is a public disgrace."

IV. NAKEDNESS AT THE SEASIDE

The Sight-invigorating Tube: In the eighteenth century, the men and women who pioneered sea-bathing in England bathed together in the nude. A print of Setterington's, published in 1735, and probably the earliest representation of an English seaside, shows a number of men and women in the water at Scarborough. They are all naked, and gaily disporting before an audience that includes two boatmen, a horseman, and a footman in charge of a bathing-machine from which his naked master is about to emerge. A few fully dressed ladies and gentlemen, and a few others undressed, are watching stolidly from the beach, and a carter with a wagon-load of timber is driving away, apparently bored with the familiar and disillusioning spectacle of the gentry unadorned.

Rowlandson's print *Summer Amusements at Margate,* published about the beginning of the nineteenth century, records an improvement in the technique of the seaside *voyeur* appropriate to the greater elegance of the age: a quartet of his typical

Englishmen, lickerish and leering, stands on a cliff with telescopes happily focused on the naked women bathing below while the aggrieved wife of one tugs at his coat-tails and is about to do him violence with a small sunshade. (Perhaps it was this practice which led Robert Blair, a minor eighteenth-century poet, to refer to a telescope as a "sight-invigorating tube".) A print of Green's dated 1813, shows women bathing naked at Scarborough, as they did in Setterington's day, and still without exciting any particular attention; the prurience of the metropolis, it seems, has not yet reached the remote north.

This freedom in the seas seems appropriate enough to an age whose First Gentleman was also its First Rake, and whose First Ladies, for a season at least, wore dresses "à la mode d'aspic" that were diaphanous enough to adorn the inspection salon of a bordello.

But surprisingly, it was a freedom that survived in part long after Victoria had ascended the throne to give her name to an age that was already in being; for the greater part of her reign, though women had retreated from the revealing muslin to the concealing velvet, and now bathed in thick flannel sacks that, as a disappointed student noted, showed "nothing but their handsome faces", men clung to their established privilege of bathing in the nude. In this respect, the Margate of Leech and the Prince Consort differed not at all from the Margate of Rowlandson and the Prince Regent. Nor was Margate unique in these abominations.

In 1841, Dr. Granville complained that the exposure of the gentlemen at Brighton was "a stain on the gentility of the Brighthelmstonians", and it was at Brighton, in the 'fifties, that an inquiring visitor, Monsieur Francis Way, had an alarming adventure:

Never shall I forget my bathe at Brighton! [he writes]. It was on a Sunday, at the time when worshippers return from church. I had been assigned a cabin in which to undress. It was a wooden construction on wheels placed at the water's edge, with steps half submerged by the waves. Getting into the sea was easy enough, as my cabin screened me from the view. Unfortunately I went for rather a long swim. The tide was going out, which made my return journey a lengthy one, and when at last I gained my depth I found that my cabin, which I had left with water lapping the hubs of the wheels, was now high and dry at fifteen paces from the sea.

To put the finishing touch on my discomfort, three ladies, a mother with her daughters, had settled themselves on stools in my direct line of approach! They seemed very respectable females and the girls were both pretty. There was no possibility of reaching my cabin without passing in front of them. They each held a prayer book and they watched me swimming about with serene unconcern.

To give them a hint without offending their modesty I advanced cautiously on all fours, raising myself by degrees as much as decency permitted. I had not, like the wise Ulysses emerging on the island of the Phoenicians, the resources of drapery in foliage. There was no seaweed on this too-tidy beach!

As the ladies did not move I concluded they had not understood my dilemma, so crawling back I started to swim again. But one cannot swim for ever, while one can sit without fatigue for hours. The ladies seemed unlikely to weary of their pose. The situation was all the more perplexing as my host, Sir Walter G., was awaiting me on the front and kept giving me unmistakable signs of impatience.

What was I to do? Remain in the water and inconvenience my host, or emerge from it and affront the ladies? I determined on the latter course. After all, why had they settled just there?

I rose slowly, like Venus from the waves. Striving to a bearing both modest and unconcerned, reminiscent of the lost traditions of innocence of a younger world, I stepped briskly past the three ladies, who made no pretence of looking away.

When at last we got home Sir Walter teased me good-
naturedly about my misadventure, and his wife told me she
knew the ladies, who were quite Puritanical! They disapproved of bathing on Sundays and had adopted that un-
expected method of discouraging Sabbath-breakers. Could
one conceive a stranger mode of teaching a transgressor to be
virtuous or of performing an act of religious fervour?

Appeal to the Thunderer: Sea-bathing became more and more
popular during the eighteen-fifties. Britain now had 8,000 miles
of railroad and hundreds of thousands of town-dwellers packed
their portmanteaux and bravely set out by rail on their first
seaside holiday. "England is suffering a sea-change," observed
the newly-founded *Saturday Review* in 1856. "A rim of paste-
board-like bathing towns is completing itself round the coast. . . .
On innumerable spots where, in 1850, there was nothing but a
fishing or a smuggling village, a whole town may be seen in
1856." And now Margate witnessed stains on its gentility similar
to those that had aroused Dr. Granville at Brighton, a decade or
so earlier. In the summer of 1856, "A Father of a Family at Present at Margate" appealed to the Editor of *The Times:*

> With a few strokes of your powerful pen you may do much
> for the cause of morality. If you were here the indecent and
> disgusting exhibitions which take place on the Marine Parade
> would shock you, as it must everyone not lost to common
> decency and propriety. I shall say no more but many families
> will bear me out in my statement if necessary.

Many families did. "I hasten to confirm the truth of the asser-
tion of a 'Father of a Family'," wrote one spokesman. "The
exhibition is truly disgusting, but what is more disgusting still
is the fact that these exhibitions are watched daily by large numbers of ladies who spend their mornings in close proximity to
scores of naked men. I can only account for this," he concluded
with a Bessemer blast of irony, "by supposing them all to be

228

artists and that they are studying from the life. The whole affair is abominable and ought to be abated. Surely, if a Society for the Suppression of Vice exists there is ample scope for its exertions."

A more realistic contribution was that of another bather who suggested "as a remedy for the undue display of the person at Margate (and indeed at other watering places) all bathers (men, of course, I am thinking about) be made to wear short trousers of a blue or any other dark-coloured linen, fastened around the waist by a running string and extending to within a couple of inches or so of the knee". This, he pointed out, was compulsory in Boulogne and in other French watering-places. The phenomenon of an outraged reader of *The Times* invoking the example of France on a question of decency, a delicious illustration of the confusions of mid-Victorian morality, was to be repeated many times in the next few years.

In 1857, Dr. J. Henry Bennet, physician-accoucheur of the Royal Free Hospital, came back from Biarritz aglow with enthusiasm for the French mode of bathing:

Both ladies and gentlemen wear a "bathing costume" [he wrote in the *Lancet*]. With the former, it consists of loose black woollen drawers, which descend to the ankles, and of a black blouse or tunic, descending below the knees, and fastened at the waist by a leathern girdle. . . . The gentlemen's dress is a kind of sailor's costume, and as custom gives them more latitude with respect to colour, material, and make, great varieties are observed. The exquisites . . . seem to take a pride in showing themselves off thus prepared for their marine gymnastics. Once in the water, all the bathers, male and female, mingle together.

At first the mingling of the sexes struck the English beholder as an infringement of propriety and decorum, but he soon realized that bathing in France was infinitely more decent then in England:

A few days after my return . . . I was at Brighton and on opening my bedroom window . . . the first sight that greeted me, immediately in front of the hotel, was half a dozen men, perfectly naked, wading about, with the water not much higher than their knees.

The *Saturday Review* looked also towards the United States for guidance in these troubled seas: "We have been told that at the American watering-places—Newport in Rhode Island, for example—ladies and gentlemen make appointments overnight to walk together into the waves next morning. . . . In the clear rocky pools of the Pyrenees, a bearded beau will sometimes be seen playing dominoes against a fair partner on a floating board. We in England are gradually introducing the same marine fusion of the sexes—only unfortunately, while in America and France everybody has an appropriate costume, the attire is confined in England to the weaker half of creation." And it seemed to the *Saturday Review* that the weaker half of creation, "in addition to those curious hats, put on a new set of manners and morals during their annual visit to the seaside."

In another issue, the *Saturday Review* wrote of the "strings of respectable women" who fringed the shores within a few yards of the bathing-machines:

There they sit, happy, innocent, undisturbed—placidly and immovably gazing at hundreds of males in the costume of Adam. There does not seem to be a notion that there is any-thing improper—there are no averted looks, no side-long glances, no blushes or shame. Naked men are treated as one of the products of the place, like lobsters, or soles, or pebbles. Hundreds of highly respectable and modest women . . . their artificial modesty blunted by custom look on the living statues so close to them as complacently and steadfastly as they would on the marble images in the Crystal Palace.

But women, too, were sometimes as uninhibited as soles or

lobsters, according to the Marquis of Westmeath, who in the summer of 1857, tried to introduce a Bill to prevent these nude exhibitions. "At this season of the year," he told the Peers, "it is the practice for women to go down to the sea-bathing places and dance in the water without any covering whatever, to the great disgust of the respectable inhabitants and visitors." Lord Westmeath's intelligence, which he said was based on reports from the magistrates of Margate, Ramsgate, and other seaside towns, does not seem to have evoked any interest in the House, and he withdrew his Bill, which would have given magistrates power to compel the wearing of suitable bathing-garments, when Lord Granville observed that it would tend to throw ridicule on legislation.

Beware of the Judas Hole!: In the following year, the blushless daughters of Albion were warned by a correspondent of *The Times* to take care when they travelled in Europe lest they be the victims of enterprising *voyeurs*. There were men, it seemed, foreigners, of course, sufficiently degraded and sufficiently audacious, to bore holes in the doors, wainscotings and ceilings of hotel bedrooms, so as to enjoy the spectacle of visiting Englishwomen getting dressed. These holes, appropriately called *Trous-Judas*, or Judas-holes, were specially trained on Englishwomen "because the traitors enjoy the malignant satisfaction of thinking that their insular modesty would be more deeply shocked if they knew what was going on". The English misses were also popular objects for contemplation because they were fair, and their scrupulous habits of cleanliness made their toilette more protracted and less guarded. They were advised to carry quantities of shawls, wraps and plaids to cover any apertures that might be discovered. The *Saturday Review*, rather more realistically, advised the travelling Englishwoman not to bother about these "wretched holes at all". "She will never know when or where she has been looked at," it pointed out. This was surely better than going about the Continent in "an unbearable state of prudery and consciousness".

"*Animated Stereoscopic Gems*": During the same summer—of 1858—*Paul Pry* denounced in its tongue-in-cheekiest manner "the disgusting depravity" of the beaches, where, it appeared, optical devices were still freely used, but now, by females.

Your prim Miss [it wrote] who would not walk through a potato field, because the potatoes had eyes, or that still more particular young lady, who wrapped a pair of trousers round the legs of a table, because the naked wood shocked her sensitive nerves, has no "compunctious visitings"—no twitches of the conscience—no religious scruples, when she borrows Charles's telescope, or Alfred's opera-glass, and "looks out" in broad noonday, surrounded by old, young, grave and gay, and brings within its focus, in full view, Adam's descendants in that state, from which our first parent was sent forth from the Garden of Eden.

"Shame Where is Thy Flush?" asked *Paul Pry*. "Left behind in London, to be worn again on a fitting occasion. . . . Even the mighty Thunderer, the Giant of Printing House Square, has not been able to suppress this yearly increasing taste for 'animated stereoscopic gems'."

"Clearly", argued the moralists of *Paul Pry*, "the indecent bathing of one person before another, whether male or female, is an obscene publication within the meaning and spirit of the act, and should assuredly be published as such. But . . . it is required that the articles seized should be destroyed, rather a hazardous experiment in this instance."

In its peroration, *Paul Pry* defined its high moral purpose: "At a time like the present, when humbug reigns triumphant and miscreants in white chokers croak for the safety of Christian England, we make no apology for showing a little of the disgusting depravity of respectability, and its seaside-bathing monstrosities.

The Unblushing Fair Sex: A more authentic protestant against these monstrosities was Dr. Thompson, author of *Health Resorts of Great Britain*, published in 1860. "How is it", asked the doctor, "that amid the well-bred visitors of Ramsgate, and indeed, of many other places, both modesty and manners seem to be left at the lodging, so that the bathers on the one hand, and the line of lookers-on, on the other, some with opera-glasses or telescopes, seem to have no more sense of decency than so many South Sea Islanders?" Brooding upon the "almost heathen indecency" of the English seaside, the doctor decided that "much of our boasted refinement is but surface deep". Nor, he pointed out sharply, was the indecency diminished "by the unblushing intrusiveness of the fair sex". Again, the example of the more modest foreigner was invoked. In most places but Britain, said Dr. Thompson, male bathers were compelled to wear some sort of decent covering. It should be imperative in Britain, too, for them to wear short drawers, which did not "in the least impede the movement of the body".

The cry was taken up by Mr. John Hulley, vice-president of the Athletic Society of Great Britain, who had followed in Dr. Bennet's footsteps, and gave an equally enthusiastic report on the "new and wholesome" habits of the French at Biarritz. The women now wore "a simple Bloomer costume consisting of jacket and loose trousers reaching to the ankle . . . list slippers . . . and a straw hat, neatly trimmed," and the men, who walked into the water with their wives on their arm and their daughters following, "simple loose baggy trousers and a skirted Garibaldi". Bathing under these conditions was a social pleasure, instead of an "unpleasant, furtive parenthesis in the day", as it was in England, where the costume considered necessary for men was "a covering of water, say about to the knees". Mr. Hulley conceded that there was something "picturesque and poetic" about this manner of veiling nudity, but "its insufficiency is obvious".

The adoption of the French system of mixed bathing, said Mr. Hulley in his long letter to *The Times*, would get rid of "habits which are a disgrace to the boasted civilization of the nineteenth century, providing sighs which are only equalled among savage tribes".

On the Effect of Cold Water: In October, 1863, William Hardman sent a characteristic report on these discussions to his Melbourne friend, Holroyd:

> The Bathing Question is one of these subjects that come under consideration every year in the season. This year Paterfamilias has been complaining loudly of the way in which shameless Britons expose their persons to curious Britonesses. Contemplative among the Nereids he parades his immodest harmlessness in absolute freedom. Paterfamilias in despair is asking for an Imperial decree, to be in force all round the shores of Britain. He would have us bathe in the French style. Turning his eyes to France, he has at last conceived some Arcadian bliss in the notion of full-dressed families bathing together all in a row, with spinsters looking on and not a blush in the horizon. They take hands, they dip, they laugh, and round about they go. I have seen them, and it must be confessed that they appear happy. But after all, they are French. Paterfamilias has forgotten to make allowances for differences of race. Rather let the preposterous exhibition of our bather go on, than condemn the Briton rushing into his native sea to feel, instead of the vigorous hug of Neptune, a clammy clutch from shoulder to knee—as sickening to his sea-senses as a paternal government to his citizen ditto. The remedy is simple; let a pretty long magisterial line be put between the machines (*bathing,* of course) of each sex. But let us have none of your damp, unpleasant, clinging garments.

There is a refreshing note of realism about Hardman's concluding observation. "Surely", he writes, "the naked Briton must be aware that the action of cold water produces an unsatisfactory effect, and leaves nothing worthy of a passing glance to the innocent but pruriently curious maiden." None the less, when George Meredith wrote to Hardman from Eastbourne in 1870, he reported "antique virgins spy-glass in hand towards the roguish spot" where half a dozen fat men at a time were scampering out of their machines, with "a glistening on the right cheek and the left. . . ."

"The Detestable Custom": Hardman was a sophisticated Londoner with a Rabelaisian gusto for life. His condemnation of the "damp, unpleasant clinging garments" into which the reformers wished to thrust the protesting hams of bathing Britons represents the typical upper-class Tory's resistance to any encroachment on his personal freedom—a freedom sanctified by tradition and therefore independent of contemporary morality. It is surprising, however, to find an unworldly country curate of the 'seventies, expressing, even more emphatically, similar views. The Rev. Francis Kilvert, a young shepherd of the Established Church, becomes lyrical when he confides to his diary the delights of plunging nakedly into the sea, and indignant when he records the attempts of society to deny him this freedom. In 1872, when Kilvert was curate of Langley Burrell, in Wiltshire, he writes of a visit to Weston-Super-Mare: "I was out early bathing from the sands. There was a delicious feeling of freedom in stripping in the open air and running down naked to the sands where the waves were curling white with foam and the red morning sunshine glowing upon the naked limbs of the bathers."

Even in the company of his mother and other ladies, he is not embarrassed by these naked limbs. Mrs. Kilvert and her son are travelling by steam-boat to Ilfracombe: "Some men were bathing, plunging from a spring diving-board in full view of the steam-boat, and one man swam round our vessel looking for all the world like a frog as he swam naked close beneath the stern in the clear blue water."

At Seaton, girls, too, were pleasantly uninhibited:

The beach was thronged, swarming, a gay merry scene, light dresses, parasols, straw hats and puggerys, lovers sitting under the shade of boats, unloved girls looking jealously on at undisguised blandishments, and girls with shoes, stockings, and drawers off wading in the tide, holding up their clothes nearly to the waist and naked from the waist downwards.

It is a charming picture, strangely at variance with the traditionally stuffy idea of Victorians at play. But the belated tide of prudery is sweeping in. It is at Seaton only a year or so later that Mr. Kilvert is introduced to the novel and nasty idea of wearing bathers:

> A boy brought me to the machine two towels, as I thought, but when I came out of the water. . . . I found that one of the rags he had given me was a pair of very short red and white striped drawers to cover my nakedness. Unaccustomed to such things and customs, I had in my ignorance bathed naked and scandalized the beach. However, some little boys who were looking at the rude naked man appeared to be much interested in the spectacle and the young ladies who were strolling near seemed to have no objection.

There is less urbanity in an entry made the following summer. Mr. Kilvert is at Shanklin, where he notes testily, "one has to adopt the detestable custom of bathing in drawers". The custom seems to him not only detestable but dangerous. "If ladies don't like to see men naked, why don't they keep away from the sight?" he asked with an asperity derived from an alarming experience:

> To-day I had a pair of drawers given me which I could not keep on. The rough waves stripped them off and tore them down round my ankles. While thus fettered I was seized and flung by a heavy sea which retreating suddenly left me lying naked on the sharp shingle from which I rose streaming with blood. After this, I took the wretched and dangerous rag off and of course there were some ladies looking at me as I came up out of the water.

The ladies, it seems, had been looking for a considerable part of the nineteenth century.

Whalebone and violets: Myself a refugee from the absolutes of Drs. Marx and Freud, I have no inclination to fix an incomprehensible label on an indeterminate age. Some savants, I know, can interpret everything that happened between 1837 and 1901, from Swinburne to the Albert Memorial from Leighton to Beecham's Pills, from Spurgeon to bustles, in terms of dialectical materialism or psycho-analysis; Mr. Jack Lindsay, indeed, in his study of Dickens, wantonly flirts with both, while, more simply, Miss Anna Kavan, an American student of these mysteries, sees in Victorian life "a manifestation of the anal complex".

But I do not altogether scorn the medicine men—and women. They have a habit of scattering bright trinkets of truth in the soggy pudding of their dogma, and their observations on the pyscho-pathology of tight-lacing seem to me of some importance. Mid-Victorian women, it must be remembered, were ardent practitioners of corsetry, and an inestimable tonnage of whales was murdered to achieve their ideal of a fifteen-inch waist.

The psycho-analysts note that some people get pleasure from thus constricting, to the point of pain, their groaning flesh. Herr Sadger, for instance, in the *Jahrbuch fur psychoanalytische Forschungen, Bd.* 5, 1913, says this pleasure derives from two sources —the actual pain of constriction and the psychological feeling of restricted freedom; and Herr Flügel, in the *International Journal of Psychoanalysis* for 1929, observes that some degree of discomfort is essential to the full gratification from the "phallic significance of clothes". A suggestive observation, and one that Miss Anna Kavan might approve, comes from a student of fashion, Mr. Hilaire Hiler, who, writing of *Costumes and Ideologies*, says:

> We believe that there may be such a thing as an anal-sadistic type of clothing which would be characterized by its tight fit, general stiffness and lack of comfort, and something

military in character. For a number of years, women maso-chists, particularly, subjected themselves to the tortures of the now happily extinct corset as they still do to the ex-tremely high-heeled shoes.

It would be absurd to say that all Victorian women who wore tight corsets were masochists. Though the origins of fashion may lie in the subconscious, those who follow its dictates often have no other compulsion than the desire to conform. But it is interesting to find respectable Victorians writing of the pleasure they experienced from the pressure of steel and whale-bone on their abdomens.

Their letters occupied a lot of space in the *Englishwomen's Domestic Magazine* at the end of the 'sixties. This magazine, one of the many successful publishing projects of Mrs. Beeton's busy husband, then had a circulation of over 60,000, and faith-fully mirrored the social and sartorial aspirations of the English middle class. It was edited by Mrs. Matilda Browne, who lived till 1936. There was so much interest in the correspondence about corsets that much of it was reprinted in a book, *The Corset and the Crinoline,* and this, too, had a big sale.

Most of the women agreed that extreme tight-lacing produced a "delightful sensation". One, whose husband had often told her that she caught him with her fifteen-inch waist, described the pleasure as "truly a reward and a luxury to enjoy". A male reader agreed: "I can quite understand a lady adopting the practice for its own sake, and the pleasure it naturally affords her," he wrote. And a widower was even more explicit:

My nieces ... respectively sixteen and seventeen years old ... have a governess who is very severe with them in the matter of tight-lacing and insists, through my orders, on the utmost amount of compression that they can bear. ... The elder ... is always anxious to help her maid and governess in their efforts with the staylace, and delights in the half-pleasure, half-pain, of the intense pressure."

There is surely a whiff of something queer about all this, but even more instructive are the letters from men who shared this passion for tight-lacing. One had a list of forty staymakers in London who made "regular corsets for gentlemen". He advised a Dublin gentleman how to order corsets by post. "In my own case, I sent the exact measurements round the chest, waist, and hips, and length before and behind, stating that I wished them to be extra long and fully boned ... the waist measure should be three or four inches less than the actual size." "Stays are worn by gentlemen a great deal more than they think", wrote another devotee, who himself wore "blue silk or scarlet French merino" corsets in winter and "Paris wove white" in summer. He liked them "as near as the same shape as the ladies as possible, ... the fullness at the top is an improvement and makes the chest look full; and why should we not have a little padding as well as the other sex?"

Another gentleman, having got accustomed to the "inconvenience and pain" agreed with a female correspondent that "the sensation of being tightly laced in an elegant, well-made, tightly-fitting pair of corsets is superb". And there was a correspondent who, to convince his sceptical friends of the benefits of tight-lacing, had worn a pair of strong, well-stiffened corsets for six weeks, "without taking them off more than for one hour in each week". He reported that for the first two or three weeks, he experienced considerable uneasiness, but soon found "a certain pleasurable feeling in it as well; and at the end of six weeks, he was delighted with the sensation". He did not say whether he had worn one of the new models advertised by Messrs. Johnson Harcham and Co., 3 and 4, Little Love-lane, Wood Street, E.C.—corsets moulded by steam and perfumed with a variety of scents, of which violet was the most popular.

Corsets were still being enthusiastically discussed in 1869, when *London Society* wrote of women who claimed to have compressed their waists to fourteen, and in two cases to thirteen, inches and who kept their corsets on all night:

But the most surprising thing of all is that these ladies, one after another, and we must add gentlemen too, declare that after a little discomfort and occasional superficial pain at first, the internal sensation of the tightest lacing in the stiffest stays is delightful and "superb".

We do not profess either to answer or explain these statements, which would be incredible if they were not so numerous.

A possible explanation was to come, many years later, from Vienna, when psycho-analysis was born. Appropriately, Vienna in the eighteen-sixties was the great academy of tight-lacing, "a stronghold of the corset", one writer called it. The Empress Elizabeth of Austria was famous for the slenderness of her waist; an object of great interest at the Exhibition of 1862 was one of her waistbands sixteen inches long. And London cognoscenti wrote with awe of the supremacy of the Viennese corsetiere.

Chapter VI

Pornography's Hydra Head

I. GROANS FROM SOAPY SAM

THE *Luxury of Divorce:* Despite the anxieties of a mutiny in India, Parliament spent much time and temper in 1857 debating a Bill to set up a Court of Divorce. Before this, divorce in England was by Act of Parliament and was as much a luxury as the saddle of reindeer or the hazelhen that were brought from Russia to give epicures "a new appetitive sensation". Even the *Illustrated London News*, reviewing the Divorce Act, conceded that "the claptrap, dear to the half-instructed, that there is one law for the rich and another for the poor, false as it is in general application, had a justification in the case of conjugal misfortune".

Some years before, Mr. Justice Maule had explained the esoteric processes of divorce to a hawker whom he was sentencing for bigamy. The hawker's wife had left him, and to provide his children with a mother, he had married again. "You have acted wrongly," said the judge, "you should have instructed your attorney to bring an action against your wife's lover for damages. That would have cost you about £100. Having proceeded thus far, you should have employed a proctor and instituted a suit in the Ecclesiastical Courts for a divorce *a mensa et thoro.* That would have cost you £200 or £300 more. When you had obtained a divorce *a mensa et thoro* you had only to obtain a private Act of Parliament for a divorce *a vinculo matrimonii.* The Bill might possibly have been opposed in all its stages in both Houses of Parliament and altogether these proceedings would cost you about £1,000."

241

"Ah, my lord," said the hawker, "I was never worth more than a thousand pence in all my life."

"That is the law and you must submit to it," said Maule J. "It is my duty to pass upon you such sentence as I think your offence deserves. That sentence is that you be imprisoned for one day, and inasmuch as the present Assize is now three days old you will be immediately discharged."

Maule's ironic judgment was quoted by Lord Campbell when the Divorce Bill was being debated, but it did not impress the Bishop of Oxford, "Soapy Sam" Wilberforce, who thought, in fact, that divorce should be confined to persons who could pay not a paltry £1,000, but £2,000. "The lower classes," said this follower of Christ, "did not demand the *privilegia* afforded to the higher and wealthier classes." The Bishop of Oxford, whose benefice was worth perhaps £10,000 a year, was supported by another well-endowed Christian, the Bishop of St. David's, and in the Commons, by Gladstone, who made twenty-seven speeches against one clause in the Bill . "Let the Lord protect the Women of England against the Priests," said *Punch*.

> Though Gladstone protests and Sam Wilberforce groans
> That what's good for a Duke is not good for a Jones

When the Bill reached the second reading the Duke of Norfolk gave notice that he would try to shelve it, contending, as a Catholic, that marriage was indissoluble. "This comes of Catholic Emancipation," said *Punch*. "We set the people free, and they seek to impose chains on us."

Some of the strenuous opposition may have come from statesmen who did not want to be denied the entertainment which the existing system provided. "When any important Bill of Divorce was under discussion," says Mr. Justin McCarthy, "the members crowded the House, the case was discussed in all its details as any clause in a Bill is now debated . . . and the time of Parliament was occupied in the edifying discussion as to whether some unhappy woman's shame was or was not clearly established."

Though the new Divorce Act wiped out some of the inequalities between a Duke and a Jones, it did not make Mrs. Jones her husband's equal. A man could now get a divorce simply by proving his wife was unfaithful; a woman had to prove that her husband had zested his infidelity with cruelty or disgusting conduct, or had deserted her for two years; this dual code survived till the nineteen-twenties.

The Act also abolished the separate action for "criminal conversation", affectionately called "crim-con". This was a common-law suit taken by a husband against his wife's lover, and damages were assessed by some mystical process that translated into sovereigns the loss he had suffered by being cuckolded.

Invention of the Crimcon-meter: One of the last actions for damages for criminal conversation before the Divorce Act became law was the case of *Lyle v. Herbert*, heard in London in August, 1857. It was notable because Mr. Lyle, attuned to the inventive spirit of the age, invoked perhaps for the first time in the history of adultery, a mechanical device to reveal his wife's infidelity. The times were appropriate to such an innovation; the air was surcharged with signs and wonders; and Mr. Lyle, who was an upholsterer, and had seen the coming of the railway, the gas-lit chandelier, and the daguerrotype, possessed an imagination that soared beyond the horse-hair and springs of his workshop and home in Charlotte Street, Fitzroy Square.

For six years he had been married to a lady "of considerable accomplishments and pleasing manners", the daughter of an Indian army officer. Their married life was affectionate and uneventful until the end of 1856, when Mr. Lyle advertised for a partner to bring fresh capital into his business. Mr. Herbert, a middle-aged investor from Croydon—he was "considerably older" than either of the Lyles—answered the advertisement and was taken into partnership. He soon found it inconvenient to travel between Croydon and London and suggested that he occupy a room in the Lyle house. This was arranged, and the partners worked together amicably. In May, 1857, Mrs. Lyle went to Brighton to visit her relatives and while she was away a telegram was delivered at her house. It was opened by Mr. Lyle who found that it was intended for Mr. Herbert, and that it had been sent by his wife to arrange a rendezvous at Euston Station that day. Mrs. Lyle did not return till the following day and Mr. Lyle began to wonder whether Mr. Herbert was interpreting the terms of his partnership rather too widely. He referred his doubts to an investigator, William Taylor, who went about his assignment with considerable zeal.

He took a room in Cumberland Street, immediately behind the Lyle residence, and installed a "blue light", specifications of which are unfortunately lacking, but with which he hoped to detect the suspects in an equivocal tableau. The mysterious blue light, however, failed. Mr. Taylor, his zeal unabated, evacuated his observation post in Cumberland Street and moved into a room in the house next door to the Lyles in Charlotte Street. (The ease with which he appears to have gained access to these highly strategic premises suggests that there was no accommodation problem in the London of 1857.) He chose a room immediately contiguous to Mrs. Lyle's bedroom, and with splendid indifference to the sanctity of property, bored a hole through the party wall to install an apparatus consisting of levers, springs and an index-hand, so contrived that the movement of the hand would indicate whether one, two, three or four persons got into Mrs. Lyle's bed.

Mr. Taylor, giving evidence on behalf of his employer, who, he said, had paid him £20 for his services, described to the court the working of this ingenious device. On the night of 18th June he and Mr. Lyle had maintained a vigil before their invention. For an hour and a half they sat in silence, drinking gin and water. Then the indicator acted (a laugh). The lever fell according to the weight (laughter). It first informed him that one person had got into bed and then that a second person had done so (renewed

244

laughter). Mr. Lyle was watching the indicator while he was looking through the hole (a roar of laughter). He immediately proceeded to the roof, entered by a trap-door, and flashed his bull's-eye lantern on Mr. Herbert and Mrs. Lyle in bed together. Mr. Herbert remained in the house after the transaction but his boots were removed. Mr. Lyle and his agent then had a brandy and cigar, and joined by four or five other people, supped on pickled salmon, gin and tea. Mr. Taylor admitted that in the excitement of the coup he had stolen a bottle of gin from his employer.

Sergeant Parry, for the defence, said it was a ridiculous and disgusting case. "Was it possible", he asked, "for anyone to hear Taylor talk about his indicator, or rather his crimcon-meter, without having his risible muscles exerted to their utmost degree?" (laughter, in which the learned Judge joined). The jury, he said, by the present state of the law would be called upon to assess the damages that a husband was entitled to for the mental anguish he had sustained. Just fancy what amount of mental anguish must have been sustained by a man who could sit for an hour and half in a room adjoining the bedroom in which he supposed his wife to be with an adulterer, drinking gin and water and waiting for an indicator to ascertain the exact period when her dishonour was completed!

The Sergeant suggested that one farthing would be quite sufficient for the witness Taylor and the plaintiff to divide between them. After a very brief retirement the jury awarded Mr. Lyle one farthing, but made no recommendation that it should be divided with his co-inventor.

II. BOUQUET OF ABOMINATIONS

Wanted: A Moral Sewers Commission: Another piece of legislation of interest to students of Victorian morals was passed in 1857; the Obscene Publications Act. This was designed to suppress London's lively trade in pornography, the headquarters of which were in Holywell Street. The *Saturday Review* was quick to note—in 1858—that:

> The great law which regulates supply and demand seems to prevail in matters of public indecency, as well as in other things of commerce. Block up one channel, and the stream will force another outlet; and so it is that the current damned up in Holywell Street, flings itself out in the Divorce Court.

And brooding over the long and lush reports of cases which the new Divorce Act had engendered, it asked, "Can it really be necessary that Holywell Street should be revived and perpetuated in the daily newspapers?" The editors obviously thought so, especially, it seemed, Mr. J. T. Delane, editor of *The Times*.

"We want a Moral Sewers Commission," said the *Saturday Review* in 1864. "To purify the Thames is something but to purify *The Times* would be a greater boon to society." And with an impassioned plunge into hyperbole it suggested that "all the foulest literature of the foulest ages, the reeking abominations of the grossest literature of France and Italy", had damaged public morality less than the "attractive and lucrative indecency" that flowed from the presses in Printing House Square:

> The unsavoury reports of the Divorce Court, the disgusting details of harlotry and vice, the filthy and nauseous annals of the brothel, the prurient letters of adulterers and adulteresses, the modes in which intrigues may be carried out, the diaries and meditations of married sinners, these are now part of our domestic life.

Love in a Gondola: In support of its charges, the *Saturday Review* waved a "bouquet of abominations" culled from less than a single week's issues of *The Times*, and to the display of which it had devoted vast areas of newsprint each day. The most conspicuous of these malodorous flowers was the case in which Vice-Admiral Codrington, a veteran of Navarino and Crimea, brought a suit for divorce against his wife, alleging that she had betrayed him with two brother officers, Lieutenant-Colonel Anderson and Lieutenant Milday, while Mrs. Codrington, denying the adulteries, pleaded in condonation that the Admiral had attempted to take improper familiarities with their friend Miss Emily Faithfull, a formidable and godly feminist, of no apparent seductiveness, who conducted a female printing press in London.

Another judicial inquiry was attracting some attention at the time, Dr. Colenso's appeal to the Privy Council against his dismissal from the See of Natal. The Bishop had questioned the historicity of the Pentateuch, including the account of the Flood, but readers of *The Times* were given a far more comprehensive report of Mrs. Codrington and her gondola, than of Noah and his Ark. When the Admiral was stationed at Valetta, Colonel Anderson had escorted Mrs. Codrington ashore almost every day and night in a gondola, and it was alleged that much of their love-making took place on these excursions. The mechanics of fornication on this fragile craft were sceptically examined by the Queen's Advocate, on Mrs. Codrington's behalf:

They were asked to believe that a lady and a gentleman of rank and education had frequently committed adultery on the narrow bench of a gondola, with four rowers in it, and a man standing at the glass door of the cabin, able to look in at any moment, and during a transit that occupied less than ten minutes. The only foundation for that monstrous story was that the boat sometimes swayed to one side or the other, "got out of trim", forsooth!

When one considers, in addition to these hazards, the difficulties of negotiating the enormous hooped skirt then fashionable, the Queen's Advocate seems to have made a strong point; but the judge, despite the "forsooth!" saw great significance in the evidence of the untrimmed boat, and a verdict was given for the Admiral on all the issues.

Mrs. Codrington's case against her husband rested on the curious circumstances that when Miss Faithfull stayed with them in their London house, Mrs. Codrington would at times leave her husband's bed and get into bed with Miss Faithfull in her communicating room. On one such occasion, she said, the Admiral had followed her, and leaping into bed between them, had attempted to rape his guest. The Admiral stoutly denied this, though admitting that he had once entered Miss Faithfull's room in his nightshirt, but only to poke the fire.

From these glimpses of private life in the Senior Service, Mr. Delane's readers could turn to the no less instructive case of *Chetwynd v. Chetwynd*, which occupied the attention of the Divorce Court for ten days. Mr. Chetwynd, second son of the Dowager Lady Chetwynd, of Longden Hall, and his wife were both characters who had galloped smack out of the pages of Surtees. He had married, at the age of forty-two, the eighteen-year-old daughter of the Honourable and Rev. Austin Talbot, "because"; as he frankly told the Court, "she was very partial to horses and a very famous rider ... generally one of the first in the hunting field". Mr. Chetwynd's enthusiasm for the hunt was such that he allowed his bride's equestrienne skill to outweigh the fact, of which he was fully aware, that she came to the altar seven months' pregnant to some unknown admirer. After their marriage, except for three intervals of child-bearing, Mrs. Chetwynd, as the judge put it, "led a life of familiarity with horse-dealers and horse-jockeys", and Mr. Chetwynd, according to the evidence, led a life of familiarity with his servants.

Squire Chetwynd was a magistrate and kept a large establishment, but he would not employ male servants and insisted on choosing the females himself. It was on the grounds of his adultery with a number of these, as well as of his cruelty to her, that Mrs. Chetwynd asked for a divorce. In a counter-petition, Mr. Chetwynd alleged that his wife had committed adultery with some of her horsy friends. One of the servants, Emma Wilkin, who said she had taken the poker to her master when he had tried to kiss her, catalogued some of his cruelties; he had thrown bread and meat at his wife; he had made their daughter, Miss Florence, kick her; he had made their son, Master Arthur, spit at her and spell W-H-O-R-E to her; and he had threatened to flog both children if, apart from this, they spoke to their mother. Mr. Chetwynd denied all these deviltries, as well as the allegations that he sat down to breakfast smelling of sour-pig-wash, and had called his wife a slimy reptile or a loathsome viper. The verdict was for Mrs. Chetwynd.

From Whitechapel to Windsor: Day by day, as the newspapers of England published, in lickerish details, these reports from the Divorce Court, the heavy damask curtains of pretence that screened the Victorian marriage-bed were rudely parted. The stories of bedroom squabbles are not in themselves important. But it is important, in a survey of the times, to realize that they were the daily reading of millions of respectable citizens.

III. UNLEASHING THE SMUT-HOUNDS

Unnecessary Development in Mayfair: In the nineteen-twenties, during one of those violent fits of morality that, as Macaulay noted, England suffers from time to time, two troubled police-men tramped into a Mayfair gallery and seized thirteen paintings by D. H. Lawrence, as well as a French translation of the *Hunting of the Snark*. The case against the foreign Snark was dropped when the police were convinced that it was a popular book in the kindergarten, but the Lawrence canvases were heaved into Marlborough Street police court and there denounced by the Crown as "horrible and filthy productions ... gross, coarse, hideous, unlovely, ... and in their nature obscene". The obscenity was in the representation of "the private parts of male and female ... grossly and unnecessarily developed, with the pubic hair exposed,"—a test by which stacks of great religious art would have to be condemned, for pubic hair was no more obscene than eyebrows to the pre-Renaissance painter.

When the defence argued—dubiously it seemed to some *amateurs*—that the pictures were works of art, the magistrate, Mr. Mead, made it clear that he knew what he liked and he didn't like art. It was, he ruled, "utterly immaterial" whether Mr. Lawrence's heavily endowed creations were works of art or not. "The most splendidly painted picture in the universe might be obscene," he said. And he warned misguided art-lovers that it was just as bad to exhibit an obscene picture in a private house as in a public place.

The prosecution of these pictures, like the action taken not long before against Miss Radclyffe Hall's novel *The Well of Loneliness* and Miss Norah James's novel *Sleeveless Errand*, was based on the Obscene Publications Act of 1857. Mr. Mead would no doubt have been surprised to learn that when this Act was passed, seventy years before the emancipation of Oxford Bags and Eton Crops, many eminent Victorians denounced it as preposterous—even though the Lord Chief Justice, Lord Campbell, who framed it, assured them that (unlike Mr. Mead) he "had not the most distant contemplation" of interfering with works of art. The history of the Act shows that in the middle of the nineteenth century, though Mr. Mudie ruled the circulating libraries and dictated to the drawing-room, there was still eloquent and enlightened opposition to his mother-of-pearl and papier-mâché gelding knife.

Mr. Birtles Points the Bone: When the Society for the Suppression of Vice was formed in 1802, its secretary, Mr. Wilberforce, announced that it would direct its attention to the profanation of the Lord's Day, blasphemous publications, obscene books, prints, etc., disorderly houses and fortune-tellers. The Society was an off-shoot of the Evangelical Movement, and its first committee included the Rev. Thomas Bowdler, who collaborated posthumously with Shakespeare, Zachary Macaulay, the father of the historian, and Mr. Hatchard the bookseller, of Piccadilly. In 1825, the Rev. J. Keate, the enthusiastic flogger from Eton, and Mrs. Hannah Moore, were members of the Society, and its agenda had been widened to include the suppression of snuff-boxes, which often had "indecent and obscene engravings, highly finished"; inside the lid and had "a large and ready market in Boarding Schools for Young Ladies".

These *objets d'art*, according to a report of the Society, were among the benefits that the ending of the Napoleonic War had brought to England: "In consequence of the renewed intercourse with the Continent . . . there has been a great influx into the country of the most obscene articles of every description, as may be inferred from the exhibition of indecent snuff-boxes in the shop-windows of the tobacconists." Some of these articles lacked even the slight functional purpose of the snuff-boxes. Mr. Birtles, the secretary of the Bristol branch of the Society, reported that he had bought, "without the least privacy on their part or mine", a variety of the most obscene devices in bone and wood, some representing a crime *"inter Christianos non nominandum"*, which they termed the *new fashion*.

The restoration of peace led also to a great influx of French whores, who established themselves in Leicester Square, Regent Street and Waterloo Place. They brought with them a taste in interior decoration that moved Baron Nicholson, then conducting *The Town*, to honest English indignation; "If the police were to search the lodgings of these filthy French harlots," he wrote, "they would find prints of the most horrible description, and paintings unmatched for bestiality. These diabolical incitements to venery are, and we trust always will be, *foreign* to Englishmen."

Mr. Nicholson's faith in the continuing fastidiousness of his countrymen was not justified. In the early 'fifties, the *Lancet* was complaining that "many of the tobacconists' shops in the most important thoroughfares have exposed in their windows the most licentious representations, as inducements to erotic passion". Pornography had become a thriving British industry, and the Vice Society's main objective. Holywell Street, named for its "sweete, wholesome and cleere" holy springs, was the centre of this unwholesome and unholy trade. It ran parallel to the Strand from St. Mary's to St. Clements Danes, and disappeared, with Wych Street, when the Strand was widened at the beginning of this century. A correspondent to *The Times* in 1857 described it as "without exception ... the most vile street in the civilized world, every shop teeming with the most indecent publications and prints".

Here William Dugdale, the Curll of the nineteenth century, the dean of mid-Victorian pornographers, had his warehouse, study, and bookshop. Repeated prison sentences did not sap his enthusiasm or inhibit his enterprise. As well as controlling the editorial and production departments of his erotic empire, he found time, when not behind bars, to make regular goodwill visits to fairs, race-meetings and markets, and to visit the two universities at least twice a year. His output was enormous. When police, on the information of the Vice Society, raided his premises in 1851, they took away 822 books, 3,870 prints, and 16 cwt. of unsewn letterpress—two heavy cartloads—all "of a most abominable description". It was Dugdale's fourth conviction, and he was sentenced to two years in the House of Correction. In 1856, when raiders seized 3,000 books from him, he had been convicted nine times. He died in prison, after having been engaged in what Mr. Mayhew calls "this infamous and diabolical traffic" for nearly forty years. His most energetic rival was Mr. Edward Duncombe, of Little St. Andrew's Street, Seven Dials, who had his sixth conviction in 1856.

O, Those Amorous Pants!: The profits of pornography were high enough to justify an occasional sojourn in gaol. Many of Dugdale's publications sold at one and a half or two guineas a volume and were pirated reprints of books published in small editions at the turn of the century. Sometimes he paid for original compositions. One of his most gifted authors was an unhappy Indian army officer, Captain Edward Sellon, who after an energetic career of debauchery among English, French,

German and Polish girls, found the greatest satisfaction in the "salacious, succulent houris of the far East", and returned to England, somewhat ruined in health and fortune, to drive the Cambridge coach. He wrote and illustrated many erotic books for Dugdale, drawing on his own experience in India and elsewhere. He shot himself in a Piccadilly hotel in 1866, after writing a poem titled NO MORE! in which he said:

> The glance of love, the heaving breast
> To my bosom so fondly prest,
> The rapturous sigh, the amorous pant,
> I shall look for, long for, want
> > No more.

There are, perhaps, in the literature of love, more felicitous phrases than "the amorous pant", but Sellon's piece must be regarded as a valedictory impromptu rather than a polished composition. It ended with two lines that he probably intended for his epitaph:

> Vivat lingam
> Non resurgam.

Turkish Delight: A characteristic of the Victorian erotic novel was the long and luxuriant title, which had the function of the modern "blurb". A typical Dugdale title-page reads:

The lustful Turk. Part the first. A History founded on Facts, containing an interesting narrative of the cruel fate of the two young English ladies, named Silvia Carey and Emily Barlow. Fully explaining how Emily Barlow and her servant Eliza Gibbs, on their passage to India, were taken prisoners by an Algerian pirate and made a present of to the Bey of Algiers; who, on the very night of their arrival, debauched Emily. Containing also, every particular of the artful plans laid by the Bey, to get possession of the person of Silvia Carey, etc., with the particulars of her becoming a victim to his libidinous desires. Which recital is also interspersed with the histories of several other ladies confined in the Bey's harem. One of which gives an account of the horrid practices then carried out in several French and Italian convents by a society of monks, established at Algiers under pretence of redeeming Christian slaves; but who, in reality, carried on an infamous traffic in young girls. Also an account of the sufferings of Eliza Gibbs from the flogging propensities of the Bey of Tunis. With many other curious circumstances, until the reduction of Algiers by Lord Exmouth; by which means these particulars became known. The whole compiled from the original letters by permission of one of the sufferers. Embellished with beautiful engravings. Published in two parts by an Arcadian, as the law directs; and to be had of all the principal booksellers in town and country. Price 2 guineas.

Dubious Stratagems of the Smut-merchants: Apart from its honest trade in pornography, Holywell Street sometimes trafficked in wares that belied their label. Dr. Acton noted "very cheap editions of *The Castle of Otranto,* Lewis's *Monk,* and . . . other innocuous romaunts, done up in obscene wrappers", and sold at high prices. "It is a good trick," he observes, "as the buyer has no remedy for the surprise."

Under the heading *Of the Sham Indecent Street-Trade,* Mr. Mayhew tells of an even more reprehensible deceit practised upon the gulls; the sale of a sealed packet "which the 'patter' of the street-seller leads his auditors to believe to be some improper or scandalous publication", but which is revealed on opening to be "portion of an old newspaper, a Christmas carol, a religious tract, or a slop-tailor's puff". (Travellers say that a similar deceit is still practised by the wily fella-heens of Port Said, who furtively press highly priced packets of "French cards" upon the inquiring tourist. When he opens his purchase in the privacy of his cabin he finds he has paid a humiliating number of piastres for a set of smudgy playing cards.)

Mr. Mayhew rightly condemns this trade as "at once repulsive and ludicrous", but one of its practitioners whom he questioned defended it warmly. Why should he be interfered with by the police, he asked, for pretending to sell what other merchants actually sold without molestation? There were shops in the Strand, Fleet Street, Holborn, Drury Lane, Wych Street, the courts near Drury Lane Theatre, Haymarket, High Street, Bloomsbury, St. Martin's Court, May's Buildings and elsewhere, "to say nothing of Holywell Street", where shameless publications were not only sold, but exposed in the windows. Was he a greater offender than these shopkeepers? His customers, he told Mr. Mayhew, were principally boys, young men, and old gentlemen. "Drunken women of the town had occasionally made loud comments on his calling, and offered to purchase, but ... fearful of a disturbance, he always hurried away." He was similarly circumspect about transactions in public-houses, where a packet might be torn open before he got clear. His "great gun" was to make up packets resembling as closely as possible those displayed in the bookshop windows. "He would then station himself at some little distance from one of these shops ... so as to encounter those who stopped to study the contents of the windows, and offer big reductions on the marked prices."

Titillation in 3D: Despite the vigilance of the Vice Society, the trade in pornography increased during the 'fifties as book-production became cheaper and more people enjoyed the benefits of literacy. Photography, released by the wet plate from the limitations of the daguerrotype, added to the resources of the pornographer; and the stereoscope, an invention of Wheatstone's and Brewster's that in the drawing-room had a severely didactic function, was now adapted to aphrodisiac ends. "There is hardly a street in London which does not contain shops in which photographs and especially stereoscopic photographs, are exposed for sale," said a writer in the *Saturday Review* in 1858. These third-dimensional studies were of women "more or less naked, and generally leering at the spectator with a conscious or elaborately unconscious impudence" and with a "brutal vulgarity and coarseness . . . as surprising as it is disgusting". The writer noted that whereas an ordinary indecent print proved only the nastiness of the artist and the vendor, an indecent photograph implied also the degradation of the model. "Decency is a matter rather of sentiment than of fixed rule and there would be far more indecency in sitting for a single time for any one of . . . (these) photographs than in adopting the profession of an artist's model."

The Mission of "Paul Pry": Emboldened by these developments, a Fleet Street publisher, Robert Martin, towards the end of 1856, started a penny weekly called *Paul Pry*. Reviving the tradition of the pornographer masquerading as moralist, which had died with Renton Nicholson's *The Town*, Mr. Martin announced that every age produced its man and the present had given birth to *Paul Pry* who was sent "to show vice its own features": He would not be threatened, intimidated or bullied, nor would he retire till his mission was fulfilled. This mission was to publish pieces about London's nighthouses and whores, reports of scandalous court cases, Holywell Street advertisements, and answers to correspondents, such as:

Green-horn—French letters are decidedly a blessing in the community. They effectively prevent the spread of venereal contagion in casual intercourse between the sexes, and in the marriage state, the increase of the family. . . . What no act of free will or legislation could effect is accomplished by the French letter.

And:

Z.A.—From one to three times a week. A day or two should always intervene. The fair average for a healthy young man would be every third day.

Paul Pry's advertising columns also showed a high missionary purpose:

Just Received from Paris
STEREOSCOPIC GEMS

A.J. begs to inform his subscribers, and the public generally, that he has just received from Paris, an entirely new assortment of Stereoscopic Slides, depicting some of the fastest, and richest scenes, in the Bagnios of the French capital, all taken from life. They have only to be seen to be appreciated; in consequence of the late seizure in Paris (see daily papers) by the gendarmes, of these warm gems, he has the greatest difficulty in obtaining as many as he wants of the right sort.

Single Slide, 5s. Set of Twenty, £4 4s. Highly coloured, 2s. per slide extra A. J. 4 Harpur St., Red Lion Square, London.

N.B.—A Catalogue, descriptive of these Warm Gems, sent on receipt of six stamps and a stamped envelope.

*   *   *

Send TWELVE POSTAGE STAMPS to A.Z., 96 Mary Street, Hampstead Road, and you will receive something slick.

*   *   *

Something Good at Last.
Aristotle's Midwifery, with Highly-Coloured Plates.
The Rake's Cabinet, with 60 Highly Finished and Coloured Engravings.

Singular Misadventure of the Right Honourable Filthy Lucre: For a while *Paul Pry* went his Messianic way without pother, mixing mild essays in salacity with brothel gossip and hints to young lechers. The watchdogs of the Vice Society must have picked up the scent immediately, but they did not pounce till he published, in his fourth month, a *jeu d'esprit* about the Right Honourable Filthy Lucre, who, after ingesting a vast quantity of "lush"—brandy, rum, gin, whisky and capillaire—invites Susan, the servant-girl, to his room, inquires, in the idiom of the day, if she will be "good-natured", and seduces her.

This process was described with a candour that even to-day would be tolerated only in a novel dealing with the love-life of a G.I. or a Marine, and Mr. Robert Martin, who published the whimsy, and Mr. William Strange, who distributed it, were both sent to gaol for selling an obscene publication.

Economics in Indecency: Mr. Strange was tried before Lord Campbell, Lord Chief Justice of England, himself an accomplished man of letters. His Honour, after reading the account of the Rt. Hon. Filthy Lucre's gallantries, expressed "astonishment and horror", particularly at the low price at which it was sold. Hitherto, he said, there had been some check to these publications, arising from the high price which was extracted for them. . . . But to sell them for one penny was a state of things which his Lordship, with great feeling, pronounced a disgrace to the country. It was no excuse, he said, that the defendant had also sold the *Household Words:* and other publications of most interesting moral, instructive and beautiful character, for which the country was indebted to Mr. Charles Dickens. The jury agreed that these cheap publications had "a far greater tendency to demoralize" than more costly ones.

The interesting doctrine that the rich are less susceptible to corruption than the poor, though scarcely empiric, soon became an axiom of Anglo-Saxon censorship. In semi-civilized countries such as Australia it is still invoked by the clerks of the Customs Departments who decide what books the Commonwealth can import. The *Decameron* and *Rabelais,* for example, are banned "in cheap editions only".

"Far more fatal than prussic acid": Lord Campbell continued to brood over *Paul Pry's* pennyworth of pornography, and when Parliament met in May he urged the House of Lords to suppress publications that he described as far more fatal than prussic acid, strychnine or arsenic. "If there were any difficulty in obtaining them from their high price," he told the Lords, "it might be of less importance." But it was the duty of the Government to take the necessary measures for immediately stopping the sale of these

licentious, obscene and disgusting penny weeklies. When the Chancellor, Lord Cranworth, said that the existing law which made it a misdemeanour to sell obscene books or prints was sufficient, Lord Campbell said he did not want to create any new offence, but to give the police more powers to seize indecent publications and destroy them.

Though the amendments he asked for were aimed solely at the rubbish of Holywell Street, at books "written for the single purpose of corrupting the morals of youth", they were strenuously opposed in both Houses. It is doubtful whether the freedom of the writer and the artist would be as vigorously defended in England to-day as it was in 1857.

In the Lords, Brougham and Lyndhurst led the attack on the proposed Bill. When Brougham reminded them that "in the works of the most eminent poets there were objectionable passages that might . . . cause them to be considered as obscene publications", Lord Campbell assured him that such works could not possibly be affected by his Bill. But Boston-born Lord Lyndhurst—he was the son of John Copley, the painter—still had doubts. What interpretation was to be put on the word "obscene"?

Suppose a man following the trade of an informer, or a policeman, sees in a window something he conceives to be a licentious print. He goes to the magistrate and describes, according to his ideas, what he saw; the magistrate thereupon issues his warrant for the seizure of the disgusting print. The officer then goes to the shop and says to the shopkeeper, "Let me look at that picture of Jupiter and Antiope." . . . He sees the picture of a woman stark naked, lying down, and a satyr standing by her with an expression on his face which shows most distinctly what are his feelings and what is his object. The informer tells the man he is going to seize the print, and to take him before a magistrate. . . . "But," says the man, "don't you know that it is a copy from a picture of one of the most

259

celebrated masters in Europe?" That does not matter; the informer seizes it as an obscene print. . . .

Our informant leaves the print shop and goes into the studio of a sculptor . . . and sees there figures of nymphs, fauns and satyrs, all perfectly naked, some of them in attitudes which I do not choose to describe. According to this Bill they may every one be seized:

Nympharumque leves cum satyris chori.

. . . In the same way the dramatists of the Restoration—Wycherly, Congreve, and the rest of them—there is not a page in any one of them which might not be seized under this Bill. One of the principal characters in one of Congreve's plays is Lady Wishfort. Dryden, too, is as bad as any of them. He has translated the worst parts of Ovid—his *Art of Love*. . . . Take, too, the whole flight of French novelists, from Crebillon *fils*, down to Paul de Kock; nothing can be more unchaste; nothing more immodest, than they are; and when my noble and learned Friend's Bill is passed, every copy of them may be committed to the bonfire. . . ."

Brougham continued his attack with an article in the *Law Magazine*, in which he said that many of the classics, now in the hands of all scholars even of tender age, contained passages "offensive to morality, indeed to common decency". In the House of Commons, John Roebuck, the man who had exposed the muddle of the Crimean War, said: "A more preposterous Bill has never been sent down from the House of Lords, and that is saying a good deal." It was an attempt to make people virtuous by Act of Parliament. It would not prevent mischief but make it by encouraging an abuse of power. Like Lord Lyndhurst he wanted to know where the line would be drawn:

The plays of Wycherly are obscene, but do you suppose you can put them down? The *Basia* of Johannes Secundus, elegantly translated by Stanley, contain some of the most obscene passages ever written. Do you hope to prevent their sale? Aristophanes, Martial, Prior, even Pope. . . . In the *Eloisa to Abelard,* one of the most brilliant poems in the English language, there are lines which I would be ashamed to read aloud. . . . Gambling houses and houses of ill-fame are to be found in some of the best streets in London, and if we are impotent to put these down, I think we will fail to put down obscene books. . . . If we arm policemen or other persons with authority to break into private houses, under pretence of searching for obscene books and prints, we institute an inquisition and begin the race of despotism. I have no faith in hypocritical pretensions to virtue and believe that by depending on the honesty and manly feelings of the people, we will do more than can be accomplished by a thousand inquisitorial and despotic acts of Parliament.

Several safeguards had to be inserted in the Act, and Lord Campbell had to repeat his assurances that it would be employed only against obvious pornography, before it was passed. Certainly, in its original sense, it would never have been invoked to suppress Miss Radclyffe Hall. But in 1868, Campbell's successor, Lord Chief Justice Cockburn, made the test of obscenity "whether the tendency of the matter charged . . . is to deprave and corrupt those whose minds are open to such immoral influences", a grotesque ruling that made it possible to suppress anything from a bible to a dictionary. The book that gave rise to this infamous judgment was one that Mr. Martin of *Paul Pry* had peddled, *The Confessional Unmasked,* a dreary but certainly not a pornographic work, one of the many popular mid-Victorian exposures of the alleged villainies of Popery. *The Confessional Unmasked,* with the *Awful Disclosures of Sister Lucy,* and Hogan's *Auricular Confessions and Nunneries,* were freely hawked in the streets of London. Another of these Christian works, *The Female Jesuit, or a Spy in the Family,* was lent by Gladstone to the Queen. "Her Majesty could hardly put it down and has been much occupied by it," Lady Augusta Bruce wrote in 1863. (It was about this time that Gladstone confided to his wife that the Queen weighed 11 stone 8 lb.— "rather much for her height"—and drank her claret strengthened —"I should have thought spoiled," said Gladstone—with whisky.

On the Complexity of Literary Taboos: At about the same time as Lord Lyndhurst was extolling the works of Crebillon *fils* and Paul de Kock, Anthony Trollope, at the request of his publisher, Longmans, was striking out some "objectionable" passages in *Barchester Towers*. One of them was "fat stomack", which, in deference to Mr. Mudie as represented by Mr. Longmans, Trollope altered to "deep chest". But this dissonance was less remarkable than the licence permitted to authors of antiquity while living writers were hog-tied to Mrs. Grundy's apron-strings. "No tribunal would censure a bookseller for supplying his customers with complete editions of the classics," said *The Times*, in an editorial approving Lord Campbell's legislation, "although much might be urged against the morality of PETRONIUS, of NONNUS, of MARTIAL, and even [the "even" is interesting] of CATULLUS AND OVID."

And no one censured the respectable Mr. Henry Bohn, of York Street, Covent Garden, for selling inexpensive translations of Petronius, Martial, Catullus, Ovid, Juvenal, Apuleius, Tribullus and Propertius, carefully annotated so that the more subtle indecencies would not be lost on the reader of limited scholarship. Whether or not Lesbia's sparrow was a simple bird or a "licentious allegory", the curious manner in which radishes were employed in the punishment of adulterers, what Catullus means when he says he is lying on his back bursting his tunic, the old Spanish custom of using urine as a cosmetic, are some of the points glossed by Mr. Bohn's editors. While Trollope was refining his guinea-and-a-half novels for the ears of the young girl, the young girl, for 5s., could acquire such snippets of erudition as "*Mentula,* synonymous with *penis,* is a nickname applied by Catullus to Mamurra, of whom he says that he is not a man, but a great thundering *mentula*". Or: "The bust of Priapus was commonly cut out of the standing trunk of a tree, and was armed with a sickle, as well as with a *phallus* of most formidable dimensions."

Tennyson objected to the word "naked" in Kingsley's pious novel *Hypatia*. No one objected to such passages as:

> *Then flinging off her dress, the imperial whore*
> *Stood, with bare breasts and gilded, at the door,*
> *And showed, Britannicus, to all who came,*
> *The womb that bore thee, in Lyscisa's name!*

in Mr. Bohn's popular Classical Library. Or, if you preferred your Juvenal in prose, in the same volume was a faithful translation by the Rev. Lewis Evans, M.A.: "The imperial harlot . . . entered the brothel . . . then took her stand with naked breasts and gilded nipples."

Why did the classics enjoy this immunity? Not because they were inaccessible to the unlettered man in the street. Mr. Bohn had changed all that. But perhaps because of the snobbery of a middle class aspiring to the aristocratic tradition. The classics remained, as it were, the property of the upper classes. Their indecencies were part of the cultural inheritance of the public schools, to which the prosperous middle class—including Dickens —now sent their sons. And clergymen like Mr. Lewis Evans translated the grossest passages without embarrassment, protected from corruption by this amulet of traditional "culture".

Miss Glitters and the Zu-Zu: Between unashamed pornography and unassailable propriety, between Dugdale and Dickens, two mid-Victorian writers occupied a remarkable zone of rebellion. Neither the raffish Surtees nor the rapturous Ouida conformed to the accepted code of the novelist, both were refreshingly unballasted by any moral purpose, and both were widely read. Surtees modestly explained that his work did not "aspire to the dignity of a novel". It certainly ignored the recognized formula, enunciated by Trollope, of making virtue alluring and vice ugly. If Surtees had any aesthetic, it was quite frankly "tarts for tart's sake". His "tolerably virtuous" Lucy Glitter, of the Astley Royal Amphitheatre, later Mrs. Sponge; Miss Spangles, of the Theatre Royal, Sadler's Wells, later Lady Scattercash; and Miss Harriet Howard, *née* Jane Brown, are pretty horse-breakers living in a lubberland of claret-cups, decanters, cigar-smoke, horses and hiccoughs, with no other motive than to enjoy it all and what the hell.

When Miss Howard invites some small boys to toffy and lollipops at Nonsuch House, where the gay conpany is relaxing after a heavy New Year's Eve, the biggest boy coyly declines without saying why; but a younger urchin, less inhibited, explains: "Mar says we hadn't. . . . Because—because she said the house was full of trumpets." And when Mr. Jorrocks suffers a rather humiliating fall, and Mrs. Blash, the pretty barber's wife, remarks: "*Hut!* he's always on his back, that old feller," Mr. Jorrocks replies gallantly: "Not 'alf so often as you are, old gal." Dr. Wingfield-Stratford says Surtees was able to maintain "a rich level of coarseness and sexual frankness" because the sporting-novel belonged to the smoke-room, not the drawing-room. But Ouida wrote deliberately for the drawing-room—with one eye on the servant-girl's attic—and her popularity was so great that even Mr. Mudie had to stock her. What did his insulated lady readers think of her lush harlots? The Zu-Zu, in *Under Two Flags*, who has been trans-lated from a garret with *bread-and-cheese* to a diamond edition of a villa where she prescibes Crème Bouzy and Parfait in succession, was a "white-skinned, bright-eyed, illiterate, avari-cious little beauty, whose face was her fortune":

She dressed perfectly but she was a vulgar little soul; drank everything from Bass's ale to rum-punch, and from cherry-brandy to absinthe; thought it was the height of wit to stifle you with cayenne slid into your vanilla ice, and the climax of repartee to cram your hat full of peach stones and lobster shells; was thoroughly avaricious, thoroughly insatiate, thoroughly heartless . . . had a coarse good nature when it cost her nothing, and was as "jolly as a grig", according to her phraseology, so long as she could stew her pigeons in champagne, drink wines and liqueurs that were beyond price, take the most dashing trap in the Park up to Flirtation Corner.

Her little toy trap, glittering with silver, has snow-white ponies and snowy reins, leopard skins and bright blue liveries, and when the Zu-Zu is not driving it, or relaxing in her boudoir with her pots of pomatum and gew-gaws of marqueterie, she is pelting the Hon. Bertie Cecil of the Life Guards with brandy cherries, or throwing half-guinea peaches at dragon-flies in the river at Richmond.

It was a strange picture of Victorian womanhood for Mr. Mudie to circulate; and the portrait of Cora Pearl in *Puck* is equally candid, though Ouida delicately calls her "Laura" Pearl.

The splendid lips had a cruel sensuality; the splendid eyes had a hard rapacity; the splendid ruddy-tinted hair shaded a brow that had the low brutal ignorance of the savage set upon it. . . . I wonder her voice did not break the spell of her beauty, it was so harsh, so coarse, so metal-like in its resonance.

IV. THE MASTER OF APHRODISIOPOLIS

Diversions of a Country Gentleman: Among those members of the House of Commons who vigorously opposed Lord Campbell's Obscene Publications Bill was the Conservative representative of Pontefract, Mr. Richard Monckton Milnes, the future Lord Houghton. Milnes, like Wilfrid Scawen Blunt, was as un-English an Englishman as England has produced—"a Yorkshire landowner who hated the land and country pursuits, preferred London to the West Riding, and Paris and Italy to both". Henry Adams called him the finest wit in London, "the man who went everywhere, knew everybody"—and, at his famous breakfast-parties at 16 Upper Brook Street—"talked of everything;" Carlyle said that if Christ were again on earth, Milnes would ask him to breakfast.

As a poet and a patron of the arts, Milnes denounced the Bill as "a clumsy method of meeting the evil, one totally alien to the habits of the country, and certain, in the end, to be disgustful to the English people." "I believe, in truth," he said, "that the Bill would never have reached its present shape if honourable members had had the manliness to state their real opinions on the subject."

No one could have spoken with greater authority, because Milnes was the most ardent collector of pornography in the British Isles, In Fryston Hall, his Yorkshire home which he gaily called "Aphrodisiopolis", he amassed a huge and handsome gallery of erotica. Swinburne, whom Milnes introduced to the writings of de Sade, wrote enthusiastically of it to Rossetti: "His erotic collection of books, engravings, etc., is unrivalled upon earth—unequalled I should imagine, in heaven." Mr. Pope-Hennessy, in his admirable biography of Milnes, catalogues some of the items:

La Pucelle with Fragonard's engravings, the illustrated Religieuse of Diderot, and Les Liaisons Dangereuses of Choderlos de Laclos. One book for which he had searched in Paris, and which was finally bought for him in 1859 and sent to London with the pages gummed together in case of discovery at the Customs, was the big edition of the alleged Caracci illustrations to Arctino's sonnets. This large quarto, L'Aretin d'Augustin Carrache ou Recueil de Postures Erotiques . . . avec texte explicatif des sujets: contains a number of engravings after water-colours supposed to be by Agostino Caracci, and to have been discovered in Italy during Napoleon's first Italian campaign, and representing classical personages making love in ways as inconvenient as they are gymnastic. Milnes also

obtained with some difficulty a good copy of Louvet de Cou-
vray's four-volume serial, *Les Amours du Chevalier de Faublas:*
and of La Riche de la Popelinière's *Tableaux de Moeurs.*
Other books in his possession included Nerciat's *Monrose:*
L'Etourdie and *Felicia L'Anti-justine* and the other works of
L'Anti-justine and the other works of Restif, *Le Jou-Jou des
Demoiselles* of Jouffreau de Lazarin, *L'Histoire des Flagellants:
Venus en Rut*, Lalmond's *Pot-Pourri de Loth:* the French trans-
lation of Cleland published in 1751 as *La Fille de Joie: La
Saladière:* an unidentifiable volume entitled *Les Yeux: le Nez
et les Tetons, Le Soupé de Julie:* the *Bibliothèque des Amants: La
Victime de l'amour: La Nouvelle Sapho:* Mirabeau's *Libertin de
Qualité, Les Travaux d'Hercule* and *Le Petit fils d'Hercule*, and
books of elegant erotic verse such as *Le Petit-Neveu de Grècourt*
printed in 1782, and its companion volume *Le Petit-Neveu de
Boccace.*

"These," says Mr. Pope-Hennessy, "with innumerable other
works of an equally resolute impropriety, went to make up the
erotic library of Richard Monckton Milnes."

Singular Use of Mr. Harris's Back: Milnes was aided in his
collecting by agents in France and Belgium. He was particularly
fortunate in his Paris representative, a former Guardsman named
Frederick Hankey, the son of a distinguished English general
and the kinsman of a Governor of the Bank of England. Hankey
was a parchment-faced, blue-eyed, elegant young man of many
sexual foibles, perhaps the simplest being his zeal for pursuing
erotica. Unlike many collectors, he was unselfish in his passion
and happy to help anyone of similar tastes. He lived with a
mistress in a crowded apartment in the rue Lafitte, opposite the
Café Anglais, surrounded by obscene statues, books bound in
human skin, and such treasures as a satin-bound copy of La
Popelinière's *Amorous Passion at Different Stages in Life* once
owned by Louis XV, a Hermaphroditus by Beccadelli, illustrated
with original drawings by Boucher, Lancret Pater and Watteau,

and a complete Sèvres dinner-service made for the Regent Philippe d'Orleans, in which every piece, from plate to salt-cellar, was ingeniously indecent. Mr. Hankey valued this set at £30,000 but the Prince of Orange to whom he offered it, though anxious to acquire it, thought the price too high to pay for a bit of titillation between courses.

Milnes could have had no more fervent pilgrim of porno-graphy than Hankey. "It is quite clear", says Mr. Pope-Hennessy after studying his correspondence with Milnes, "that had it not been for Frederick Hankey's assiduity, the Fryston erotica would never have been assembled at all."   Nor would it have been assembled had not Hankey been as ingenious in transmitting his purchases as he was indefatigable in making them.   Small items were smuggled through the English Customs in the pocket of a valet's overcoat. Bulkier ones sometimes enjoyed, like Harriette Wilson's letters from Paris, and Lady Holland's Dutch herrings, the impregnable protection of the British diplomatic bag. Once, a Queen's Messenger included erotica for Milnes with despatches for Lord Palmerston. But the most important medium was the complaisant manager of Covent Garden, Mr. Harris, who visited Paris frequently, and apparently had some anatomical qualifications for book-running. "He is not only most devoted to me," Hankey wrote, "but a very good hand at passing quarto volumes as he has done *several* times for me in the *bend* of his *back*." In this pliant back were concealed Milne's two obscene Louis Quinze statuettes in Sèvres *pâté tendre,* and perhaps the Lesbian tableau by Pradier which Swin-burne liked.

Another cultivated amateur of pornography was the scholar and traveller Henry Spencer Ashbee, who bequeathed to the British Museum, together with his magnificent Cervantic library, a considerable collection of erotica. In his diary, which Mr. Pope-Hennessy quotes, he records an afternoon and evening spent among Hankey's "unique volumes". "He has given himself up body and soul to the erotic mania, thinks of nothing else, lives for nothing else," Ashbee wrote. "Nothing is bawdy enough for him whether in expression, thought or design."

The *Saturday Review* may have had men like Milnes and Ashbee in mind when it wrote, in 1872: "The passion for notoriety, the rage for distinction of any kind, sometimes plays strange pranks, but it is difficult to realize the elation of the man whose bosom swells with the proud consciousness that he is pointed out in society as possessing a finer collection of nasty books and prurient pictures than anyone else."

Journey to the Land of Might-have-been: What would have happened to Monckton Milnes' groaning shelves of bawdry if Florence Nightingale had become the mistress of Fryston Hall? I know of no more beguiling speculation in all Victorian history than this, nor is it wildly fanciful. Mr. and Mrs. Nightingale were delighted when the eligible Milnes fell in love with their daughter, whom he met in 1842; he was a brilliant and popular *litterateur*, host and politician, of thirty-three, and she a demure and serious young woman of twenty-two. Milnes proposed marriage several times, and after five years their acquaintance had matured sufficiently for him to mesmerize Dr. Buckland's tame bear, Tig, so Florence could fondle it. But by then she had come to the conclusion that life was "no holiday game . . . nor a clever book", whereas Milne was unashamedly enjoying it both as a game to play and a book to contemplate; and in 1854, when Florence was emptying the twenty chamber-pots that the War Office had provided for the 2,000 men in Scutari hospital, Milnes had married the less purposive Annabel Crewe and was filling his bookshelves with erotica. "If she had married me," he wrote some years later, "there would have been a heroine less in the world and certainly not a hero the more."

Florence Nightingale, besides her instinct for dedication, must have had some exoteric qualities, for Dr. Benjamin Jowett, the plump and sardonic Master of Balliol, also fell in love with her.

269

V. COCK-A-HOOP ON A DUNGHILL

Lord Campbell died in 1861, four years after his Obscene Publications Act became law. "Its success," he had written in his diary at the time, "has been most brilliant. Holywell Street, which had long set law and decency at defiance, has capitulated after several assaults." But in 1868, the *Saturday Review* reported that, as far as London went, the Act was a "dead letter":

> At the present moment the dunghill is in full heat, seething and steaming with all its old pestilence. . . . Six shops in Holywell Street and three in Wych Street . . . exhibit books and pictures and filthy wares of all unspeakable kinds, in the most open way, and without the slightest attempt at disguise or concealment.

A year later, it gave some details of the organization of Holywell Street, still "a filthy by-word and a public scandal". There was "a brotherhood in this gang; a guild of vendors of obscenities . . . with "a close and compact alliance, offensive and defensive", and common funds to defy the law. One book sold covered the loss of six confiscated:

> It now appears that the business is so lucrative—a guinea a volume being the ordinary price of these pornographic productions—that the trade is worked scientifically. When one dealer is committed for trial, he absconds and his pals pay his forfeited bail, and the case comes to an end.

Had he lived to read this, Lord Campbell might have had sad doubts about the possibility of sterilizing morals by statute. He would have known even more painful disillusion had he lived to see the legislation he had aimed solely at Holywell Street being used to assail a novel by Zola or a scientific study by Havelock Ellis, or, in our own century, the writings of a James Joyce or a D. H. Lawrence.

"*. . .and so, poor wicked nineteenth century: farewell.*"
—Wilfrid Scawen Blunt.

INDEX